"All too often, when it comes to the Bible, familiarity generates apathy. Yet, as the fountainhead and inexhaustible reservoir of the Christian life, the Word of God should be the believer's most treasured resource. Through the lens of Psalm 119, Pastor Kniep not only sounds a clarion call to return to a love for God's revelation, but provides a step by step prescription of helpful strategies to shed light upon the biblical pathway. Pastors and church leaders will find *Loving God's Word* to be thoroughly biblical and eminently practical, a truly timeless resource that will enhance their own zeal for the Word of God and ignite the passions of others."

—Irv Busenitz, Th.D., Author, Professor and V.P. of Academic Admin.,
The Master's Seminary

"Many Christians are shriveling up from spiritual malnutrition. Lack of disciplined Bible reading, Scripture memory, and meditation have led to multitudes of spiritual anorexics. What is the cure? Pastor Seth Kniep's book, *Loving God's Word: Seven Strategies for Slaying Bible Apathy*, is certainly an antidote. With vivid illustrations and simple explanations, Pastor Kniep argues for Bible gluttony. The format of the book is unique. The reader is taken on a spiritual quest through Psalm 119, the nuclear warhead of Psalms on this subject. Richly devotional, thoroughly practical, and easily accessible to all, *Loving God's Word* is a panacea for spiritual anorexia. A perfect resource for personal devotions or group Bible studies."

—Pastor Jack Hughes, D.Min., Author, Pastor of Calvary Bible Church, Burbank

"Seth Kniep's excellent study on Psalm 119 is appropriately titled, *Loving God's Word*. In it he combines personal anecdotes, inspired teaching and probing questions to lead the Bible student into the kind of meaningful spiritual exercise that can change his or her life. Kniep's love and reverence is contagious in this book. I urge you to read the book and catch his passion!"

—Steve Gallagher, Author, Biblical Counselor and President of Pure Life
Ministries

"Our Lord stated that "man does not live by bread alone but by every word that proceeds from the mouth of God" (Matthew 4:4), but the daily energetic reading of God's Word is what many fail to do these days. I welcome Seth Kniep's book, *Loving God's Word: Seven Strategies for Slaying Bible Apathy*. His book does what the title promises. It provokes you to thirst after God's Word in the likeness of the author of Psalm 119, which is the subject of Kniep's exposition. *Loving God's Word* is more than an exposition of Psalm 119; it is exposition with artful illustration and personal application which results in exciting the passion for God's Word.

If your heart has grown apathetic to the reading and practicing of the Word of God, you will find this book a special help in priming the pump of your affections so that God's Word will become alive once more in your soul. Even those acquainted with the profitable use of the Word of God will find this volume a useful ar͟ ͟ ͟ ͟ ͟ ͟ ͟ ͟t͟o͟o͟l in their quest to stay zealous of God and His Word. I thank Seth for his ͟ ͟ ͟ ͟recommend this stirring volume to those who endeavoᴦ

—Alex D. Montoya., Th.M., Pastor, Author, Professor,

LOVING GOD'S WORD

7 STRATEGIES FOR SLAYING BIBLE APATHY

SETH KNIEP

LIFESONG
PUBLISHERS

Somis, CA

ISBN: 978-0-9718306-8-4
Copyright 2007 by Seth Kniep

Published by LifeSong Publishers
P.O. Box 183, Somis, CA 93066-0183
805-655-5644
www.lifesongpublishers.com

Unless otherwise noted, all Bible quotations are from the New American Standard Bible.

Scripture taken from the NEW AMERICAN STANDARD BIBLE. Copyright 1960, 1962, 1963, 1968, 1971, 1972, 1973, 1975, 1977, 1995 by the Lockman Foundation. Used by permission.

Cover and chapter head design by Jon Walusiak and Josh Huhn at Design Point.

Library of Congress Cataloging-in-Publication Data

Kniep, Seth, 1977-
  Loving God's word : 7 strategies for slaying Bible apathy / by Seth Kniep.
      p. cm.
  Summary: "A verse-by-verse exposition of Psalm 119 divided into seven strategies for practically living and loving God's Word"–Provided by publisher.
  Includes bibliographical references.
  ISBN-13: 978-0-9718306-8-4 (pbk.)
  1. Bible. O.T. Psalms CXIX–Criticism, interpretation, etc. 2. Bible. O.T. Psalms CXIX–Commentaries. I. Title.
  BS1450119th .K55 2007
  223'.2077–dc22

                              2006037479

It is strange that of all the pieces of the Bible which my mother taught me, that which cost me most to learn, and which was to my child's mind chiefly repulsive, the 119th Psalm, has now become of all most precious to me in its overflowing and glorious passion of love for the law of God.

~ Mr. Ruskin ~

This sacred ode is a little Bible, the Scriptures condensed, a mass of Bibline, Holy Writ rewritten in holy emotions and actions. Blessed are they who can read and understand these saintly aphorisms; they shall find golden apples in this true Hesperides, and come to reckon that this Psalm, like the whole Scripture which it praises, is a pearl island, or, better still, a garden of sweet flowers.

~ Charles Haddon Spurgeon ~

To eight men who met with me every Monday at 5 a.m.
to study the Word
to make war upon sin
and to worship our Lord and Savior Jesus Christ:

Tom Barker
Gil Bussanich
Lee Craven
Rich Iadevaia
Ian Martin
David Massey
Ernie Mockary
Jesse Rodriguez

A special thank you to Joe Molinari and Laurie Donahue
for their priceless editorial input.

Contents

PREFACE   11

INTRODUCTION: PRICELESS AS GOLD, PRACTICAL AS TOOLS   13

CHAPTER 1: WHY LOVE GOD'S WORD?   19

CHAPTER 2: FOUR QUESTIONS FOR THE LOVER OF THE WORD   37

STRATEGY #1: EMBARK ON GOD'S WORD AS THE PATH TO KNOWING GOD   47

     CHAPTER 3: HOW TO BE A LOVER OF THE WORD   49
     PSALM 119:1-8

     CHAPTER 4: THE BIBLE ZEALOT   59
     Psalm 119:113-120

     CHAPTER 5: FRESH GROUND OR INSTANT–
     EXPERIENCING THE WORD OF GOD   71
     PSALM 119:137-144

STRATEGY #2: REVERE GOD'S WORD WITH AWESOME WONDER   81

     CHAPTER 6: THE MAGNIFICENT WORD OF GOD   83
     PSALM 119:25-32

     CHAPTER 7: MINING THE TREASURE HOUSE OF WISDOM   95
     PSALM 119:97-104

     CHAPTER 8: WHAT GOD'S WORD WILL DO TO YOU   105
     PSALM 119:129-136

STRATEGY #3: CLING TO GOD'S WORD LIKE A ROCK IN A STORM   115

     CHAPTER 9: WHAT TO DO WHEN THE SUFFERING IS UNBEARABLE   117
     PSALM 119:81-88

     CHAPTER 10: THE WORD: YOUR SURVIVAL KIT FOR STAYING ALIVE   125
     PSALM 119:89-96

     CHAPTER 11: WHAT TO DO WHEN YOU NEED HELP FROM GOD   133
     PSALM 119:153-160

STRATEGY #4: FOLLOW GOD'S WORD AS A GUIDE IN PRAYER   145

     CHAPTER 12: HOW GOD CAN HELP YOU KEEP HIS WORD   147
     PSALM 119:33-40

     CHAPTER 13: HOW TO PRAY USING GOD'S WORD   155
     PSALM 119:73-80

     CHAPTER 14: DIVINE INSTANT MESSAGING   163
     PSALM 119:145-152

STRATEGY #5: SHINE GOD'S WORD ON YOUR HEART AND LIFE   171

     CHAPTER 15: ENTER THE COLLEGE OF CHRISTIAN LIVING   173
     PSALM 119:65-72

CHAPTER 16: HOW TO BE DOMINATED BY THE WORD OF GOD
PSALM 119:105-112   181

CHAPTER 17: DEAD ORTHODOXY OR LIVING TRUTH–
THE IMPORTANCE OF THE AFFECTIONS
PSALM 119:161-168   191

CHAPTER 18: HOW TO WORSHIP A HOLY GOD IN AN UNHOLY WORLD   203
PSALM 119:169-176

STRATEGY #6: FLEE TO GOD'S WORD AS A REFUGE FROM PERSECUTION   215

CHAPTER 19: GOD'S WORD: A REFUGE FOR THE BROKEN-HEARTED   217
PSALM 119:17-24

CHAPTER 20: HOW TO REMEMBER GOD'S WORD WHEN YOU SUFFER
THE ATTACKS OF YOUR ENEMIES
PSALM 119:49-56   227

CHAPTER 21: ARE YOU QUALIFIED FOR DIVINE DELIVERANCE?   237
PSALM 119:121-128

STRATEGY #7: RESOLVE TO LIVE GOD'S WORD NOW AND FOREVER   247

CHAPTER 22: RESOLVE TO APPLY   249
PSALM 119:9-16

CHAPTER 23: THE PARADOX OF OBEDIENCE   263
PSALM 119:41-48

CHAPTER 24: 8 RESOLUTIONS OF THE MAN OR WOMAN OF GOD   273
PSALM 119:57-64

FINAL WORD FROM THE AUTHOR   281

LOVING GOD'S WORD OUTLINE   283
Twenty-five lesson outlines for preachers, teachers, and small group leaders

PREFACE

The more we store our minds with heavenly truth, the more deeply shall we be in love with it. The more we see the exceeding riches of the Bible the more will our love exceed measure, and exceed expression.[1]

~ Charles Spurgeon ~

THE NAKED TRUTH

Do you burn with undying love for God's Word? Search long and you'll find few questions more important. Build stupendous cathedrals, listen to spellbinding sermons, sing with breathtaking choirs and witness striking testimonies; still you'll find all these are like dust on your shoes compared to the thirst-quenching satisfaction of loving God's Word. **Genuine, affectionate and faithful love for the Word of God will mold a heart that is captivated by Christ, unweakened by temptation and unwavering in resolve.** On the other hand, **feeble love for God's Word produces feeble Christian living.** When the Word is not loved, sin grows like a hideous monster, quenching joy and confining the believer to a dungeon of emptiness. But when you treasure Christ's Word above even your own life, sin shrivels and joy is immeasurable. Were the oceans made of ink, you could drain them dry writing for a million years on the scroll of the sky and still not record all the blessings to be reaped by loving God's Word.

To burn with love for God's Holy Scriptures means to love His book with intensity, to love this Book like no other.

This Book contains the mind of God, the state of man, the way of salvation, the doom of sinners, and the happiness of believers. Its doctrine is holy, its precepts are binding, its histories are true, and its decisions are immutable. Read it to be wise, believe it to be saved, and practice it to be holy. It contains light to direct you, food to support you, and comfort to cheer you. It is the traveler's map, the pilgrim's staff, the pilot's compass, the soldier's sword and the Christian's charter. Here heaven is opened, and the gates of hell disclosed. Christ is its grand subject, our good its design, and the glory of God its end. It should fill the memory, rule the heart, and guide the feet. Read it slowly, frequently and prayerfully. It is a mine of wealth, health to the soul and a river of pleasure. It is given to you here in this life, will be opened at the Judgment, and is established

---

1   Charles H. Spurgeon, *The Treasury of David: Classic Reflections on the Wisdom of the Psalms*, vol. 3 (Peabody: Hendrickson Publishers, n. d.), 425.

forever. It involves the highest responsibility, will reward the greatest labor, and condemn all who trifle with its contents.[2]

Gazillions of Christian self-help programs, Christian health seminars, Christian financial guides, Christian Q&A books, Christian place mats, and even stickers for your bumper or ornaments to hang on your mirror deck the halls of Christian stores, yet one truth remains simple but critical: victorious, happy and satisfied Christian living is impossible without cherishing the simple and pure Word of God. And that is what this book is all about.

> **THE WORD "CHERISH"**
>
> Read the famous "love" chapter of the Bible, 1 Corinthians 13, (in the 1611 King James Version), and you will not find the word "love" but "charity." In the Elizabethan language of the 1600's, people spoke differently, using the word "cherish" instead of "love."

---

2   Author unknown.

Precious as Gold: Practical as Tools

The miners of the California gold rush wouldn't have rushed if this precious metal was not also practical. People love gold not only because of its beauty and shine, but because it can be turned into money to buy houses, land, and lots of high-returning stocks and bonds.

In the same way, God's Word is as practical as it is precious. Thomas Watson underscored its value when he wrote, "Islands of spices, coasts of pearl, rocks of diamonds, these are but the riches that reprobates may have. But the Word gives us those riches which angels have.[3]" At the same time, this precious Book is of immense practical value to the believer. Both the first and the fortieth Presidents of the United States of America understood this. George Washington, said, "It is impossible to righteously govern the world without God and the Bible," and Ronald Reagan pronounced, "Within the covers of one single book, the Bible, are all the answers to all the problems that face us today—if only we would read and believe."

If God's Word is as practical as it is precious, it should influence every part of our lives. Loving God's Word does not mean simply "doing your devotions." Anyone can "do" devotions. Muslims bow toward Mecca, Jews supplicate at the praying wall, and Yoga students meditate on their "inner voice." The phrase "do your devotions" has been reduced to a remedial ritual to absolve guilt for not doing your daily ceremonies. We must not use God's Word like a nightly toothpaste to chase away the plaque of guilt. Knowing God's Word is about knowing a Person, the Almighty, awesome God of the universe who is too holy to be looked upon and so gracious that He did not spare His Son a torturous death so that we can have eternal life. The believer who views time in God's Word as just another appointment on his Outlook calendar has terribly abused the purpose of the Bible.

Husbands, how would your wife feel if the only time you spoke to her was

---

[3] Thomas Watson, *Heaven Taken By Storm* (Morgan: Soli Deo Gloria Publications, 1992), 13.

during your daily fifteen minute "marriage devotion time?" And if you refused to call her, think about her, pray for her, or touch her the rest of the day and night until the next "fifteen minute marriage devotion" time, what would happen to your marriage? It would fade out like an isolated burning coal.

Although scheduling daily time for Bible study is essential, the influence of the Word of God is not meant to be relegated to an item on a to do list, compartmentalized to one small section of the day. The purpose of Bible study time is to fill you with truth so that it can disseminate into your soul the rest of the day. Years ago, I helped my father and brother build a house on the west coast. Because the building was far from grocery stores, my brother and I would stock up on Ranchers candies every Sunday so that we could enjoy them throughout the week. We knew if we didn't stock up on Sunday, we would be candy-less all week long. Likewise you must stock up on the Word of God. In the middle of a hectic life with so many responsibilities pulling you every which way, you have to set aside protected time to be in the Word. If you don't plan in advance, time in the Word gets postponed, the end of the week arrives and you feel the pain of spiritual malnourishment when you realize that you haven't cracked your Bible all week long. Back on the coast, my brother and I would pop in a candy and suck on it for hours until it was nothing but a reduced sliver of sugar, food coloring, and high fructose corn syrup. No sooner would one disappear that we'd pop in another. In a similar way, God wants you to enjoy the savoring flavor of His Word all throughout the day. Spurgeon stated, "Take a text, and lay it on your tongue like a wafer made with honey, and let it melt in your mouth all the day. If you do this, and meditate upon it, you will be surprised to notice how the various events of life will help to open up that text."

As you finish your time in study and close the Bible to go on with your day, realize that your "devotion time" has not ended but just begun! How long would a mountain climber last if he spent an hour packing his gear but forgot to bring it on his expedition? The close of your study time begins hours of daily devotion as you mentally dip into those wonderful truths throughout the day and marinate your decision-making with divine truth!

I know of some believers who write a passage on a 3x5 card, stick it on their dashboard and see it every time they turn the key. I have a another friend who was so harassed by off-colored jokes by his co-workers that he brought his Bible to work with him and read it every lunch break.

Go to work with the Word in your heart, praying to the God of the Word and obeying the commands of the Word. Let it help you in temptation, encourage you in dark places, and give you strength when you feel weak. Let it be so gratifying to your soul that all other temptations lose their flavor! Let it permeate your mind, run through your blood, protect your thoughts, and influence your decisions. The believer who holds the Word of God before his mind's eye all through the day will find it hard to give sin a glance of attention.

Eleanor Schmidt relates in *Reader's Digest* how her doctor recommended surgery and referred her to a specialist. Arriving early for her appointment, she found the door unlocked and the young surgeon behind the desk deeply engrossed in reading, so she cleared her throat. Startled, he looked up and closed the book. Suddenly, she realized that his book was the Bible. "Does reading the Bible help you before or after an operation?" she asked. Her fears were dispelled by his soft, one-word answer: "During."

ANCIENT BUT RELEVANT

Within the pages of this book you will find seven strategies to nurture a deeper love for God's Word and it all starts with the heart of the author of Psalm 119. But before you wonder what a 176-verse, 3,000 year old poem written by a man who never saw a car or threw a bowling ball has to do with you, understand that God declares the relevance of His Word to every believer: *"All Scripture is inspired by God and is profitable for teaching, for reproof, for correction, and for training in righteousness so that man of God may be adequately equipped for every good work" (2 Tim 3:16).*

Paul says that all Scripture is profitable! Yes, even the genealogies and temple laws. This word "profitable" means useful, advantageous, or practical. The God-breathed Scriptures were designed to be practiced.

You may then wonder, "But the psalmist comes from another era in time. How can I relate to a man who passed away 3,000 years ago?" Man's need has not changed in the last 3,000 years. The psalmist struggled with the same passions of the flesh that you battle. The advancement of technology, communication, and modern culture may deceive you into believing that man's nature has somehow improved or his needs changed, but being more civilized does not equal being more righteous. If anything, modern advancement in travel, communication, and warfare has fooled man into thinking that he is now somehow morally better for it, yet his nature has not changed. He struggles with the same sins, needs the same Savior, and will only find strength in the same Word.

My goal is not to impress you with a skillful homily, or tickle you with flattering quips and nifty clichés. Instead, I want to take you on a journey. A journey to the heart of a man who loved God's Word with every cell in his being. We will watch how he made God's Word the lifeblood of his soul. We will try to understand why his heart throbbed in dripping affection for truth, at times so hard that he felt it would break (Ps 119:145).

I cannot plant love for God's Word in the soil of your heart. Only the Holy Spirit can do that. But by explaining the text and showing you the psalmist's unbelievable passion for truth, it is my prayer that God will use this book to set you on the right path to knowing and loving His precious Word.

Today many pastors plague their pulpits with a cloud of frilly anecdotes instead of crystal truth. They use the Word as a launching pad for opinion instead of the centerpiece of worship. But the Word of God should be made so clear that you can feel it's pricking arrows and taste its invigorating waters. If your soul feels wilted and dry, may the Holy Spirit use His Word to stoke the dying embers of your hardened heart and fan a blaze so fierce that others cannot come near without igniting themselves. And if you already deeply love God's Word, may God use the following pages to enrich your affection for the Bible yet more. If God uses the remaining words of this book to mold your heart half as much as he has used Psalm 119 to mold mine, then my mission has accomplished its purpose ten times over.

> [God's Word is] a store of manna for God's pilgrim children...The great cause of neglecting the Scriptures is not want of time, but want of heart, some idol taking the place of Christ. Satan has been marvelously wise to entice away God's people from the Scripture. A child of God who neglects the Scriptures cannot make it his business to please the Lord of Glory; cannot make Him Lord of the conscience; ruler of the heart; the joy, portion, and treasure of the soul...If the Bible be used aright by anyone, it will be to him the most pleasant book in the world.[4]
> ~ Robert C. Chapman ~

May His words be more pleasant to you than life itself.

---

[4]   Robert L. Peterson and Alexander Strauch, *Agape Leadership: Lessons in Spiritual Leadership From the Life of R. C. Chapman* (Littleton: Lewis and Roth Publishers, 1991), 15-16.

PART ONE:
MOTIVES, STUMBLING BLOCKS,
TOOLS AND QUESTIONS

I

Why Love God's Word?

While studying in the Holy Lands, a seminary professor met a man who claimed to have memorized the entire Old Testament—in Hebrew! Needless to say, the astonished professor asked for a demonstration. A few days later they sat together in the man's home.

"Where shall we begin?" asked the man.

"Psalm 1," replied the professor who was an avid student of the psalms.

Opening his Hebrew Bible to Psalm 1, the professor followed along for two hours as the man recited chapter after chapter of the Old Testament Hebrew from memory. But the big shocker was yet to come. As they talked some more, the man admitted that he was an atheist! [1]

This man is living proof that some humans can know Scripture by memory better than most Christians and yet be completely dead to its meaning. Even the most wicked men can learn the Bible but not love its Author. The atheist loved the Bible for the wrong reason, as do many believers today.

Think of the students, parents, husbands and wives who cringe at the shout from the pulpit, "Read your Bible!" and then run home to read in order to relieve their conscience without asking, "Why am I doing this?" If you asked them, no doubt they'd answer, "Because it's what Christians are supposed to do." That's like the teacher telling the student who asked why he must study math, "Because that's what students do." The teacher has just created the most unmotivated student in the world. Christians like this will read God's Word with as much interest as people read software agreements.

WRONG MOTIVES

The believer must understand why he is to treasure God's Word. If you love the Word of God only because "that's what Christians do," then you have not loved it but abused it. Every believer who sets his heart to study God's Word

---

1   Jack Kuhatschek, *Taking The Guesswork Out of Applying The Bible* (Downers Grove: InterVarsity, 1991), 16.

will be tempted to do it for wrong motives, and though his sails may look good for a season, if his motives are not on course, his ship will soon be run aground. Check your motive when you open this great Book and see if you love it more than just for the sake of loving it, or do you battle one of the following unhealthy motives for spending time in God's Word?

1. Duteous obligation. This is the motive of the Christian who studies only because he must. It's like going to work on Monday morning or studying for a test all night long. The only thing that gets him into the Word is sheer duty or obligation. His pastor cries out, "Read your Bible!" His Sunday School teacher commands, "Get in the Word!" His parents order, "Memorize verses!" These burdens crush his conscience until his only escape from the shackles of guilt is compliance. This even happens to a pastor or teacher who finds himself studying God's Word only for sermon preparation. The joy and excitement he once felt as a new believer when he poured over the Word, inhaling every precious drop, has turned to dry sand. He studies only because "that is what pastors do," but love for God's Word has grown cold. Even the new convert may begin his new life in Christ with cheerful reading of the Word, but when the motivation is only "because it's my duty," the joy quickly erodes and Bible study becomes as detested as crawling out of bed before the sun comes up.

Husbands, if one evening you showed up on your wife's doorstep with anniversary flowers and she gives you a big hug and says, "Oh Honey, why did you?" and you say, "Because I'm supposed to," she'd be insulted. (Isn't that right wives?)

God is not pleased when you wearily obey His Word in legalistic obligation like stepping on the stair master after seven years of too much eating. God intends for you to enjoy what you read, to be thrilled with every word! In Stephen Charnock's words, "Christ loves not melancholy and phlegmatic [a sluggish temperament] service."[2]

There is another unhealthy motive for spending time in the Bible.

2. Arrogant ambition. This is the motive of the believer who worships knowledge. He has placed Bible knowledge on the throne of worship instead of the Author of the Bible. Every Bible study, every sermon, every Bible reading time is for the sole purpose of storing Bible truth in his cerebral hard drive so that he can parade his learning and defeat all who contradict his views. He has fallen more in love with truth than the Christ of truth. His condition is diagnosed perfectly by the Lord Jesus Christ in Revelation 2:2-4:

---

2   Stephen Charnock quoted by Spurgeon, 438

WHY LOVE GOD'S WORD?

I know your deeds and your toil and perseverance, and that you cannot tolerate evil men, and you put to the test those who call themselves apostles, and they are not, and you found them to be false; and you have perseverance and have endured for My name's sake, and have not grown weary. But I have this against you, that you have left your first love.

These believers remind me of the great Bible study movement under Ezra which deteriorated into a school where rabbis fanatically worshipped the bare letters of Scripture and considered them magical. Some even claimed that God Himself spent three hours daily studying the letters of the Law![3] They committed the sin of bibliolatry: worshipping Scripture instead of its Author.

Some Christians are known better for what they stand against than what they stand for. There is a time and place to know the doctrines of cults and heretics, but it is noteworthy that when the New Testament authors battled false doctrines, they spent more time exposing the character of the false teacher than the details of his false doctrine (1 Tim 4:1-5; 2 Pet 2; Jude 5-16). Likewise, they gave more attention to exhorting the church to stand strong on the rock of the doctrines handed on to them (1 Tim 4:6-11; 2 Pet 3:1-2; Jude 17-23) than exposing the error of the heresies threatening the flock. It would take a thousand lifetimes to learn all the errors of all the heretics, but when you know the real thing, the counterfeit is quickly obvious when held alongside the truth. Agents of the Secret Service are not trained to recognize all the counterfeit bills. This would take months and years. Instead, their trainers teach them how to recognize a genuine dollar bill, making all forged copies obvious.

It is a sad day when the believer is only known for what he stands against.

I'm non-charismatic	I'm non-denominational	I'm non-Arminian
I'm non-Calvinistic	I'm non-free will	I'm non-predestination
I'm non-allegorical.	I'm non-literal	I'm non-dispensational
I'm non-Reformed.	I'm non-amillennial	I'm non-psychology

Although it is good to stand against many of these things, it is equally important—if not more important—to know what you stand *for*. Even if you soundly condemn every false doctrine that has ever existed, until you stand upon the Word of God, you stand upon a foundation of quicksand. Many have built their foundation upon the ruin of their enemies instead of the foundation of Truth. They have created a vacuum, sucking out bad doctrines but failed to

---

3   Paul Lee Tan, *The Interpretation of Prophecy* (Rockville: Assurance Publishers, 1974), 41.

replace them with the Lord Jesus Christ.

When the believer does this he lives off of criticism. His passion is fueled by anger towards those who disagree with him. He is better at criticizing those who practice man-centered evangelism than at telling unbelievers who Christ is. He studies not for love of God but for love of study. His haughty, arrogant, and negative attitude is hidden under the mask of "being biblical."

Take away false doctrines and this kind of preacher has nothing to preach about! No more enemies to shoot down. He might as well retire and go to Tahiti. And what is the problem? He is no longer preaching for Christ and salvation from sin. The topic for every sermon is prompted by those who disagree with his church's doctrinal statement. People who sit in this kind of church will slowly start to measure their personal righteousness against other believers who have different doctrines. Christ is no longer the measure and source of righteousness. Paul said, "For I determined to know nothing among you except Jesus Christ, and Him crucified!" (1 Cor 2:2). This does not mean that Paul was anti-doctrinal. Above all things Paul commanded the young pastors, Titus and Timothy, to teach, defend, and treasure the doctrine of God's Word. But we must not forget that Paul preached the Word of Christ because he loved the Christ of the Word. When one's love for Christ is chief, his hatred for false doctrine will be rightly placed. He will not live to find people he disagrees with, but will live to help others become like the very Christ who died for them. Hatred for false doctrine is to be fueled by love for Christ, not by affection for debate. While false doctrine must be exposed and eliminated and the Bible reserves the most flaming rebukes for those who lead the sheep astray, in our passion for being right we must not go overboard. Although we should not be afraid of speaking of our convictions in doctrines not related to salvation, let us not wield greater skill in criticizing those who disagree than repenting of our own daily sins.

Martyn Lloyd Jones, the great expositor of England's Westminster Chapel, once confronted a man who struggled with this. While guest-preaching in Toronto, Canada, he met T. T. Shields of Jarvis Street Baptist Church, the leading orthodox preacher of that city. Although in theology Shields and Lloyd-Jones stood close, Lloyd-Jones felt that Shields was too critical of those who disagreed with him.

In author Iain Murray's words, "Rather than helping young Christians by the strength of his polemics against liberal Protestants and Roman Catholics, Lloyd-Jones believed that Shields was losing the opportunity to influence those whose first need was to be given positive teaching."

Martyn Lloyd-Jones continues the story: "Shields came to fetch me and we had lunch. We talked on general subjects and then we went to sit in the garden. There, as we drank coffee, he suddenly turned to me and said, 'Are you a great reader of Joseph Parker?'

'No, I am not.'

'Why?'

'I get nothing from him.'

'Man! What's the matter with you?'

'Well, it's all very well to make these criticisms of the liberals but he doesn't help me spiritually.'

'Surely you are helped by the way he makes mincemeat of the liberals?'

'No, I am not. You can make mincemeat of the liberals and still be in trouble in your own soul.'

'Well,' said Shields, 'I read Joseph Parker every Sunday morning. He winds me up—puts me right.'"

On the drive home, Lloyd-Jones graciously appealed to Shields to forsake his critical spirit and start giving people the gospel, winning them over for Christ instead of using his pulpit as a machine gun to level his opponents. Shield's 59 year old eyes filled with tears as he confessed that no man had spoken to him in this way before. He decided he would call his board for a meeting on the next evening and tell them exactly what Lloyd-Jones suggested. If they agreed with Lloyd-Jones, then he would do as Lloyd-Jones says. If they disagreed, then he would not change. The meeting took place and the men told Shields not to listen to Lloyd-Jones' advice.

Years later, Shields drove away some of his warmest supporters and eventually finished his ministry with a congregation greatly reduced in size.[4]

3. Personal selfishness. This believer only sees the Bible as a self-help manual to give him tips on how to be more successful in this life or to make him feel better about himself when he is down. He treats the Bible like atheists treat God when a natural disaster hits and they cry out to heaven for help. He searches the Scriptures, looking for parts that make him feel good, but ignores the weightier doctrines. To him the Bible is not a revelation of God's person, but a fast ticket to promotion. He practices the flip-and-guess method of closing his eyes, leafing through the pages, and letting his finger fall on some random verse which he is convinced "came straight from God." He forces every passage into immediate application before he even knows who is writing, to whom it is being written, or even the point of the verse, slaughtering proper interpretation. He is more interested in himself than the Author and he looks for what he can get from the text before even considering what its author is trying to say. He is no different than the man who marries only for sex and uses his wife only as an object of

4   Iain H. Murray, *D. Martyn Lloyd-Jones: The First Forty Years* 1899-1939 (Carlisle: The Banner of Truth Trust, 2002), 271-273.

pleasure, tossing her back on the shelf when finished. This is not love, but abuse, and his only goal is to satisfy his lustful desires. To him the Bible is not "God's Word to man" but "my road to happiness." Scripture is ointment for his wounds to use when he's feeling down, but rarely bread and water to his soul for daily sustenance for life and godliness.

So what is the right motive for knowing God's Word? One day a scribe stood amazed as Jesus responded with confidence and wisdom to every schemed question his enemies directed at Him. Being able to withhold himself no longer, he stepped forward and asked Christ, "What commandment is the foremost of all?"

"The foremost is 'Hear O Israel! The LORD our God is one LORD; and you shall love the LORD your God with all your heart, and with all your soul, and with all your mind, and with all your strength.' The second is this, 'You shall love your neighbor as yourself.' There is no other commandment greater than these."

Readily agreeing that God is one God, the scribe added: "To love Him with all the heart and with all the understanding and with all the strength, and to love one's neighbor as himself, is much more than all burnt offerings and sacrifices" (Mark 12:33).

Jesus' response is the kind of response every believer wishes for when talking to God incarnate: "You are not far from the kingdom of God" (Mark 12:34). Wow! Imagine the moment. Christ saved His most charring censures for the Pharisees. Even after this event, He would spend 36 verses of singeing chides to warn the people about the hypocrisy of the Pharisees (Matt 23:1-36). The gospels spare no words singling out this menacing group of evil men, and even the name "Pharisee" has become an icon of hypocrisy. And yet out from the snake nest of the hypocrites comes one man who can summarize the Old Testament law with such accuracy that Christ commends him for it! Every time I read this passage I re-read it just to relive this unforgettable page of history: *Christ commends a Pharisee!*

But why? This man's words reflected a heart of understanding. The Pharisee had not missed the boat while searching for the oars. He was not so engrossed with the minutia of laws that he overlooked God's one big point: *you are to love God with everything in you.* This is the greatest commandment and the chief requirement of every human. This serves God's ultimate purpose to glorify and enjoy Himself forever. If you miss this one, then you've missed the whole Bible. Grind every command, every law, and every instruction of the Old Testament into a single ounce of truth and it will be one thing: *Love! God first and man second.*

All of Scripture is permeated with the great theme of God's great love for mankind through Jesus Christ His Son, and the summarized duty of man in response is to love God with all his heart, soul, strength, and mind. This means you are to love God with every cell in your body, every thought of your brain, every word of your mouth, every ounce of your strength, and every intention of your heart! Love is so important, that Paul says in 1 Corinthians 13 that even if you possess all the Christian virtues of Scripture but do not have love, you have nothing.

But how can the Christian love God with all his heart? The Christian can express love for God in thousands of ways, but loving God starts with one thing: loving the Word of God. It's quite simple: **You are to love the Word of God so that you will love the God of the Word.** You cannot separate the two and still grow in Christ anymore than you can remove oxygen from water and still have H_2O.

PSALM 119
33 ACTIONS AND ONE MEANING

At this point you may be thinking, *I agree we should not study God's Word out of duteous obligation, arrogant ambition, or relentless selfishness. And I agree that the chief motive for loving God's Word is to love God. But what exactly does it look like to love God's Word?*

You spend time with people you love. You think about them all day. You want to be with them, talk with them, care for them, protect them, defend them, adore them, speak highly of them and tell others about them. You may even plan your day around them.

The psalmist of Psalm 119 gives a similar description of what it means to love God's Word in 176 verses. And he does so with no fewer than 33 verbs.

GOD'S WORD IS TO BE:

ACTION	VERSE	ACTION	VERSE
Accepted	65, 75	Meditated upon	15, 23, 27, 48, 77, 78, 97, 99, 100, 148
Appreciated	62	Observed	2, 22, 33, 56, 69, 100, 115, 145
Beheld	18	Pursued	45, 94, 157
Believed	76	Proclaimed	13, 46
Clung to	31, 87	Rejoiced in	14, 111, 162
Considered	95	Regarded	15, 117
Delighted in	16, 24, 47, 70, 77, 92, 143, 174	Remembered	16, 52, 61, 83, 93, 109, 141, 153, 176

Followed	24, 30, 32, 51, 59, 102, 105, 110, 173	Revered	38, 48, 86, 89, 91, 96, 98, 99, 120, 128, 129, 137, 138, 152, 160, 161, 164, 172
Hoped in	49, 52	Spoken of	43
Influenced by	80	Sung	54
Inherited	111	Tasted	103
Kept	4, 5, 8, 9, 17, 44, 55, 57, 60, 63, 67, 88, 101, 106, 134, 146, 166, 167, 168	Treasured	11, 72
Looked upon	6	Trusted	25, 28, 37, 40, 41, 42, 50, 58, 107, 116, 149, 154, 156, 165, 170, 175
Learned	7, 12, 18, 26, 33, 64, 66, 68, 71, 73, 102, 108, 124, 135, 171	Understood	27, 34, 73, 104, 125, 130, 144, 169
Longed for	20, 40, 82, 123, 131	Waited for	43, 74, 81, 114, 147
Loved	47, 48, 97, 113, 119, 127, 140, 159, 163, 167	Walked in	35
Obeyed	1, 3, 112		

Inject all these actions into your daily living from now until your last day and with your final breath you can say with confidence, "I loved God's Word!" Do not let this daunting list intimidate you. God didn't give His people a Word they could not keep. The Apostle John wrote, "For this is the love of God that we keep His commandments and His commandments are not burdensome" (1 John 5:3).

A WELL OF REFRESHMENT

Do you burn with passionate affection for God's Word? If you do not love the Word of God, you will find it very difficult to gain victory over sin. This is not a pattern of perfection but a pattern of growth. Look back over the last 12 months of your life and answer this question honestly: How much have I grown? You cannot grow in Christ without growing in your love for His Word. Loving God's Word can keep you from sin. When my wife was just 12 years old, her mother wrote these words on the inside cover of her Bible:

> THIS BOOK WILL KEEP YOU FROM SIN,
> OR SIN WILL KEEP YOU FROM THIS BOOK.

Loving the Word will keep you from sin like delighting in intimacy with your spouse can keep you from adultery. In Proverbs 5, Solomon tells the young man tempted with infidelity to "Drink water from your own cistern and fresh water from your own well. Let your fountain be blessed and rejoice in the wife of your youth. As a loving hind and a graceful doe, let her breasts satisfy you at all times. Be exhilarated always with her love" (Prov 5:15, 18, 19). Relishing the sexual delicacies of marriage is an antidote to adultery. A married man can flee pornography, fantasies, and flirting not only by turning his eyes away *from* temptation but *to* his wife, just as a parched man in Death Valley would savor a fresh well.

Humans are motivated by two factors: to alleviate pain, or to increase pleasure. We are a pleasure seeking, pain-hating race. When you find pleasure in God's Word like a husband in his own wife, temptations and enticements lose their power. It's hard to sin while savoring the sweet spring water of the Scriptures.

I once read the story of a dissident soviet Jew, Anatoli Shcharansky, who knew this kind of satisfaction. He sent his wife from Russia to freedom in Israel where he would join her as soon as possible. He kissed her goodbye with the parting words, "I'll see you soon in Jerusalem." But Anatoli was detained and finally imprisoned. It seemed their reunion in Jerusalem would not only be postponed but may never occur. During long years in Russian prisons and work camps, Anatoli was stripped of his personal belongings. His only possession was a miniature copy of the Psalms. Once during his imprisonment, his refusal to release the book to the authorities cost him 130 days in solitary confinement. Finally, twelve years after parting with his wife, he was offered freedom. In February 1986, as the world watched, Shcharansky was allowed to walk away from Russian guards toward those who would take him to Jerusalem. But in the final moments of captivity, the guards tried again to confiscate the Psalms book. Anatoli threw himself face down in the snow and refused to walk on to freedom without it. Those words had kept him alive during imprisonment, and he would not go on to freedom without them. He'd rather live as a condemned prisoner, never seeing his wife again, than part with God's Word.

As Americans, we have the mentality that we deserve freedom. As much as I appreciate freedom, there may come a day when I must choose between prison with the Word or freedom without it. God has not promised His people physical freedom, but spiritual freedom. God stands under no obligation to remove all persecution, but He has guaranteed the strength to endure it (1 Pet 2:21-25; 4:19; 1 Cor 10:13). People will suffer unbearable persecution just to hold onto something they treasure. Would you do the same just to read the Bible? Do you wake up each morning looking forward to your time in God's Word? Are you eager to get to church to hear the Word preached? Do you love to drive your car because that's your one chance to listen to iPod-casting sermons or Bible reading MP3's?

If loving God's Word is a campaign against sin and a source of unspeakable joy, then why don't more believers love it?

ROUGH ROAD: FOR BIBLE FANATICS ONLY

Extreme racers bike, paddle, and run practically nonstop for five to six days through several hundred miles of jungles, mountains, lakes, and raging rapids with only a few hours of sleep. Marathoners push hard, tri-athletes push harder, but no one tests the limits of the human body and mind like the extreme racers. They frequently lose up to ten pounds of water, fat and muscle in one race and burn calories and electrolytes faster than they can use them. At the finish line, their organs are faltering, their muscles deteriorating, and some of them even hallucinate. And then they come back for more.[5] That's endurance with an obsession. If only 100 believers were obsessed with God's Word with the fervency of an extreme racer, the world would be turned upside down!

But loving the Word does not come easy. Nothing worth gaining comes pain-free. Ask anyone to tell you about the easy road to the heights of success and he'll ask you what planet you were born on. Likewise, the path to loving God's Word is riddled with foot traps and stumbling blocks that can be avoided.

STUMBLING BLOCKS TO LOVING GOD'S WORD

Temptations distract it. Let's face it. In spite of an outstanding foundation, America is not the "Christian Disneyland" so many wish for. Among billboards inviting you to lust, bosses tempting you to commit mutiny, and foods so delicious you have to change your belt size if you yield to your desires, the many faces of temptation make loving God's Word sometimes feel impossible.

But God has promised the believer that no temptation is too strong. "No temptation has overtaken you but such as is common to man; and God is faithful, who will not allow you to be tempted beyond what you are able, but with the temptation will provide the way of escape also, so that you will be able to endure it" (1 Cor 10:13). That's not a suggestion, but a guarantee. God will not push you beyond your limits. And when He does allow you to encounter temptation, take courage; it is for your good. Temptations are potential blessings because without them, you wouldn't feel the need to cry out to God for help. God is most pleased when He is most glorified and you glorify Him when you desperately need His strength. Instead of letting the world draw you away from God, let the very sight of temptation cause you to flee to God, more deeply entrenching your love for God's Word.

Junk food de-flavors it. Worker bees live off a diet of pollen and honey, and they live for only six weeks. But the queen bee feeds upon the royal jelly from birth, giving her a lifespan of six years. What are you feeding on? Is your daily food the life-changing power of the Word of God or junk food? Body-worshipping magazines, books parading anti-Scriptural ideals, man-centered

---

5   Alice Park, "Can You Push Yourself Too Hard?" *Time Magazine*, (June 6, 2005), 69..

music, and time-wasting soap operas are just a few of many paths to *mind pollution*. If you keep up a regular diet of the garbage of this world you will have no appetite for God's Word. You must guard your heart with all diligence "for from it flow the springs of life" (Prov 4:23). Protect what you watch, listen to, and read. *You can no more hunger for God's Word while eating junk food than a man can crave Brussels sprouts after sating himself on candy bars.* Your eyes and ears are gateways of food for your soul; don't fill them with poison.

Have you ever gone a day without a meal? Probably not intentionally, unless you were fasting. But when Satan tempted Christ to turn stones into bread loaves, Christ atomized the attack with the simple statement, "Man shall not live on bread alone but on every word that proceeds out of the mouth of God" (Matt 4:4). In the face of agonizing hunger, Christ still treasured God's Word above physical food. I once did a 40 hour famine for a fund raising program that delivered food and the gospel to starving children. The first few hours my hunger was intense. But after the first 24 hours of slow starvation my hunger dropped and my body grew shaky and weak. I had gone so long without food that my body had moved beyond hunger pains. This will happen to the Christian who stops giving himself a daily intake of the Bible. After a while, he no longer feels the hunger and it becomes much easier to live without. This is a dangerous way to live.

False doctrines muddle it. We live in an era entrenched in postmodernism, relativism, and man-centered theology. So-called Christian doctrines such as annihilationism (hell is not forever), open theism (God does not know all things), or The New Perspective (denies the biblical definition of justification) have crept into our churches. In this sea of error by professing evangelicals, how can the believer steer his ship straight? Nothing but a return to loving the pure and clean Word of God will spare the believer from the tragedy of going off-course. As the psalmist says, "Your commandments make me wiser than my enemies, for they are ever mine. I have more insight than all my teachers, for Your testimonies are my meditation. I understand more than the aged, because I have observed Your precepts" (Ps 119:98-100).

Modern culture belittles it. To an unbeliever, the gospel is complete foolishness and the thought of one putting all his hope and trust in a 2,000-3,500 year old Book is moronic. But do not let this discourage you, for Paul already addressed this two millennia ago in 1 Corinthians 1:18, "For the word of the cross is foolishness to those who are perishing, but to us who are being saved it is the power of God." The world will never admire the Bible beyond viewing it as a classic piece of literature.

In January of 1984, as a man painted the home of an 89 year old lady in Spokane, Washington, he admired her large family Bible prominently displayed on the coffee table. Noticing his interest the lady commented that it was 116 years old and a priceless heirloom.

"How remarkable!" the man said, and then added, "It doesn't matter how old the Bible might be, what's on the inside is what matters."

The lady replied, "Oh, I know. That sure is the truth. Why, we have recorded in the Bible all the family records and births and marriages and deaths that go so far back we could never replace them." The lady could not see any value in God's Word beyond this life. To her it was nothing more than an ancient artifact of family records.

The world will never think correctly about God's Word. But take heart, for God delights in using the foolish things of this world to shame the wise (1 Cor 1:27) so that all the world will some day know that it was not man's intelligence or charisma that brought people to salvation, but the pure wisdom and power of God (1 Cor 1:29-30).

The influence of modern culture has even been inoculated into some Christian circles, circles where the letters after a man's name carry more weight than his love for the Savior. Circles where ministry position matters more than truth, and "who's who" in Christianity is more discussed than Christ. Some even look down upon a man or woman who weeps over his sin and sings for his salvation as he studies God's Word. Some would have you think that emotions are primitive and unsophisticated. As a result, Christians who fear men more than God squelch their emotions to find acceptance, and God's Word quickly becomes cold to their heart. Solomon's words are timely: "The fear of man brings a snare, but he who trusts in the LORD will be exalted" (Prov 29:25). We need not please others, only God. Make it your ambition to love God's Word with all your heart, soul, and mind. Perhaps God will use your influence to save others from cold ritualism.

Time strangles it. With Roomba robot vacuums cleaning your carpet, diabetics who can beam glucose readings from home to their physician by means of a wireless armband and the new Paparazzi model watch made by Swatch that updates its wearer with the latest news every 15 minutes, you'd think that extra time would be abundant these days. But spending time in God's Word has become more infrequent and difficult than ever before.

After a quick breakfast, dropping off the kids for school, a day with customers at the office, cleaning the car, preparing dinner, attending your church fellowship, catching up on emails, and trying to spend time with your family in the wee hours of the fading daylight, where do you find time to study God's Word?

I can tell you with conviction that it's not a question of time, but of priority. When a Christian states that he does not have time to study God's Word, what he really means is that there are other things in his life that he is not willing to say "no" to. Do you have time to watch TV, surf the internet, chat on the phone, go out to dinner, go to the movies, or take a vacation? To play golf? To read the paper? We have no problem filling our time with "stuff." But how important is all that "stuff" when you pass through the pearly gates of heaven? Life is a vapor; maximize the short breath of your days by investing in things you can take to heaven (James 4:14).

God's has promised that His "divine power has granted to us everything pertaining to life and godliness" (2 Pet 1:3). If God has given you the resources, then He most certainly has given you the time to use those resources. It may take sacrifice, but never will the day come when you say, "I regret the cost."

THREE TOOLS FOR ONE PROJECT

One day, while standing in a grocery shop of a large manufacturing town just west of Scotland, Alexander Wallace noticed an elderly, frail widow staggering in to make a few purchases. She was the classic Noah Webster definition of "poor."

This day was a dark one for the big town. Nearly every weaving loom was stopped. The meals of highly respected tradesmen now depended on public charity, and only a trifle of money was given each day only to the most poor and needy.

Clutching her meager allowance of a few copper coins in her withered hands, she carefully allotted each penny to her most basic needs until she came to the last one. Pinching that coin between her bony fingers and with a heroic expression of contentment and cheerful resignation on her wrinkled face, she said, "Now I must buy oil with this that I may see to read my Bible during these long dark nights. For it is my only comfort now when every other comfort has gone away."[6] Without youth and wealth, this lady found all of her strength in the Word of God she cherished.

Whether you be widowed or wealthy, king or slave, prince or pauper or pastor or layman, you too can treasure the Word of God. You do not have to be a great preacher, attend seminary, Bible College or know every dispensation of dispensationalism or every covenant of covenant theology in order to love this Great Book as the widow did. All you need are three things: the Holy Spirit in your heart, the Word of God in your mind, and a broken heart before the Lord.

The Holy Spirit In Your Heart. The Holy Spirit opens your heart to the treasure chest of God's pearls of truth so that you can pick up each diamond,

---

6   Alexander Wallace, quoted by Charles H. Spurgeon, *The Treasury of David: Classic Reflections on the Wisdom of the Psalms,* vol. 3 (Peabody: Hendrickson Publishers, n. d.), 324-325.

hold it, feel it, and experience its awesome sparkle. In Ephesians 5:17 Paul calls the Word of God the "sword of the Spirit." What good is a sword without a skilled soldier to swing it? Completely useless. You can no better comprehend the full force of God's Word without the Holy Spirit than a sword can win a war with no soldier to brandish it. This is why unbelievers are dead to the Word. Thomas Watson stated, "The same Scripture which to them is a dead letter, should be to thee a savior of life."[7]

If you are a Christian, the Holy Spirit lives within you. Praying the sinner's prayer, stepping forward to an altar call, signing a card, or going to church all your life does not save you. True salvation comes by turning away from your sin and putting your whole faith in Jesus Christ as the full and worthy sacrifice for all your sins. Once this happens, God puts His Holy Spirit in you to guide, strengthen, protect, and grow you.

John the Apostle wrote, "As for you, the anointing which you received from Him abides in you, and you have no need for anyone to teach you; but as His anointing teaches you about all things, and is true and is not a lie, and just as it has taught you, you abide in Him" (1 John 2:27). This "anointing" is God's Holy Spirit. Does this mean we should fire the preachers, dismiss the teachers and find a private oasis where we can study the Bible for ourselves? Not at all! John is saying that every bit of your Bible understanding—whether it be through teacher or preacher, Bible study or personal devotions—you receive by the power of the Holy Spirit. The Bible preacher is no more effective than the Holy Spirit working through Him. Without the Holy Spirit, he's a puppet without a hand.

Your personal time in the Word is fruitless apart from God's Holy Spirit within you. The German reformer, Martin Luther, said, "The more you distrust yourself and your thoughts, the better a theologian and a Christian you will become."[8] This leaves you with only one option: you must seek, pray for and trust the help of the Holy Spirit, or loving God's Word will be more impossible than flying a wingless airplane.

William Tyndale said, "I will cause a boy who drives a plow to know more of the scriptures than the pope." Tyndale understood that a pope, in all his pomp and glory, cannot understand a single syllable of truth apart from God's Holy Spirit, whereas a plow boy can learn mountains of Scripture if just the Spirit of God helps him.

Some view God's Word as a magic brew that produces automatic godliness, as if learning Bible passages and memorizing verses will perform an enchanting spell that automates perfect holiness and turns the believer into

---

7   Thomas Watson quoted by Spurgeon, 245.
8   Dan McCartney and Charles Clayton, *Let the Reader Understand* (Wheaton: Victor Books, 1994), 95.

a super-Christian. This belief is a setup for big disappointment. God's Word changes lives by the power of the Holy Spirit just as a sword brings victory by the power of the soldier swinging it. It is supernatural but not mystical.

The Word of God In Your Mind. In order to love the God of the Word, you must possess the Word of God. But unfortunately, we live in a day where this simple truth is not so simple. Millions of professing believers have been victimized by the lie that you can love God apart from loving His Word. This false notion was condemned by Martin Luther five hundred years ago:

> God is everywhere. However, He does not want you to reach out for Him everywhere but only in the Word. Reach out for it and you will grasp Him aright. Otherwise you are tempting God and setting up idolatry. That is why He has established a certain method for us. This teaches us how and where we are to look for Him and find Him, namely, in the Word.

Those who trade truth for experience are like Aesop's dog who crossed a bridge with a bone in his mouth and looking into the water he saw another dog with a bone that looked better. So he dropped the bone he was carrying to get the other and, of course, he lost both. He gave up the reality for the reflection.[1] And so it is with one who gives up God's Word for fanatical experiences and mental impressions which Paul warned the believer of in Colossians 2:18: "Let no one keep defrauding you of your prize by delighting in self-abasement and the worship of the angels, taking his stand on visions he has seen, inflated without cause by his fleshly mind."

The greatest commandment is not to love the Bible with all your heart, soul, and strength, but to love God supremely. And yet no soul will love God without also loving His Word. The two are inseparable. The man who tries to know God without His Word is a mindless fool. But the man who diligently studies the Scriptures but is cold toward its Author does no better than the demons (James 2:19).

The Bible leaves no room for loving God without also loving His Word. Jesus told His disciples, "He who has My commandments and keeps them is the one who loves Me; and he who loves Me will be loved by My Father, and I will love him and will disclose Myself to him" (John 14:21). Simply said, if you love God, you will love His Word and you cannot claim love for a Word that you do not obey.

Just in case one of His disciples didn't get it, Jesus repeats Himself three verses later, but this time in the negative, "He who does not love Me does not

---

1   John F. MacArthur, Jr. *Charismatic Chaos* (Grand Rapids: Zondervan Publishing House, 1992), 34.

keep My words; and the word which you hear is not Mine, but the Father's who sent Me" (John 14:24).

But some object: "I'm not one of those Bible-thumping legalists who go around quoting Bible verses. I have a personal relationship with God and don't need to read His Word to know Him." This can be compared to one who says, "I love my wife but I don't care what she says."

If your spouse embarked on a two month trip across the ocean, would you read the letters she sent? If you tossed them in the garbage, your friends would rightly diagnose you with a serious mental malfunction or a hatred for your life-mate. In a similar way, God has written a love letter to you. This letter is packed with cliff hanging stories, affectionate letters, melodies of praise, and sobering narratives. God wrote them all for the single purpose of helping you to know Him. God's Word is His way of telling you about Himself, and your love for Him will be shown by how much you savor what He has to tell you.

No book is more worthy of your full attention and ardent devotion than the Bible. I have yet to meet a Christian who complains that he loves it too much.

A Broken Heart Before The Lord. When country crooners twang, "You broke my heart," they're talking about a shattered romance. That's different than a humble spirit—the kind of spirit that has tasted its own dust and felt the glory and greatness of God. The more you realize your own unworthiness and His greatness and tender mercy, the more easily you will grow in affection for His Book.

Being broken does not come without cost. As a teenager I was a basketball fanatic. One day while playing full court, I jumped to block the opponent's shot. Gravity sent my entire bodyweight down onto my left foot which rolled inward over the foot of my opponent until my foot was at a right angle to my calf. In three minutes my ankle was bigger than my thigh. X-rays showed it wasn't broken but I'll never forget my doctor's words: "It would have been better if it had broken. Breaks heal better." Eight weeks on crutches proved his point. God is good at breaking vessels. Then He can reset them so they heal the way He wants. Look for a single man or woman in Scripture who burned with zeal for God's Word without previously being broken and you won't find one.

- Paul wasn't ready to be a missionary until God broke him on the road to Damascus (Acts 9:1-8.)
- Peter didn't preach God's Word like a warrior until he suffered the guilt of denying Christ three times (Luke 22:54-62).
- Joseph did not possess the character for second in command of Egypt until he lay locked up in prison as a falsely accused rapist (Gen 39:7-23).

• God made Moses a fugitive for forty years before he made him leader of a 2.5 million congregation to lead out of slavery and to give the entire Law of God (Exodus 2).

Every day the world tells us that what matters is on the surface: How tan your skin is, how deep your pockets are, how white your teeth are. Remember when Samuel traveled to Bethlehem to anoint one of Jesse's sons as the next king of Israel? It must have been an impressive scene with all the elders of Bethlehem collected in Jesse's house to see whom God would pick. When Eliab, Jesse's first son passed by, Samuel couldn't believe his eyes. Eliab towered above the others with brawny muscles, wide shoulders, and handsome appearance. *Surely this is the man God wants to be king!* Samuel thought (1 Samuel 16:6). But God had shocking news for Samuel. Just like Samuel we live in a world where people judge others by the package instead of the product. Talk to marketing specialists and you will learn that the right look on a package can triple sales in just a matter of months.

Suddenly God interrupted Samuel's shallow thinking, "Do not look at his appearance or at the height of his stature, because I have rejected him; for God sees not as man sees, for man looks at the outward appearance, but the LORD looks at the heart" (1 Sam 16:7).

Six more sons passed by. As the last one walked by Samuel said, "The LORD has not chosen these." An awkward chill of silence must have followed. What? Not *one* of Jesse's sons is qualified for the kingship? And then Samuel broke the silence, "Are these all the children?"

But wait, there is one more. But he's too young! He's just a young teenager who has never fought in battle. He's never marched in a platoon.

And Jesse responded, "There remains yet the youngest, and behold, he is tending the sheep." Just a sheep herder. A lamb caretaker. He watched wooly animals so intelligent they'd walk off a cliff if you told them to.

But Samuel was persistent, "Send and bring him; for we will not sit down until he comes here" (1 Sam 16:11). After what must have been a long wait, a young ruddy teenager with beautiful eyes and handsome face broke through the doorway (1 Sam 16:12). How ironic that God explains David's looks right after He stated that external features carry no weight on qualifying a man for kingship! But this was icing on the cake. God did not choose David for his looks. And that is why He told Samuel, "Arise, anoint him, for this is he" (1 Sam 16:12). But why, God? Why him? Because what matters to God is the heart! And David met that qualification (Acts 13:22).

It was not until Job lost his wealth, all his children, and his own health to the point of wishing for death that he could finally say "I know that You can do all things, and that no purpose of Yours can be thwarted...Therefore I have declared that which I did not understand, things too wonderful for me, which I did not know...I have heard of You by the hearing of the ear; But now my eye sees You; Therefore I retract, And I repent in dust and ashes" (Job 42:2-6).

Carlos P. Romulo, the five-foot, four-inch former ambassador from the Philippines, was attending a reception held in Fort Worth when one of his lanky Texan hosts addressed him. "How does it feel to be in the midst of all these six-footers?"

"Like a dime among nickels," replied Romulo.[2] Romulo touched a profound truth. What matters is on the inside. If your heart is broken before God, you are ready to love God's Word, for a broken heart is a ready heart. An ancient saint grasped this concept beautifully in his prayer:

> Lord, high and holy, meek an lowly, let me learn by paradox that the way down is the way up, that to be low is to be high, that the broken heart is the healed heart, that the contrite spirit is the rejoicing spirit, that the repenting soul is the victorious soul, that to have nothing is to possess everything, that to bear the cross is to wear the crown, that to give is to receive. Let me find thy light in my darkness, thy joy in my sorrow, thy grace in my sin, thy riches in my poverty, thy glory in my valley, thy life in my death.[3]

With these three ingredients, the Holy Spirit, the Word of God, and a broken heart, your love for God's Word can grow twenty fold as you study Psalm 119 until that great day when you stand before the Author Himself.

---

2   *Readers Digest,* (July 2004), 141.
3   John MacArthur, *Hard to Believe* (Nashville: Thomas Nelson Publishers, 2003), 5.

CHAPTER

2

Four Questions for the Lover of the Word

I beseech you to let your Bibles be everything to you. Carry this matchless treasure with you continually, and read it, and read it, and read it again and again. Turn to its pages by day and by night. Let its narratives mingle with your dreams; let its precepts color your lives; let its promises cheer your darkness, let its divine illumination make glad your life. As you love God, love this Book which is the Book of God, and the God of books, as it has rightly been called; and may God make this Book to be your comfort when you pass through the valley of death-shade, and may you in heaven have for ever to praise him who revealed himself to you through the page of this blessed Book!

~ Charles Spurgeon ~

Psalm 119 stands like an oak tree among acorns compared to other chapters of the Bible when it comes to loving, living, and depending on the Word of God. An old commentator was not in error when he called it "a holy alphabet for Zion's scholars."[4]

But before we examine the soil of the massive text of Psalm 119, let's take a helicopter view of the layout of this grand chapter. As you scan the landscape, you will want to ask yourself *four questions about your love for God's Word.*

Question #1: Do I make God's Word my priority?

Just as a great painting represents a great painter, a great book reflects a great writer. So who wrote Psalm 119?

Commentators and theologians have debated this question for years. The traditional position points to David, the King of Israel. Others suggest Daniel, Ezra the priest, or even King Hezekiah. But the psalm does not provide enough evidence to make any one view absolute. While we don't know for sure who

---

4   John Richard Sampey, "Psalms" in *The International Standard Bible Encyclopedia*, vol. 4, edited by James Orr et. al. (Grand Rapids: William B. Eerdmans Publishing Company, 1939), 2492.

wrote it, we do know that the psalmist makes the Word of God his priority! Why else would he write 176 lines of Bible-exalting poetry! Every passage in this giant masterpiece discusses God's Word except for three verses (90, 121, 122). You will not find another passage in Scripture that talks so much about the Word of God.

Many have been shocked at the length of this chapter but the surprise evaporates when they see this psalmist's love for God's Word. As seven years of labor to receive Rachel seemed but a few days to Jacob (Gen 29:20), so a whole library of words from God should seem but very brief to those who love Him dearly.

Some have criticized Psalm 119 for its repetitive themes. But men who make these accusations reveal the hollowness of their own soul. They are like the scientist who studies snowflakes and concludes, "They're all the same!" and forsakes the project to spare himself boredom. But were he to look closer, he'd soon discover that out of one billion flakes, not two can be found to be exactly alike. On this Spurgeon comments, "Our author never repeats himself: though he runs up and down the same scale, his music has an infinite variety."[5]

And so it is with the Word of God. Yes, the themes are repeated again and again, but take a closer look and you will see that "each verse is a distinct pearl" as Spurgeon says. "Each blade of grass in this field has its own drop of heavenly dew."

But why does the psalmist give Scripture so much priority? Saint Augustine of Hippo answered the question 1600 years ago, "When the Bible speaks, God speaks!" When you read God's Word, you are hearing God's voice.

When Kimberly and I were engaged, we'd talk on the phone until late into the night and found it extremely difficult to end our conversation. Several times we'd fall asleep with the phone still resting on our ear until suddenly an "off the hook" beep jerked us out of slumber and we'd finally hang up. If you love someone, their words are dear to you. What would you communicate to your spouse if one day you grumbled, "When you talk to me, please keep it short, because I'm busy?" Yet we have said the same thing to God when we claim to have no time for Bible study or complain that a sermon is too long. Thomas Watson said it well:

> We give great attention to the last speeches of friends. A parent's dying words are received as oracles. Oh, let all this provoke us to diligence in hearing. Let us think, "This may be the last time that Aaron's bell shall sound in our ears and before another day is passed we may be in

---

5   Spurgeon, 257.

another world."[6]

Pulpits across America have conditioned Christians to fifteen minute sermonettes and ten minute pep talks. A sermon longer than twenty minutes breaks the attention tolerance limit. Consider the Puritans who listened attentively to preaching four to five hours straight. After the Israelites returned from Babylon and finished the construction of the new Jerusalem walls, Ezra, the priest and scribe, led them in a time of worship. Standing at a wooden podium (the first pulpit mentioned in all history; Neh 8:4!), Ezra read the Word from "early morning until midday" (Neh 8:3). That's five to six hours of reading! And the people were not sitting on cushioned chairs in air-conditioned buildings. Oh, to be so hungry for truth that you are disappointed when the sermon ends!

What are your priorities? You can rate your priorities by calculating how much time you spend on a given activity. Although time is not always an exact measurement of priority, it does reveal what you value. How much time do you spend reading the news, watching TV, working at your job, talking to your spouse or reading to your children? A man who never sees his family cannot be a family man. A man who works bare minimum hours will never be a company man. Would it be a lie if you were called a "Bible man" or "Bible woman?" Map out how you spend every hour of each day, and the answer will be clear.

Question #2: Do I put God's Word in my memory?

Noted Bible teacher, E. Schuyler English told the story of Michael Billester, a Bible distributor who visited a small hamlet in Poland shortly before World War II. Billester gave one Bible to one villager who read it and converted to Christ. The new believer gave the Book to other villagers who also repented and believed. This cycle continued until 200 people had placed their faith in Jesus Christ, all through the work of one Bible! When Billester returned in 1940, the group of new converts met together for a worship service in which he was to preach the Word. He normally asked for testimonies, but this time he requested several in the audience to recite verses of Scripture. One man stood and said, "Perhaps we have misunderstood. Did you mean verses or chapters?" These villagers had not memorized a few select verses of the Bible but whole chapters and books! Thirteen people knew Matthew, Luke, and half of Genesis, and another person had committed the entire book of Psalms to memory. These new villagers did not underestimate the value of Bible memory!

If you chose one chapter in the Bible to memorize, what would it be? Few would select Psalm 119, after all, it's 176 verses! Yet, the acrostic form of this Psalm shows that it was written to be memorized. Jews who treasured God's

6   Watson, *Heaven Taken by Storm*, 18.

Word dearly placed great emphasis on Bible memory. But how did they handle such a massive chapter?

The author of Psalm 119 penned this great masterpiece in twenty-two sections. Each section contains eight verses of poetry, and the first word of every verse begins with the same letter. For example, every verse in the first eight-verse section begins with Aleph (the first letter of the Hebrew alphabet). Every verse of the second eight-verse section begins with Beth (the second Hebrew letter) and so forth. In an English Bible you will find that each section of eight verses is entitled by a letter of the Hebrew alphabet, beginning with Aleph and ending with the last Hebrew letter, Tav. This acrostic style gave the Hebrew mind pegs on which to hang each eight verse strophe on the alphabet from their own language. Even Jewish children would memorize long sections of Scripture. Jesus, having been trained in the Mosaic Law, would have been required to memorize many Old Testament passages at a very young age.

The style of Psalm 119 has taught us an invaluable lesson. Memorization of Scripture is priceless. In verse eleven the Psalmist writes, "Your word I have treasured in my heart, that I may not sin against You" (Ps 119:11). The Hebrew word for "treasure" was used to depict someone storing away precious diamonds or jewels. God's Word is more precious than any jewel and is to be stored in our hearts so we can retrieve it at any time.

Memorizing the Bible for the sole purpose of regurgitating verses is Bible abuse. When this happens, the believer reduces Scripture to raw, cold data and Bible memory has become a means to an end. Store God's Word in your mind and you will be able to rely on it for strength, remember it for meditation, obey it for growth, and quote it for evangelizing any time, night or day. You cannot obey, think about or meditate on a passage that is not in your head. It's hard to study your Bible while stuck in traffic, writing business reports, or puffing on the treadmill. So in your study time, grab a few verses, repeat them until you know them well, and you will be equipped to carry God's Word in your heart all day long!

Question #3: Do I love God's Word dearly?

Psalm 119 is well-known for focusing on God's Word. But the point is often overlooked that this entire Psalm is a prayer! The Psalmist is not talking to the reader about the Bible, but to God about His Word. In the first three verses he uses the distant third person: "How blessed are those" (vs 1 and 2); "They also do no unrighteousness" (vs 3); "They walk in His ways" (vs 3). But suddenly in verse 4 he looks up to heaven and cries out, "You have ordained Your precepts that we should keep them diligently. Oh that my ways may be established to keep Your statutes!" (Ps 119:4-5). To think about the Word without breaking forth in prayer is unthinkable to the mind of the psalmist. A woman deeply in love with her husband does not just talk *about* him but also *to* him. Likewise, the psalmist's study of the Word moves him to break forth in ceaseless prayer and praise.

Believers who fall more in love with the Word of God than the God of the Word commit the sin of bibliolatry. Yes, it is true that if someone loves God he will love His Word. Yet at the same time, some men fall deeper in love with the discipline of study than the communion of fellowship. Studying the Book is no longer the means to know the Author but is the end itself. The Word has become their god. They have loved truth more than the Lord of truth. Refuse to separate Bible study from prayer, and you will focus on God more than His Word. Bible study fills your mind with truth and prayer expresses that truth back to God. Just as every river ends up in the sea, so every Bible study should blossom into a flood of praise and prayer. George Mueller said, "After a very few minutes [of meditating on God's Word] my soul has been led to confession, or to thanksgiving, or to intercession, or to supplication." *That* is the purpose of God's Word!

A lady attended a Scottish church and enjoyed it thoroughly. After inquiring who the preacher was, she was told it was Mr. Ebenezer Erskine. So when next Sunday arrived, she was off to hear Mr. Ebenezer Erskine. But the service was dull and drab and she did not enjoy it at all. After the service ended she told Mr. Erskine of her experiences these last two Sundays. He responded, "Ah! Madam, the first Sabbath you came to meet the Lord Jesus Christ, and you had a blessing; but the second Sabbath you came to hear Ebenezer Erskine, and you had no blessing and you had no right to expect any."[7] When you listen to the Word what are you listening for? Only more Bible facts? Or do you listen to hear its Author?

God talks to you through Scripture, and through prayer you talk to Him. How long would a relationship last if you only listened and never responded? The psalmist is not content to talk abstractly about God's Word. He prays it with fervency and passion. Studying the Word will not only increase your prayers, but it will also guide them. In the words of E. M. Bounds, "Prayer exalts the Word of God and gives it preeminence in those who faithfully and wholeheartedly call upon the name of the Lord." He continues:

> Prayer invariably generates a love for the Word of God. Prayer leads people to obey the Word of God and puts into the obedient heart a joy unspeakable. Praying people and Bible-reading people are the same sort of folk. The God of the Bible and the God of prayer are one. God

---

7   Charles Spurgeon, *Lectures to My Students* (Grand Rapids: Zondervan Publishing House, 1954), 405.

speaks to man in the Bible; man speaks to God in prayer. One reads the Bible to discover God's will. He prays in order to receive power to do that will. Bible reading and praying are the distinguishing traits of those who strive to know and please God. [8]

The Word will correct your thinking about yourself, other Christians, the world, and most importantly the God to Whom you pray. How could anyone expect to understand the answer he receives from God if he does not discern how He thinks, what He wants, or Who He is?

Years ago, when I pastored high school students, I discovered that a common prayer request was for their grades. Now what would happen if the student spent his study time selling doughnuts instead of taking classes? When the college asks for his transcript and finds instead of high school courses, "sold doughnuts for three years," how would the enrollment officer respond?

"Yes, but I sold big fat donuts filled with jelly, and others with little crunchy white sprinkles all over the top!" The student would be laughed off the campus. He did not understand what the college wanted, and therefore he could not receive from the college what he desired. In the same way, you must understand God if you want to pray in His will so that you may receive what you ask for (John 14:13; 1 John 3:22).

Dick Eastman, a man who committed one hour every day of his adult life to the discipline of prayer, said this: "Our prayer time, no matter how intense, is never truly complete without the divine nourishment available only from God's Word."[9] God delights in hearing us remind Him of His own Word, and it gives our prayers content, purpose, and biblical direction. Those who are full of God's Word will be moved to far more conversation with God than those who rarely study it. Many have said that familiarity breeds contempt. Although often true of people, it works conversely with God's Word. Like salt water, the Word leaves you wanting more and like fresh water it satisfies your thirst. Spurgeon said that John Bunyan was so full of the Bible that if you cut him he'd bleed Bible verses. May our prayers be the same.

Question #4: Do I face God's person seriously?

The world's fastest reader, Paul Scheele, reads 200,000 words per minute. At 300 words a page that's 666 words a minute, eleven pages a second. His reading comprehension is so impressive that people ask him, "Do you know the author?" We should know God's Word so well that people ask us the same question when we talk about the Bible. It's one thing to know a book. It's another

---

8   E. M. Bounds, The Necessity of Prayer in *E. M. Bounds on Prayer*, book two (New Kensington: Whitaker House, 1997), 181.

9   Dick Eastman, *The Hour That Changes the World* (Grand Rapids: Baker Books, 1999), 55.

to know the Author of the book.

The psalmist of Psalm 119 does not let the Book eclipse the Author. He uses no fewer than eight different Hebrew words to describe God's Word. Translated into English, he calls it God's law, testimonies, ways, precepts, statutes, commandments, judgments/ordinances, and word. That's one imposing list! But why does the psalmist use eight different terms to say the same thing? *Because the psalmist wants to express the full depth and breadth of God's revelation.*

THE EIGHT WORDS USED FOR SCRIPTURE IN PSALM 119

ENGLISH TERM	HEBREW TERM	MEANING	EMPHASIS
Law	*Torah*	From a root meaning *to instruct* or *to teach.*	God's standard of perfect righteousness. Often refers to the entire body of Scripture from Genesis to Deuteronomy.
Testimonies	*Eduth* or *Edah*	To *testify* or *give witness of.*	God's Word testifies of his attributes and acts. Highlights God's perfect reputation.
Ways	*Derek*	*Ways* or *paths.*	Points to God's ways which are always perfect.
Precepts	*Piqqud*	General term for *command.*	Underscores God's authority and right to tell His creation what to do.
Statutes	*Choq*	Usually refers to a *specific order* or *prescribed task.*	Emphasizes God's precision and the boundaries He gives.
Commandments	*Mitsvah*	*Give charge* or *take command.* The Jewish "Bar-Mitzvah" comes from this word	Almost synonymous with precepts and statutes
Judgments/ Ordinances	*Mishpat*	To *judge* or *govern.*	Accents God's right to rule and judge the world.
Word	*Imrah* or *Dabar*	What God *says.*	Paints the picture of God as the speaker.

This graph categorizes the different lexical nuances of these eight terms but as with all words in Scripture, the immediate context of each word's usage will determine its final meaning.

These words together communicate one all-encompassing theme: The revelation of God. When we read God's Word we are reading God's revelation of Himself, His person, His acts, and His character. The telescope through which we can see God above and the kingdom in which He dwells, is the Word of God. It shows us God's redemptive plan of salvation through Jesus Christ His Son. The Bible makes the reality of heaven above a knowable truth on earth.

No doubt these eight different terms decorate the psalm with poetical variety. And it is also true that each word carries a different nuance as seen in the graph above. Yet, these eight terms are intermingled so that only the context will determine their individual meanings.

We may consider ourselves "biblical Christians." We may learn our Bible verses, study our lessons, and shout "amens" when good sermons are preached.

But we must beware lest we find ourselves in the quandary of an ancient ruler whose wife died. Broken in tears, he decided to honor her death by constructing a gorgeous house in which to place her corpse. Pouring countless hours and money into this project, he built a structure that made the most elegant buildings look like shacks. But one day as he ambled through the future home of his wife's corpse, he tripped over a large box sitting in the middle of the room. Kicking it he yelled, "Get this out of here!" To his great chagrin, it was too late when he realized that the box contained the body of his own wife.

Sometimes the believer can get so bogged down in the study that he grows blind to the big picture. If we ravenously study the Bible for increased knowledge alone, pursuing a self-image of Scriptural intelligence, we can easily forget the purpose behind it all: to know its Author.

God gives you His Word to confront you with His person. If the Book becomes more valuable to you than its author, you have traded pearls for plastic. Take warning lest you treat God's Word like a textbook until it no longer touches your heart or brings you into contact with the Author. Do not forget that the *Word* is the *Word of God*. God originated it, God wrote it, and God gave it to you so that you may know Him. Do not separate the Word from the writer of the Word. The demons know it well, and yet they hate God fiercely (James 2:19). **The Word of God was given to you so that you may know the God of the Word.**

As for us, we cast anchor in the haven of the word of God. Here is our peace, our strength, our life, our motive, our hope, our happiness. God's Word is our ultimatum. Here we have it. Our understanding cries, "I have found it;" our conscience asserts that here is the truth; and our heart finds here a support to which all her affections can cling; and hence we rest content.
~ Charles Spurgeon ~

PART TWO:

SEVEN STRATEGIES FOR SLAYING BIBLE APATHY

Embark on God's Word as the Path to Knowing God
Psalm 119:1-8, 57-64, 113-120, 137-144

Many roads crisscross the state of Texas, but only one led to our home. It was called Old Paris Road. Twenty minutes of driving over jarring bumps and maneuvering around pot holes and you'd be there. The road was so bad you'd think the road service company went out of business during the Great Depression. Nevertheless, it was the only way home. In the same way God has given us a map to His kingdom. This map has but one road and one destination. It is not an easy road. It is checkered with painful trials and high standards. But it is the only way because it is the Word of God.

You will find many other maps in this world—Watchtower Publications, the Book of Mormon, the Holy Koran and Rabbinic Traditions. But in the end, these writings will not withstand the test of fire. Their ashes will be a screaming testimony that they were mere concoctions devised in the mind of Satan to lead many astray. And they hold one thing in common: all who follow them will end up in the same lake of fire. John Macarthur writes:

> Scripture is comprehensive, containing everything necessary for one's spiritual life. Scripture is surer than a human experience that one may look to in proving God's power and presence. Scripture contains divine principles that are the best guide for character and conduct. Scripture is lucid rather than mystifying so that it enlightens the eyes. Scripture is void of any flaws and therefore lasts forever. Scripture is true regarding all things that matter, making it capable of producing comprehensive righteousness. Because it meets every need in life, Scripture is infinitely more precious than any solutions this world has to offer.[1]

The psalmist of Psalm 119 fills page after page with admiration for God's Word because he knows that the only path to knowing God is through His

---

1   John MacArthur, "The Sufficiency of Scripture" in The Master's Seminary Journal, 15:2 (2004):15.

Word. In this first strategy we will discover how to be a lover of the Word (119:1-8), what a Bible zealot looks like (119:113-120), and how to experience the Word (119:137-144).

3

How to Be a Lover of the Word
Psalm 119:1-8

The year was A.D. 303 and Roman emperor, Diocletian, issued a decree which he hoped would extinguish the spreading flames of Christianity. One of his primary objectives was the seizure and destruction of the Christian Scriptures. Later that year, officials enforced the decree in North Africa, targeting Felix, Bishop of Tibjuca (a village near Carthage). The mayor of this town ordered Felix to hand over his Scriptures. But Felix refused to surrender the Word of God at the insistence of men. Roman authorities finally shipped Felix to Italy where he paid for his stubbornness with his life. On August 30, as the record states, "with pious obstinacy" he laid down his life rather than surrender his Gospels.[1]

When a man gives his life for the Word, he has passed the ultimate test of true love. To die for something is to sacrifice for a thing worth more to him than his own life. (John 15:13)

Ask a thousand Americans and statistically nine hundred of them will tell you that they have a Bible, but less than half of them ever take it off the shelf.[2] What good is a Bible if you don't know how to use it? The Bible was not made to fill a spot on your shelf or to collect dust. It was made to sanctify and purify you, the believer. As Howard Hendricks said, "Dusty Bibles always lead to dirty lives."[3]

We need churches filled with men and women madly devoted to the Word of God. Until we are lovers of the Book we will never be a people of God. And if we are not a people of God, our lives will be futile and end in dark disappointment.

What does the believer who loves God's Word look like? No place in the Bible answers this question better than the first eight verses of Psalm 119. From

---

1   Bruce L. Shelley, *Christian Theology in Plain Language* (Nashville: Word Publishing, 1985), 41.
2   ChristianityToday.com, http://www.christianitytoday.com/tcw/6w6/6w6114.html, July 19, 2005.
3   Howard G. Hendricks and William D. Hendricks, *Living By the Book* (Chicago: Moody Press, 1991), 9.

this passage we find four actions which can move us toward becoming lovers of the Word. To be a lover of the Word you must...

1. Walk as a believer of the Word with devotion (vss 1-3).

> HOW BLESSED ARE THOSE WHOSE WAY IS BLAMELESS, WHO WALK IN THE LAW OF THE LORD. HOW BLESSED ARE THOSE WHO OBSERVE HIS TESTIMONIES, WHO SEEK HIM WITH ALL THEIR HEART. THEY ALSO DO NO UNRIGHTEOUSNESS; THEY WALK IN HIS WAYS (119:1-3).

The psalmist opens this masterpiece with the words "How blessed!" He repeats it again in verse 2. The most basic meaning of this Hebrew word is "happy." The psalmist says, "How happy are those who live blameless lives in obedience to God's law!"

When Leah's maid, Zilpah, gave birth to her second little boy, Leah shouted, "'Happy am I! For women will call me happy.' So she named him Asher." (Gen 30:13). The word "Asher" is the same word used in the first two verses of Psalm 119. When Leah named her son "Asher" she named him the "happy one." A blessed man is a happy man.

But the psalmist calls those who keep God's law "happy" for another reason. It's because they keep the Word of God! Show me a miserable Christian and I'll show you a Christian who does not obey God's Word. Bible-obeying people are happy people.

• Paul was a Bible-obeying man. And what did he say three times while sitting in a slimy dungeon? *Rejoice!* (Phil 1:18; 3:1; 4:4).

• After enduring a beating with rods and being chained in shackles, what did Paul and Silas do? *They sang!* (Acts 16:25).

• Jeremiah preached among wicked Jews who threw him in a pit of mud and rejected God's commands. He lived in a world that had turned against God's law and yet, in spite of their rampant wickedness, he could say with conviction: "Your words were found and I ate them, and Your words became for me a *joy* and the *delight of my heart*" (Jer 15:16).

Why are Bible obeying people happy people? Because they live in the will of God! The source of all joy is the Creator (1 Ch 16:27; Ne 12:43; Ps 16:11; 43:4; Gal 5:22; 1 Thess 1:16), and therefore the only way to live a life of true joy is when you are living in a way that pleases Him. As preacher and author, Dr. Jack Hughes once said, "Don't be a grumpy Gestapo, weaned on a dill pickle who says, 'I worship in the solemn assembly.'" There's nothing spiritual about looking like a weeping willow.

How can you identify a happy Christian who walks as a believer of the Word? The Psalmist answers this question. The one who walks as a believer of the Word is:

- *Blameless in reputation*

The psalmist says the happy, blessed man is one "whose way is blameless" (1:1). "Blameless" does not mean perfect. The Bible calls many men "blameless" (Gen 6:9; Job 1:1) and yet no man is sinless (Gen 6:5). In this case, a blameless person does not have a gross defaming character trait. His reputation is not spoiled by some heinous sin or habitual indulgence.

It is commonly said, "Where there is smoke, there is usually fire." Gene Getz has written, "If there is smoke of sin in your life then you need to ask yourself where it's coming from."[4] Throw heaps of water on the fire of your sin before it grows into an enormous blaze.

- *Active in obedience*

The psalmist goes on to say that happy people are those who walk "in the law of the Lord" (1:1). The happy man does not just talk about the Word, he lives it. Beware lest you grow better at talking about the Word than obeying it. Your talk may convince humans, but it won't convince God. Talking about God's Word does not impress God. He's looking for doers. The apostle John writes "Little children, let us not love with word or with tongue, but in deed and truth" (1 John 3:18). James, the brother of our Lord, pens the following:

> Therefore, putting aside all filthiness and all that remains of wickedness, in humility receive the word implanted, which is able to save your souls. But prove yourselves doers of the word, and not merely hearers who delude themselves. For if anyone is a hearer of the word and not a doer, he is like a man who looks at his natural face in a mirror; for once he has looked at himself and gone away, he has immediately forgotten what kind of person he was. But one who looks intently at the perfect law, the law of liberty, and abides by it, not having become a forgetful hearer but an effectual doer, this man will be blessed in what he does (James 1:22-25).

In Psalm 119, skip down to verse three and you find the same theme. The psalmist describes those happy people who love God's Word as those who "do no unrighteousness" (119:3). Once again, this does not mean sinlessness, for Solomon himself said, "There is no man who does not sin" (1 Kings 8:46).

The term "unrighteousness" here means "evil." The believer who truly

---

4   Gene Getz, *Elders and Leaders* (Chicago: Moody, 2003), 142.

believes in God's Word does not commit intentional evil acts. He is an upright godly person.

- *Protective of Scripture*

Blessed people also "observe His testimonies" (1:2). This word "observe" is the same word used of a watchman who guards the city by keeping on the lookout. He guards and protects.

Do you protect that which is valuable to you? I doubt you put your DVD players on the back porch, or leave your wallet on the front steps of your house. If you live in a big city like Los Angeles you lock your car.

Ever since the law was first given to Moses at Mt. Sinai, Satan has attacked God's Word through deceiving doctrines that sound good and scholarly. The Pelagians ignored man's depravity. The liberals attacked inspiration. Some charismatics twisted the ministry of the Holy Spirit. The Open Theists attacked God's omniscience. And now the New Perspectives are attacking the cross.

Too often we more ardently protect our perishable earthly belongings than the eternal, precious words of God's truth. One month ago I met a lady who went to a Texaco gas station to purchase gas. The worker at the station swiped her credit card through a tracker device and stole the number on the card. By the time she left, he had pulled $5,000 from her account. She was outraged. But would you be as upset if it was someone contradicting the clear teaching of Scripture? Would you pull out the sword of God's Word and fight for its truth—even at the cost of your own life?

- *Superlative in devotion*

The psalmist describes these happy people as those "who seek Him with all their heart" (119:2). The term "heart" is a very broad term in the Old and New Testaments. "Heart" does not just mean your affections. It does not just mean your will. It does not just mean your loyalty. Nor does it just mean your imagination, your purpose, your understanding, your mind, or your ability. It means all of the above.

Do you seek God with all your heart? No Christian can seek God more until he loves himself less. It means that all that is dear to you will be of infinitely less worth to you than God Himself. It means that you will be able to say with Jerome, "If my parents should persuade me to deny Christ, if my wife should go to charm me with her embraces, I would forsake all and flee to Christ."[5]

---

5   Watson, 93.

2. Embrace the purpose of the Word with conviction (vss 4-5).

YOU HAVE ORDAINED YOUR PRECEPTS
THAT WE SHOULD KEEP THEM DILIGENTLY (119:4).

At first glance this point looks very similar to the first, but there is a significant difference. The first point dealt with walking in obedience to the Word while the second deals with understanding the purpose of the Word. The faith of many has been shipwrecked on the reef of misunderstanding why God's Word was given to us. And here the psalmist gives us the purpose of God's Word. God has "ordained" (commanded) His precepts, that we should keep them diligently.

A. W. Tozer recalls a passage in the Hindu writings which said, "You who are busy learning texts and not living them are like the man counting other people's cattle without having a single heifer of his own."[6] Likewise, what benefit is there in learning God's Word with no intention of embracing its commands? He who loves God's Word will keep it. Study the Word, read the Word, memorize the Word, sing the Word and listen to the Word all you want, but until it is kept, you have prostituted its purpose. Now watch what the psalmist does in verse 5:

OH THAT MY WAYS MAY BE ESTABLISHED TO
KEEP YOUR STATUTES! (119:5)

Here he turns from discussing the need for God's Word to be kept, to a personal cry that God would strengthen him to keep it. He has moved from the distant third person in verses 1-4 to the personal second person in verses 5-6. His words become a prayer to God, revealing his deep desire to keep and obey God's precious Word.

The psalmist is not one who spouts the theological truth that we need God but feels nothing. Instead he craves the Word of God and hungers for its strength. His cry for help is real and genuine because he knows his weakness.

3. Receive the blessings of the Word with thanksgiving (vss 6-7).

THEN I SHALL NOT BE ASHAMED WHEN I LOOK UPON
ALL YOUR COMMANDMENTS. I SHALL GIVE THANKS TO YOU
WITH UPRIGHTNESS OF HEART, WHEN I LEARN
YOUR RIGHTEOUS JUDGMENTS (119:6-7).

Obedience always produces blessing. Let this motivate you in the face of your next temptation. Verse 6 illustrates the blessing of no more shame. "Then...after I have walked as a believer of the Word and embraced the purpose of the word,

---

6   A. W. Tozer, *Essays on Spiritual Perfection* in *The Tozer Pulpit*, vol. 1, edited and compiled by Gerald B. Smith (Camp Hill: Christian Publications), 39.

then...I shall not be ashamed!"

The Word illumines the inner crevices of the sinner's heart, revealing its dark motives and evil crafts, moving the sinner to run away and ignore his guilt or to repent and be forgiven (James 1:23-24; 1 John 1:9). Every time you read God's Word, you have the option to let it convict you and change you, or to forget your condition and return to your wickedness. Obedience to God's Word never fails to erase shame and yield great confidence.

The blessing is not only removed shame but also deep thanksgiving, as the psalmist says in verse 7. When a believer walks in the Word and embraces the purpose of the Word, shame not only disappears but a heart of thanksgiving overflows. And this heart is not fake, nor shallow, but "upright" (vs 7). In the original language, "upright" means literally to be "smooth" or "straight." Notice that this thanksgiving is a result of learning God's "righteous judgments"(vs 7). All of God's orders and all His decrees are perfectly righteous, without spot. Does your heart overflow with thanksgiving when you learn God's orders and decrees?

William Cooper once read of a godly man who sat looking up to heaven with tears in his eyes. "Why are you crying?" a bypasser asked.

He answered, "I admire the Lord's mercy to me, that He did not make me a toad." The bypasser looked down to see a toad sitting at his feet."[7] How much more reason do we have to give thanks when we consider our food, water, house, clothing, church, the Word, and even our salvation!

4. Ask God to help you obey the Word with resolve (vs 8).

I SHALL KEEP YOUR STATUTES (119:8A).

Many have come to God's Word, listened to what it teaches, understood what it meant, seen their own condition of sin, even agreed that they need to change, and then walked away with no resolve to obey. But consider the words of Joshua to Israel as he stood on the brink of his own death: "Choose for yourselves today whom you will serve" (Josh 24:15). Many men and women are afraid to make a solid and complete decision. They hate the stigma that comes with denying God, yet they fear the cost of completely choosing to follow God. They are mortified at the thought of being thoroughly wicked or thoroughly Christlike. So they choose the middle road, just godly enough to feel good but just sinful enough so that they don't have to forsake their favorite sins.

Christ rebuked people of this stock in the church of Laodicea: "I know your deeds, that you are neither cold nor hot; "I wish that you were cold or hot. So because you are lukewarm, and neither hot nor cold, I will spit you out of

---

[7]   William Cooper, "Why All Should be Thankful," *Free Grace Broadcaster*, 3.

My mouth" (Rev 3:15-16).

It is not God's desire for you to live a life of mediocrity. "Mediocre" literally means "halfway to the peak." It illustrates the climber who makes it halfway up the mountain and then gives up. Choose today whether you will camp your tent in the valley of sin or build your fortress on the mountain of God's Word, but don't be content to live somewhere in between. Drop to your knees and ask God, "Am I willing to follow You with a whole heart? What is it in my life that I can't stand the thought of forsaking?" Allow Him to show you. And then ask God for strength to follow Him with a whole heart, and He will grant it abundantly, for His grace is sufficient (2 Cor 12:9).

We come to the Psalmist's final words in this section:

DO NOT FORSAKE ME UTTERLY (119:8B)

Why would the psalmist say this? Does he not know the great faithfulness of God? Does he not understand the infinite mercy of God's compassion? Yes, he does, but he also faces two other truths: his weakness and God's justice. The psalmist knows that he is weak and therefore only God can help him to keep God's Word; he also knows that he is sinful and therefore God has the full right to forsake him forever.

Every true believer feels forsaken by God at times when he sins. He may be under great pressure to compromise and does not sense God's strength or when he is tormented by great trials, he cannot see God's right arm of help. But God never forsakes His children.

If the psalmist is too weak to obey and too sinful to be accepted by God, then why does he cry out to God? Because he knows that God is both strong and gracious—strong enough to help him keep the Word and gracious enough to forgive him of all his trespasses.

In this chapter we looked at four ways to become a true lover of God's Word:

1) Walk as a believer of the Word (vss 1-3).
2) Embrace the purpose of the Word (vss 4-5).
3) Receive the blessings of the Word (vss 6-7).
4) Resolve to keep the Word (vs 8).

A general prepared for battle against a powerful enemy. The messenger boy entered his tent. "Messenger boy, what's the news?"

"It's bad news, sir!" said the messenger.

"Well, tell me quickly," replied the general.

"The enemy, sir. We have only 10,000 men. They have 20,000."

"Very well," responded the general with confidence, "then we shall double our efforts against them and win!" But before he finished speaking another messenger boy entered the tent, panting heavily.

"General," gasped the new messenger boy. "The news is worse."

"Why, tell me," urged the general.

"We were wrong in our first report. We have only 10,000 men but the enemy has 30,000!"

"Very well then, we shall triple our efforts and have the victory!" answered the general with determination. But before he finished speaking yet another messenger boy entered.

"General, the news is yet worse."

"Well, what this time?" asked the general.

"We have only 10,000 men but the enemy is marching 40,000 men against our camp at this very moment."

"Aha!" said the general. "Then we shall get on our knees and ask the LORD of hosts for strength to win!"

And that is exactly what you must ask of the Lord so that you may be a lover of His Word. Ask Him for victory and He will not turn His shoulder (1 Cor 10:12; 2 Pet 1:3).

QUESTIONS FOR CONTEMPLATION

1. What do these verses teach you about those who are blessed?

2. What is the psalmist's heart desire? What does he pray for?

3. In one sentence, write the theme of this passage (be more specific than "The Word"!)

4. According to vss 5-6, when and why will the psalmist not be ashamed?

5. How does the psalmist respond when he learns of God's righteous judgments in verse 7?

6. Why do you think he ends this section by crying out: "Do not forsake me utterly!"?

7. How has this passage influenced your thought life? Be specific.

4

The Bible Zealot
Psalm 119:113-120

Of all the people feared in New Testament times, few were dreaded more than the "knife men." A knife man would subtly enter a crowd with a dagger beneath his cloak, softly make his way toward a prominent Roman collaborator, and suddenly plunge the blade into the man before quickly disappearing back into the swarm.[1]

These men were called zealots because of their great zeal for political freedom from Rome. It was a zeal driven by bitter hatred and political fanaticism. But there is a different kind of zealot. He is not a political extremist. No, this man's zeal burns from above. He is a zealot for God. J. C. Ryle describes him well:

> Zeal in religion is a burning desire to please God, to do His will and to advance His glory in the world in every possible way. It is a desire which no man feels by nature—which the Spirit puts in the heart of every believer when he is converted—but which some believers feel so much more strongly than others that they alone deserve to be called "zealous" men...
>
> A zealous man in religion is preeminently a man of one thing. It is not enough to say that he is earnest, hearty, uncompromising, thorough going, whole-hearted, fervent in spirit. He only sees one thing, he cares for one thing, he lives for one thing, he is swallowed up in one thing; and that one thing is to please God.
>
> Whether he lives, or whether he dies—whether he has health, or whether he has sickness—whether he is rich, or whether he is poor— whether he pleases man, or whether he gives offense—whether he is

---

1   Everett Ferguson, *Backgrounds of Early Christianity* (Grand Rapids: William B. Eerdmans Publishing Company, 2003), 532.

thought wise, or whether he is thought foolish—whether he gets blame, or whether he gets praise—whether he gets honor, or whether he gets shame—for all this the zealous man cares nothing at all.

He burns for one thing; and that one thing is to please God, and to advance God's glory. If he is consumed in the very burning, he cares not for it—he is content. He feels that, like a lamp, he is made to burn; and if consumed in burning, he has but done the work for which God appointed him. Such a one will always find a sphere. If he cannot work, and give money, he will cry and sigh and pray...If he cannot fight in the valley with Joshua, he will do the work of Moses, Aaron, and Hur on the hill (Ex 17:9-13). If he is cut off from working himself, he will give the Lord no rest till help is raised up from another quarter, and the work is done. This is what I mean when I speak of "zeal" in religion.

Zeal is not a character trait you are born with. It's a choice. Zeal comes from the will, and will grows from convictions forged in the house of God's Word. You can choose to be a deflated balloon of apathy. Or you can be zealous—zealous for God and His Word.

But what does that look like? Here are three sketches of a Bible zealot.

1. A Bible zealot deeply desires God's holiness (vss 113, 115, 118, 119).

> I HATE THOSE WHO ARE DOUBLE-MINDED,
> BUT I LOVE YOUR LAW (119:113).

The psalmist leaves no room for partial emotion. His holy hatred toward the hypocrites burns as hot as his love for God's precious law. The term "double-minded" means to have a divided mind—a mind that lives two lives at odds with one another. It is the person whose hands and mouth live in contradiction.

But why would the psalmist hate the hypocrites? Does this not contradict Christ's instructions in Matthew 5:43-44, "You have heard that it was said, 'You shall love your neighbor and hate your enemy. But I say to you, love your enemies and pray for those who persecute you...'"?

Two things we know for sure: Godly men love their enemies, (Matt 5:43-44) and godly men hate those who hate God (Ps 139:21-22).

This apparent contradiction is no more incongruous than man's accountability to be saved (Acts 17:30), even though he cannot and will not seek God unless God first seeks him (John 6:65; Acts 13:48; Rom 3:10-18). Righteous hatred for those who hate God is not a personally-motivated, vindictive, bitter hatred. It is a holy hatred. It is a hatred motivated by love towards God. It is no less just than the cry of the martyrs for God's vengeance upon their persecutors in Revelation 6:10. If someone attacked your three year old child, would you stand by and say, "I'm supposed to love you so do what you want and when you're finished I'll give you the gospel"?

If you love your child, you will defend him, even to the point of inflicting harm upon the attacker to stop him, powered by every cell in your body, until your child is safe. That's holy hatred. What motivated you to attack this assailant? Your love for your child. As one author says, "To see evil and not be alarmed by it is a sign that there is something terribly wrong with us."[2]

Revenge towards those who offend, persecute or inconvenience you is not holy hatred. Holy hatred is always driven by zeal—not for personal pride, but for God's glory. You cannot say "I love God" and not be offended when someone shames Him with a double-life.

But when Christ said "Love your enemies" (Matt 5:44), He was addressing Jews who looked down upon anyone who was not of their faith. The Jews had more than discriminated against the Gentiles—they treated them with disgust. There was nothing holy about it. They refused to walk through Samaria, the nation of half-Jews, even if it greatly inconvenienced them (John 4:4,9). It was not holy hatred, but arrogant pride. Paul speaks of this hatred in Titus 3:3, "For we also once were foolish ourselves, disobedient, deceived, enslaved to various lusts and pleasures, spending our life in malice and envy, hateful, hating one another."

Claiming love for God and yet feeling no righteous anger when sinners blaspheme His name is as double-minded as the hypocrites in this psalm. It would be more ludicrous than a soldier who fights for the enemy while wearing the uniform of his country, or a treasure collector who serves tea to a pack of thieves while they rob his riches. William Cooper writes:

> He that loves a tree, hates the worm that consumes it; he that loves a garment, hates the moth that eats it; he that loveth life, abhorreth death; and he that loves the Lord hates every thing that offends him. Let men take heed to this, who are in love [with] their sins: how can the love of God be in them?[3]

But note that the psalmist is not just opposed to those who hate God, but to those who claim to love God and live the opposite. A man who loves God with his mouth but hates him with his deeds is worse than someone who lives in open rebellion.

Christ reserved his most flaming rebukes for the Pharisees, whom he called blind guides, fools, blind men, white-washed tombs, serpents, and a brood of

2   *Hard Sayings of the Bible,* editors Walter C. Kaiser Jr., Peter H. Davids, F. F. Bruce, and Manfred T. Brauch (Downers Grove: InterVarsity Press, 1996), 282.
3   William Cooper Quoted by Spurgeon, *Treasury,* 377.

vipers (Matt 23:13-36). Is that holy hatred? Without a doubt. The same Pharisees He died for out of divine love (John 3:16), He also hated for their hypocrisy. As Solomon writes, there is a "time to love and a time to hate" (Eccl 3:8).

Here is a summary of the differences between sinful and godly hatred.

Sinful hatred is:
- Motivated by one's own pride. "I will get you back because you hurt me."
- Self-centered and godless. God's holiness, God's justice, and God's righteousness are not regarded. Instead of calling out to God for His justice, the offended wants his own justice.

But godly hatred is always:
- Motivated by zeal for God's holiness. It is really the fruit of his own love for God.
- Offended only because God was offended. The concern is for God's glory, not his own.
- Concerned not for his vindication but for God's vindication.
- God-centered. It seeks God's will and God's glory in the matter. The believer moved by godly hate refuses to take the account into his own hands.

A great example of this is King David. David, the very man who cried out, "Do I not hate those who hate You, O LORD? And do I not loathe those who rise up against you?" (Ps 139:21) is the man who refused to avenge Saul over and over again (1 Sam 24, 26). And even at Saul's death, instead of rejoicing in the fall of his enemy (Prov 24:17-18), he wrote him a beautiful eulogy (2 Sam 1:17-27), and cut down an Amalekite for lying about killing "the Lord's anointed" (2 Sam 1:14-16).

DEPART FROM ME, EVILDOERS, THAT I MAY OBSERVE THE COMMANDMENTS OF MY GOD (119:115).

These evildoers are a distraction to the psalmist's obedience. The psalmist wants nothing to do with their evil ways so he can fully focus upon keeping the commandments of his God. By calling God "my God" he makes it clear that his God is different from the god of these evildoers.

The psalmist's zeal is so great that he will keep no company with anything that comes between him and his God. He knew the company he kept would shape his convictions and influence his actions. Even the most impervious man will be influenced by those he spends time with, thus godly company is imperative for godly living.

Few things are more precious than a true friend who cherishes the Word you cherish and worships the God you worship. It is the friend to whom you can confess your sins and ask for prayer. It is the friend you can trust with even the most sensitive information. When he stumbles, this friend will welcome your rebuke and return it likewise when you stumble. It is the friend who "sticks closer than a brother" (Prov 18:24).

Notice that the psalmist is most urgent in removing anything that may distract him from obeying God's Word. He does not tell the ungodly to depart because they make him uncomfortable or do not suit his tastes. No, he sees them as a threat to his own faithfulness, a distraction from his commitment to honor God. George Swinnock wrote,

> When David would marry himself to God's commands, to love them, and live with them, for better for worse, all his days, he is forced to give a bill of divorce to wicked companions, knowing that otherwise the match could never be made.[4]

We should be as John the Apostle who bolted from the bath house the moment he realized that the false teacher Cerinthus was inside. As believers we are called to remove anything that threatens our obedience to God. This could be as simple as interruptions to your study of the Word. Satan will use every tool possible to turn your eyes away from the Word of God. W. E. Sangster of Westminster Central Hall in London understood this danger when people repeatedly entered his office and distracted him from his sermon preparation. He devised an ingenious method of dealing with distractions. In the words of Stephen Olford:

> He made such occasions an opportunity for trying out his sermon. After the initial introductions and pleasantries, Dr. Sangster would say something like this: "My dear friends, I am so excited about Sunday's sermon that I must share some of the thoughts and blessings that God has given to me." And with that opening statement he would launch right into a full discourse![5]

YOU HAVE REJECTED ALL THOSE WHO WANDER FROM YOUR STATUTES, FOR THEIR DECEITFULNESS IS USELESS (119:118).

Just as there can be no law without consequences, there can be no holiness without wrath. The psalmist exalts God's justice and holds it forth like a lamp in the night that all may see His righteousness. When God rejects those who reject Him, He gives them exactly what they have requested. They have signed their name to the document of rebellion and now God delivers the consequences in

---

4   George Swinnock quoted by Spurgeon, 362.
5   Stephen Olford, *Anointed Expository Preaching* (Nashville: Broadman and Holman, 1998), 63.

full.

This word "useless" comes from a word that means to "deal treacherously with." The ungodly delight in deceiving others and leading them away from God's law. This is the epitome of treachery. A more wicked deed could not be done than to lead others away from the God of the universe and into open rebellion that will result in their eternal damnation. In Christ's own words, "But whoever causes one of these little ones who believe in Me to stumble, it would be better for him to have a heavy millstone hung around his neck, and to be drowned in the depth of the sea" (Matt 18:6; cf. James 5:20).

You can almost smell the smoke of God's wrath as the psalmist burns with God's indignation. He is so close to God that you will never find him asking the question, "God, if you are a loving God, how could You punish sinners?" No. He understands God's holiness and knows that this in no way contradicts His undying love. The sign of a mature Christian is one who can "amen" both God's unfailing love and His fierce wrath.

YOU HAVE REMOVED ALL THE WICKED OF THE EARTH LIKE DROSS; THEREFORE I LOVE YOUR TESTIMONIES (119:119).

The psalmist's sense of God's holiness has not waned in this verse. The wicked are to the earth like dross is to silver: impure, worthless, and poisonous. The earth is polluted by the presence of the wicked, but God will burn them out like dross melts from silver.

The psalmist speaks with a prophetic tone, as if the removal of the wicked has already been done. He is so sure of God's judgment upon the wicked that he speaks as if it were a past event. This passage finds its final fulfillment in Christ's second coming when unbelievers' corpses will spread so far and wide that God's angel will call out to all vultures for a giant feast (Rev 19:17-19). It is for this reason that the psalmist loves God's testimonies. He loves them for they uphold what is clean and disdain all filth.

2. A Bible zealot rests in God's protection (vss 114, 116, 117).

To "rest" doesn't sound very zealous. And the political zealot of the New Testament would applaud this objection—but not the Bible zealot. No believer is zealous who is not also utterly dependent on His God.

YOU ARE MY HIDING PLACE AND MY SHIELD; I WAIT FOR YOUR WORD (119:114).

Hiding places were very important in the psalmist's day. When an enemy gained victory, the only alternatives were death or to escape to a hiding place.

But the psalmist did not need to run from his persecutors. The Lord was his hiding place. King David testified that no matter where he went, God was ever present (Ps 139:7-9). That's a horrific thought if you are God's enemy. But for those who love and honor God, it is true comfort. God is our hiding place of safety and our shield of protection.

In the psalmist's day, shields were as important as hiding places. Archaeology confirms that some armies rode their chariots with three men: one drove the chariot, one held a bow with arrows, and the third grasped a shield which was used to protect his two companions. Fighting without a shield in the psalmist's day would be as mindless as welding metal without protection goggles today.

Often, the believer will try to find solace in his sin and comfort in his vices. Under the moment of trial he will often flee to his own lusts and would rather put on the chains of sin, with which he has grown far too intimate, than find refuge under the wing of God. He thinks that by yielding to his sinful desires, he may find a balm that soothes the wounds of life. Though this hiding place looks like a warm house of comfort and reprieve, he will soon discover that it is a pit of pythons filled with dead men's bones.

Satan offers the believer hiding places with friendly titles and inviting doorways. But inside, the believer will become a target for his flaming darts. He finds destruction if he seeks refuge in anything but God.

It is often harder to stand firm under the bitter winds of trial, than to run to one's cave of cowardice. But the psalmist refuses to run to his own devices. And though he is afflicted by his enemies (113, 115), he refuses to fret and instead waits patiently for God's Word. The psalmist's hope is neither in himself nor his own methods, but in God.

SUSTAIN ME ACCORDING TO YOUR WORD THAT I MAY LIVE; AND DO NOT LET ME BE ASHAMED OF MY HOPE (119:116).

The psalmist is weak and weary. He begs God to sustain him just as He has promised so that he can live. His weariness is so great that he feels he will die without God's help.

And then he pleads, "Do not let me be ashamed of my hope." In other words, "Do not let me my hope turn into disappointment, for that would bring me shame." His hope is in God's promise to sustain him, and if that sustenance breaks out from underneath him, his bold hope will wilt into his own humiliation.

UPHOLD ME THAT I MAY BE SAFE... (119:117A).

The psalmist pleads for God's upholding, for it keeps him safe. Not long after the 9/11 tragedy in New York, the Tom Bradley terminal at the Los Angeles Airport was completely shut down because someone threw a wrapped fruitcake in the trash and a passerby thought it was a bomb.

Around the same time, a plane traveling from Houston to Los Angeles had to make a forced landing because the flight attendant and a passenger got into a fight over a pillow. She asked him to show his ID, he wouldn't, and everybody panicked. We live in a very insecure world. Imagine living without belief in a sovereign God. Imagine the emptiness of life and the terror of death in a place with no God to turn to. The psalmist does not need to imagine any such thing for he knows that God will keep him safe. His God is the same God who heard the prayers of Daniel from the deadly den of lions so that Daniel could later say, "O king, live forever! My God sent His angel and shut the lions' mouths and they have not harmed me, inasmuch as I was found innocent before Him; and also toward you, O king, I have committed no crime" (Dan 6:21-22).

...THAT I MAY HAVE REGARD FOR YOUR STATUTES CONTINUALLY (119:117B).

The safety that God brings comforts the psalmist so that he can regard God's Word in peace. This word "regard" means "to gaze." I remember the first time I met my wife, Kimberly. I gazed. I shook her hand and time stood still. The world around me froze like ice and I just stared in amazement. The psalmist loves God's Word so much that he is captivated by it!

But take careful note of why the psalmist prays for safety—so that He may gaze at God's Word! Our prayer requests are often filtered through the grid of our selfish motives. We want deliverance, safety, and security so that we don't have to suffer discomfort. The end goal of our prayer request is for ourselves while God's glory is irrelevant. But when was the last time you prayed, "God deliver me from this trial so that I may more faithfully observe your law! God rescue me from my pain so that I can focus more clearly on applying Your Word!"? Were every believer to pray with these motives, a revival unheard of since the Reformation would sweep the globe.

3. A Bible zealot shudders in God's presence (vs 120).

MY FLESH TREMBLES FOR FEAR OF YOU, AND I AM AFRAID OF YOUR JUDGMENTS (119:120).

This word "tremble" means to "bristle up" or "to creep." It is the same word used of Job's flesh which "bristled up" when he was struck with fear (Job 4:15).

The God for whose holiness the psalmist is on fire and the God in whose protection the psalmist confides is also the God who causes him to tremble with great fear. Why? Because the psalmist understands God's holiness. He knows that God is holy and just and He judges the unholy.

In its most reduced form, "holiness" means set apart. Although it is true that God's people are called "holy ones" because their sin is forgiven and they live in obedience to Him, God is still more holy than His saints on earth. He is more holy than His sinless angels. He is more holy than we will ever be even in our resurrected bodies. This is because at its core, holiness does not mean "sinless" but "set apart." God is set apart from His creation because He was not created. Thus, the closer you draw to God, the more you will tremble at His holiness like Isaiah did 2700 years ago (Is 6).

Just as obedience is motivated by love for God's law, it is also motivated by fear of God's judgments. Thirty seconds of meditation on the horrors of hell can do as much good for the believer as thirty seconds of contemplation on God's love.

We are to fear the act of sinning. The thought of God's burning righteousness should make us fearful to turn against Him. This does not mean we cannot come to Him for forgiveness. He will never abandon the repentant believer. But just as a son both loves and fears his father, so we should tremble before the throne of the Almighty One.

A few years ago I was listening to a Christian radio show where struggling believers call in for "spiritual" advice. The caller said, "Sometimes I'm tempted to get angry at God. And then my husband tells me I shouldn't."

I almost drove off the road when I heard the host's response, "I think God expects us to get a little angry at Him sometimes."

This demonstrates the prevailing flippant attitude many Christians have about the sovereign Creator of the universe. Their attitude is not the attitude of Abraham over whom terror and great darkness fell when God's presence neared (Gen 15:12). It is not the attitude of Joshua who fell on his face when he realized he was speaking to the captain of the host of the LORD (Josh 5:13-15). It is not the attitude of Isaiah who cried out, "Woe is me, for I am ruined!" when he faced the presence of God in the temple (Is 6:5). The zealous believer will shudder when he stands before the throne of God's holiness.

Henry Martyn completed a brilliant education which could have earned him a high-paying, lifelong career. But when he sensed God calling him to be a missionary to India, he forsook his career and prepared for his trip across the seas. But there was one problem. He was engaged to a woman named Lydia who did not share his affections for India. He finally realized it must be "Lydia or India," and with these words he made his final decision: "My dear Lydia and my duty called me different ways, yet God has not forsaken me. I am born for God only, and Christ is nearer to me than father or mother or sister." So he went to India to "burn out for God."[6]

That's Christian zeal!

In this chapter we have drawn three sketches of a Bible zealot:

1) A Bible zealot burns for God's holiness (vss 113, 115, 118, 119).
2) A Bible zealot rests in God's protection (vss 114, 116, 117).
3) A Bible zealot shudders in God's presence (vs 120).

---

6   Ibid., 302.

QUESTIONS FOR CONTEMPLATION

1. Why does the psalmist hate those who are double-minded? Should we hate those who are double-minded? Is there room for a holy hatred in the Christian life? (see also Psalm 139:21-22). If not, why? If so, when and how and to what degree?

2. What does verse 114 teach you about what God can do for the believer?

3. What is the psalmist's motive in verse 115 for telling evildoers to depart from him?

4. What are his prayer requests in verses 116-117? Why does he pray these? At what moments in your life do you most need God to do these kinds of things for you?

5. What has God done in verses 118-119? Why has God done these things?

6. In verse 120, this psalmist who is very close to God trembles before Him. Why? Is this a sign that he is far from God? Why or why not?

7. Out of this entire passage what is the one most important principle you learned?

5

Fresh Ground or Instant: Experiencing the Word of God
Psalm 119:137-144

A legend from the year 850 AD tells that a goat herder, Kaldi of Ethiopia, was tending his goats one day when he noticed that the goats that ate red berries from a little shrub were much friskier and more playful than those that did not. And so Kaldi did what any bored goat shepherd would do: he tried one himself. Minutes later he began to feel happier, and thus the first coffee bean was discovered![1]

Today, coffee is the world's most celebrated beverage on earth—more than 400 billion cups are consumed every year. It is one of the world's most popular commodities, second only to oil.[2]

But in 1938 something happened. The Nestle company invented instant coffee to help the Brazilian government solve it's coffee surplus problem.[3] But many coffee diehards refused to lower their caffeine standards to an instant coffee mix and continued to put their coffee through the old percolating procedure. Like David Letterman, they believed that "decaffeinated coffee is useless warm brown water."[4]

Many of us have become like those instant coffee drinkers. We don't want to spend the hours of labor, meditation, and soaking up of God's Word required to make a mature Christian. We are "instant" Christians when it comes to Bible study. We want immediate results with little labor and lightning fast Bible facts with no meditation.

This is the greatest danger of our current information age. Never before have we had the availability of thousands of books, commentaries, dictionaries and encyclopedias at the simple click of a mouse. What took Bible students an hour to find in Luther's day, we can have in three seconds. It is now easier to

---

1   "Koffee Korner," http://www.koffeekorner.com/koffeehistory.htm, May 18, 2005.
2   Ibid.
3   Ibid.
4   "Koffee Korner," http://www.koffeekorner.com/quotes.htm, May 18, 2005.

get more for less; but this can have tragic results. Many people who do not love God and who do not treasure His Word can acquire more Bible knowledge than people who lived 500 years ago. And they do so without enduring the tedious labor required to gain the same information.

But there is a tremendous value in that invested time, for nothing can replace the extended meditation in God's Book. After writing a six volume commentary on the book of Hebrews, John Owen (a man who knew English, Hebrew, Greek, and Aramaic) concluded that the most valuable tools for learning the Scriptures were prayer and meditation. And you can't do either well without investing time.

The Word of God was never meant to feed your brain alone. It was also created to feed your soul. Until you have wrestled with, endured pain with, prayed with, and suffered with the text of God's holy Word, you cannot say that God's Word has percolated through your mind and heart.

When was the last time the Word of God filtered through you? I don't mean when was the last time you attended a Bible study, memorized a verse or listened to a good sermon. When was the last time the Word of God broke you to tears over your sin, or filled you with shouting joy over God's goodness to you? When last did your heart glow so hot with praise for God it almost burst? When were you last so full of God's Word that the pores of your skin emitted its fragrance?

I am speaking of those moments that the Word of God breaks through the calloused walls of your heart and floods you with a sense of God's presence that falls nothing short of supernatural elation or when you see a sinner breakdown with mixed joy and sorrow as he repents of his sins and puts his faith in Jesus Christ.

These are things that cannot be written on paper or sketched in diagrams. They are inexpressible in human language, for nothing compares with the supernatural experience of being flooded with and fed by the Holy Scriptures!

If you have not experienced the Word of God in this way, you may be wondering if you are a "fresh ground" or "instant" Christian. The answer lies in Psalm 119:137-144. The believer whose soul has been soaked by the Word of God will take three steps:

1. He will embrace the holy character of God (vs 137).

> RIGHTEOUS ARE YOU, O LORD, AND
> UPRIGHT ARE YOUR JUDGMENTS (119:137).

The Hebrew language uses an extra word to make this passage extremely direct. "Righteous are **You** O Lord!" God's person is righteous and His judgments are upright. Notice how the psalmist cannot separate the Word of God from the God of the Word. What the Word says of God is always true, and everything about God's person perfectly agrees with the Word.

At its root, "God is righteous" simply means that God is always right. The protestors protest and the atheists will debate, but in spite of all that man may say, God is always right. Bring every human into the court of judgment and you will find fault. Bring in the most godly pastors or the most sanctified martyrs and you will find fault. Bring in the most theologically perfect devotionals or exegetical commentaries written by man and in time you will come across some error. And often the more pious a religious man grows, the more arrogantly he thinks. But there is not a germ of imperfection found in God, for He is always right.

God is altogether righteous in every way, never sinning, never erring, never doing a single deed or thinking a single thought that contains even a grain of imperfection. This is a terrifying thought for the sinful creature. Who can stand with head held high in the burning presence of the Holy One? What sin-stained creature would be so bold as to lift his eyes in the presence of the sinless and mighty God of the universe?

Yet it is also a sea of comfort to the believer. When all the world around screams that God is not fair or that life is unjust, remember that God rules this world and ordains all that happens in it. And since God is righteous, what He is doing is always right and is always for the believer's ultimate good. Because He is sovereign, He may even use the unjust lashes of the wicked to help you love Him more.

In 602, a man named Phocas rebelled against the Byzantine Emperor Maurice and took over the kingdom. As Maurice was led out to execution, each of his five sons was executed before his father's eyes. At each fatal blow Maurice said, "Righteous art thou, O Lord, and upright are thy judgments."[5] Maurice's serene poise was unbelievable. How could a father exalt God at every blow that ended the life of his sons? Because he knew that in spite of man's error, God's person is righteous and His judgments are upright.

Paul the apostle understood this, too. That is why he could say, "Do all things without grumbling or disputing" (Phil 2:14). The only day you have a right to complain is the day God errs, and that day, my friend, will never come.

---

5   Neale and Littledale quoted by Spurgeon, 394.

2. He will revere the perfect deeds of God (vs 138).

YOU HAVE COMMANDED YOUR TESTIMONIES IN
RIGHTEOUSNESS AND EXCEEDING FAITHFULNESS (119:138).
The psalmist moves from stating the **fact** of God's righteousness to explaining the **act** of God's righteousness. God is not passively righteous. He does not just sit in heaven for an eternity of inert drowsiness. He commands His perfect testimonies, and He commands them in righteousness. This word "righteousness" describes His act of commanding, and the motive of His act is pure.

Many sinful men have used the pure Word of God as a sword of cruelty. They have shouted holy truths from hearts of murderous slander. But you will not find this in God's actions. Every word He gives and every command He makes is done in sinless perfection with motives so holy they would blind the naked eye.

But God's command is not only righteous, but also done in "exceeding faithfulness." The psalmist is on a chain of superlatives here. (How else do you describe the holy character of God? No human language can do it justice.) He does not just say that God commands in faithfulness, but in exceeding faithfulness. This word "exceeding" can be translated as "abundant," "much," or even "force." The idea is that God's faithfulness is indescribably abundant.

But what is God faithful to? Himself. There is no entity higher than God's throne so if He is faithful, then He must be faithful to His own Word. What great comfort this can bring to every child of God! In spite of our shattered promises, broken oaths, and canceled vows, God will never lie, never deceive, and never mislead one of His children. God has not failed to keep even the smallest of His promises to us. Every single one will be fulfilled to the end.

3. He will possess the cherished Word of God (vss 139-144).

From verses 139-144, the psalmist expresses how the Word affects his life. He does not state isolated facts about God's Word, but communicates what it is doing to him. We like to separate ourselves from Scripture. We like to talk about what it says as if we were some data-gathering machine spitting out information. Many Bible students and believers are Word warriors and knights of truth as they debate doctrine. But it can become cold, impersonal and dead to their affections. The Word has run through their head but not their heart. They have closed, locked, and sealed the door to their heart so the Word cannot get in.

Beloved, the Word is not only to be a testimony of our mouth, but also a testimony of our life! We can speak abstractly about its facts and figures, but we must also speak about it experientially, expressing what it does through and to us.

A believer must balance **know**ing Scripture and *applying* Scripture. A believer who loves to talk about doctrine but thinks little of applying it can become cold, lifeless, and arrogant. He can be like a cocky marine who received all the training but never knew the grit of white-knuckling a grenade while his comrades are blown to pieces just feet from his fox-hole. At the same time, the believer who lives to experience God but never studies His Word lives a life of mushy sentimentalism. His passion can become emotion-driven fluff that changes direction as fast as a wind vane. We must both know and apply the Scriptures.

MY ZEAL HAS CONSUMED ME, BECAUSE MY ADVERSARIES HAVE FORGOTTEN YOUR WORDS (119:139).

George Swinnock said, "Zeal is the heat or intension of the affections; it is a holy warmth, whereby our love and anger are drawn out to the utmost for God, and His glory."[6] The psalmist's zeal, his burning passion for God's glory, has consumed—literally possessed—him. He is so in love with God's Word that to see his enemies forgetting God's words bothers him to the point of emotional exhaustion. He feels wasted and dried up over others' disobedience! We often feel wasted over our own sin, but how often do we feel that way over the sins of others?

YOUR WORD IS VERY PURE, THEREFORE YOUR SERVANT LOVES IT (119:140).

The psalmist's high view of God's Word does not only produce consuming zeal, but also endearing love. The enormity of his pain over those who break God's Word is equal to the profundity of his love for the purity of God's Word. When you love something intensely, the object of your love can be a source of both dark sorrow and rapturous joy. You could not say that a man who shrugs at his wife's adultery truly loves her. Nor could you say that a man who never holds, cuddles, kisses, or serves his wife truly cares for her. If he loves her dearly, her sin will bring him deep grief and her godliness will bring him elated joy. Likewise, the psalmist is so in love with God's Word that to see it honored thrills him and to see it broken pains him.

But why does the psalmist love God's Word so much? The verse tells us, "Your word is very pure, therefore your servant loves it." This verse is a window straight into the heart of the psalmist.

Many will love God's Word only because their parents love it. It is simply an emblem of their family tradition. Others will love God's Word only because

---

6   Swinnock quoted by Spurgeon, 394.

their church loves it. In order to be accepted in the church they must accept the church's book, therefore they accept God's Word. If the church suddenly threw out the Bible and embraced the book of a different religion, so would the people whose love was never for the Word itself but for acceptance in their religious circle.

But those whose hearts have been transformed by the blood of Christ and the mercy of God love purity and therefore, when they find that this book is pure, they cling to it with all their soul! Its purity makes them shout for joy!

In the final four verses the psalmist begins to reveal his condition of suffering, and he compares the desperation of his suffering to the comfort and encouragement of God's Word. The more he suffers, the more sufficient God's Word is proven to be. God's Word is the anchor of his soul.

I AM SMALL AND DESPISED, YET I DO NOT FORGET YOUR PRECEPTS (119:141).

The psalmist feels he is neither liked nor respected. He feels he is little and disregarded in the world's eyes. This is a good place to be. God often uses the unjust persecutions of the wicked to remind us that compared to God's holy majesty we are but specks of dust on the window sill that pass with the next breeze. When we face that reality, the precepts of God's Word mean more to us than life itself.

The Word is not precious to many a believer because he does not get low enough to look up to it. He is not willing to shrink his pride. He is always looking down on the Bible as if it were some optional instruction manual on how to have a better life. The Word is important to him but not vital, significant but not imperative. He affirms its inspiration and applauds its inerrancy, but does not crave it like a poisoned man craves the antidote, or a starving man yearns for bread.

Books about Christians who have suffered years of torture for refusing to blaspheme the name of Christ fill the shelves of countless libraries. After release from prison, they later testified that through many hours of torture, God's Word became dearer to them than their own life. Scriptures they had long forgotten suddenly flooded their minds during hours of excruciating pain. Likewise, some of David's most fervent psalms were written during his persecution by Saul.

Like lungs without oxygen is the believer without the Word of God. You must come low if you want to look high to the Word of God.

YOUR RIGHTEOUSNESS IS AN EVERLASTING RIGHTEOUSNESS, AND YOUR LAW IS TRUTH (119:142).

God is completely trustworthy in everything. God has not one single misdemeanor, lie, or unjust action on His record and His record is a very, very long one. God's righteousness is not momentary. It does not rise with the sun and disappear with its setting. It does not come like a storm and leave when the weather changes. Unlike man's, God's righteousness is eternal. There never was a day when it did not exist and if you try to reach the end of God's righteousness, you will not find it.

Consistency over a long period of time proves faithfulness. If God put His actions on a resume, the paper would have no beginning and no end, for His righteousness is eternal.

Whether you lose your job, fall into bankruptcy, or get diagnosed with terminal cancer, you still can trust God, whose righteousness has not and will not change.

The psalmist also says that God's law is truth. God's law never lies. The psalmist exalts God's righteousness and law in the middle of fierce suffering to remind both the reader and himself that God is worthy to be trusted completely.

TROUBLE AND ANGUISH HAVE COME UPON ME, YET YOUR COMMANDMENTS ARE MY DELIGHT (119:143).

Strangely, this word "trouble" actually means "narrow." The psalmist is metaphorically bound in a tight place where he feels suffocated and claustrophobic. Yet, in the midst of this trouble and anguish he cries out with the ever comforting reminder that God's commandments are his delight!

Try explaining that to an unbeliever. What fool can feel delight in the midst of trouble and anguish? The same fool whose soul is saturated in God's Word! I am positively convinced that the more this psalmist suffers, the more he loves God's Word. Every blow of persecution drives him deeper and deeper into his love for God's Law.

The irony is that his love for the Word is the cause for his persecution. If eating a certain food caused your face to swell and your eyes to temporarily lose vision you would learn to detest that food. Why? Because it causes you pain. But the very Word that brings persecution to the psalmist only makes him love it more. And the more he loves it, the more his enemies persecute him for it, and the more they persecute him the more he drinks from its strength and loves it!

YOUR TESTIMONIES ARE RIGHTEOUS FOREVER; GIVE ME UNDERSTANDING THAT I MAY LIVE (119:144).

Again the psalmist exalts God's Word calling it eternally righteous. The believer is not to doubt the righteousness of God's testimonies for one instant, for never will there be a day where he will find them to be unrighteous.

As he has done many times before, the psalmist asks for understanding while under the trial of persecution. Although the psalmist knows the character of God's Word, he does not fully understand it. He knows that God alone can give him the understanding he needs in the midst of turmoil. The Word is his single hope so that he does not die of despair. His very life is dependent on the Word of God.

In this chapter we have looked at three steps that can help you to experience God's Word:

1) Embrace the holy character of God (vs 137).
2) Revere the perfect deeds of God (vs 138).
3) Possess the cherished Word of God (vss 139-144).

Many truths are lost because ministers pour their wines into sieves, either into leaky memories or feathery minds. Meditation is like a soaking rain that goes to the root of the tree and makes it bring forth fruit.
~ Thomas Watson ~

QUESTIONS FOR CONTEMPLATION

1. Why is studying the Word of God not enough? Why is it so important to experience the Word as well?

2. What does it mean to possess God's Word?

3. Go through the verses and note how the psalmist feels about God's Word. Now compare these feelings to yours. Do you feel the same way about the Word of God? What needs to change in your life so that your affection for God's Word will grow?

STRATEGY 2

Revere God's Word with Awesome Wonder
Psalm 119:25-32, 97-104, 129-136

The Jewish scribes revered the Holy Scriptures with almost unbelievable admiration. Copyists of the Old Testament manuscripts washed their entire body and put on full Jewish dress before copying the Scriptures. Unless the pen was newly dipped in ink, the scribe could not write the name of God, and should a king address him while writing this name, he was not to take notice of him.[1]

The scribes from the Qumran community (where the Dead Sea scrolls were found) were even stricter. When writing God's name, they were required move into a separate room, appoint a different scribe and use a separate pen. Even if he had copied 10,000 lines of Scripture, if he erred in writing God's name, he was required to start completely over from page one after giving the manuscript in error a special burial by placing it in a sealed bottle in its own separate cave.

Although their reverence of God's Word sometimes grew so radical that it turned into bibliolatry (worship of the Bible), their awe for the Holy Scriptures should make many a Christian blush with shame for treating God's Book, having no match in purity, power, and authority, with such flippancy. This is why Charles Haddon Spurgeon said of the Bible:

> As no other voice can, it melts me to tears, it humbles me in the dust, it fires me with enthusiasm, it fills me with pleasure, it elevates me to holiness. Every faculty of my being owns the power of the sacred Word. It sweetens my memory, it brightens my hope, it stimulates my imagination, it directs my judgment, it commands my will, and it cheers my heart.

In the next three chapters, we will look at three different strophes of Psalm

---

1   Norman L. Geisler, *A General Introduction to the Bible* (Chicago, 1986), 348-349.

119 that uncover the psalmist's remarkable esteem for the pages of Scripture: The Magnificent Word of God (119:25-32), Mining the Treasure House of Wisdom (119:97-104), and What God's Word Will Do to You (119:129-136).

The Magnificent Word of God
Psalm 119:25-32

World famous paintings by seventeenth century Dutch Masters were exhibited at a prominent South African museum in the month of September 2004. But this painting exhibition stood out from the others because no one could actually see the paintings. Calling it a "flip" exhibition, each painting was flipped so that its face was to the wall. Perhaps in an effort to justify its absurdity, Andres Lamprecht, the man behind this idea, called it "conceptual art intervention."[1]

This is exactly how unbelievers see the Word: in pure blindness. Satan has covered their eyes with blindness so that they cannot see the light of the gospel and believe (2 Cor 4:4). God's Word is dead to them. They cannot see its glory nor feel its cleansing power unless God removes the scales from their eyes and lets them see the truth.

If you are a Christian, that was exactly your predicament before you bent your knee to Christ. Blind, biased, and running as fast as you could toward hell, God in His great mercy chose to open your eyes, convict you of sin and let you see that Christ will either be your Savior or your Judge. You repented of your wickedness and put your whole faith in Jesus Christ's atonement for your sins, and now you can say with confidence that you have all that you need for growing in your understanding of God's Word (1 John 2:27). God mercifully opened your eyes and made you a new creature, changing you from His arch enemy to his adopted son or daughter and now you can refresh yourself in the fruit of His Word at any time.

How we take it for granted. We grow so accustomed to hearing, reading, and learning from His Word that we no longer have an appetite for it. When apathy is present, we tragically lose hunger and appreciation for God's Word.

I want to re-whet your appetite for the food of God's Word by giving you seven reasons why God's Word is so wonderful from Psalm 119:25-32.

---

1   *World Magazine* (August 14, 2004): 9.

1. God's Word is wonderful because it revives the dead (vs 25).

MY SOUL CLEAVES TO THE DUST...(119:25A).

Israel and the surrounding area is one of the dustiest areas in the world. Desert sandstorms are deadly. Dust, the most undesirable of the raw materials of God's creation, tastes horrible, burns your eyes, and finds its way into every nook and cranny of your house. In spite of its abundance, in King Solomon's house and in his glorious temple, not a single piece of furniture was made from dirt (1 Kings 6 and 7). In fact, only the cheapest of homes were made of mud with straw roofs.

In Jewish culture when a man suffered unendurable grief he tore his clothes, dropped to the ground and covered his head with dust. Dust belongs on the bottom of shoes. Dust is where dead bodies are laid to rot. And dust is where the psalmist's soul now lies. Note that he is not just rolling in the dirt, but cleaving to it. People cleave to the things they hope in. The most the psalmist can hope in is the powdery dust of the earth. He is dead in his affections for God, dead in his love for man, dead in his passion for holy living. But praise God that is not the end of the verse!

...REVIVE ME ACCORDING TO YOUR WORD (119:25B).

This word "revive" means "to make alive." The same Word of God that created the heavens and the earth and the same Word that called Lazarus from the dead is the same Word that refreshes your weary soul.

Just one mouthful of muddy water has revived men stranded in the blazing desert to get them to an oasis. How much more will the living water of God's Word renew your weary heart!

My first job was at age twelve, landscaping for five dollars an hour—a lot of money to a twelve year old boy. Because I was new, the foreman officially dubbed me the "Mole Man." I moved rocks, hauled sand, spread mulch and pushed a wheelbarrow until my hands were so blistered I couldn't make a fist. I labored in scorching heat, rising to 120 degrees Fahrenheit on some days.

One day I sat down for lunch, tired, thirsty and starving. The foreman suddenly produced a little container with the inscription, "Tapioca Pudding." I'm sure you have enjoyed juicy Popsicles or a refreshing slurpy in your lifetime, but there is nothing like cool tapioca pudding on a hot day. In three bites it was gone, and I found myself staring into the lunch box looking for more. The tapioca would not have tasted so refreshing had I not been suffering in the dry heat of summer. Nor would the psalmist delight in the refreshment of God's Word so fervently had his soul not cleaved to the dust.

2. God's Word is wonderful because it teaches the ignorant (vs 26).

I HAVE TOLD OF MY WAYS... (119:26A).

The psalmist's life is open to God. He does not foolishly think he can withhold things from the all-knowing God. Nor is he so arrogant that he only talks to God about the big problems. No, he talks to God about everything!

"My ways" means all the psalmist's life. It includes his victories and his failures, his acts of kindness and his deeds of cruelty, his virtues and his sins, his high times and his low times, things he craves and things he detests. The Christian close to God talks to Him about everything.

As you grow in affection for your life mate, so does your pleasure in talking to him or her. Even the little things like: "Today my lips were chapped so I tried that new Chapstick®." Or... "That was a delicious apple you put in my lunch today!" The motive is not simply to give information to your spouse, but rather because you love spending time with and conversing with your best friend.

Why would the psalmist have such confidence in talking to God about everything? Because he knows that God is gracious and loving. Matthew Henry wrote, "It is an unspeakable comfort to a gracious soul to think with what tenderness all its complaints are received by a gracious God."[2] If you are convinced that you care about yourself, know that God cares for you infinitely more.

When you talk to God about your deepest hurts and darkest temptations, you admit that you know that He understands perfectly and can bring you comfort and deliver you from temptation (Luke 11:4). As Paul told the Philippians, "Be anxious for nothing, but in everything by prayer and supplication with thanksgiving let your requests be made known to God" (Phil 4:6).

...AND YOU HAVE ANSWERED ME (119:26B).

The psalmist doesn't just talk to God—God talks back! He did not hear His voice nor did he see a vision. Then how did He answer him? Through His Word. God does not just hear you, He answers you. Would you like to know God more intimately? Then talk to Him about everything. Would you like to hear from God? Then read His Word.

...TEACH ME YOUR STATUTES (119:26C).

The psalmist does not just want to hear God's Word, he desires to understand it. Being a new and ignorant believer—or even a long time believer with little maturity in Christ—can be very frustrating. You may ask, "Where do I start?

---

2   Matthew Henry, *Matthew Henry's Commentary on the Whole Bible: Complete and Unabridged in One Volume* (Peabody: Hendrickson, 1996), n. p.

Theology books? But I need to study verse by verse passages to get the details. Oh, yes, and I also need the big picture so I better take a Bible survey class. And what about how we got our Bible? But didn't my pastor say I need to memorize it too? Oh, and what about theology proper? What about pneumatology, hamartiology, and anthropology? And bibliology, demonology, and Christology?" The choices are so many and so good. But here the psalmist shows you where to start: begin by asking God to teach you. Notice that the psalmist recognizes that God is the teacher: *"teach me Your statutes" (vs 26)*.

How does God teach you? God teaches you by His Spirit. Whether you are learning from a Bible teacher, small group, sermons, theology books, or your own personal study time, it is the Holy Spirit who works through these methods to open your understanding to the Word of God.

> As for you, the anointing which you received from Him abides in you, and you have no need for anyone to teach you; but as His anointing teaches you about all things, and is true and is not a lie, and just as it has taught you, you abide in Him (1 John 2:27).

Years ago the great German reformer, Martin Luther said, "Be assured that no one will make a doctor of the Holy Scripture save only the Holy Ghost from heaven." All the best Bible teachers in the world will teach you nothing until the Holy Spirit teaches them.

You may be wondering, "How do I get God to teach me?" It's not a very complicated process. ***Ask Him.*** "Open my eyes, that I may behold wonderful things from Your law" (Psalm 119:118). The same God who opened the eyes of Elisha's servant to scores of horses and chariots of fire is the same God who dwells in your heart and helps you every time you study His Word (1 Kings 6:15-17).

3. God's Word is wonderful because it uplifts the downcast (vs 27).

MAKE ME UNDERSTAND THE WAY OF YOUR PRECEPTS (119:27A). The psalmist suffers ignorance. He craves to understand the path of God's commandments. He wants to know more than the fact of God's command. He wants to claim an intimate understanding of it.

On top of my refrigerator at home sits a turtle which we named "Mr. Turtle." (I know, what an original name!) If I had you over for dinner you could look at that turtle, hold that turtle and call him by his special name. You could even say, "I know that turtle." But as his master, I understand him. I know what he wants when he starts scraping the side of his aquarium. I know how he feels when he's still. I know what he's looking for when my four year old son drops him in the bathtub and he goes swimming like a fish. You know him, but I understand him. The psalmist wants more than head knowledge. He craves intimate understanding.

But why, psalmist, do you long to understand the way of God's precepts?

...SO I WILL MEDITATE ON YOUR WONDERS (119:27B).
Understanding God's Word results in meditation on God's awesome person. The psalmist is taken from depression to glory, from the pit of mud to the ninth cloud. The chief cause of misery in the believer's life is an intense focus upon his own self. Misery results when he is too in love with his own person to take time to meditate on God's person, too conceited with his own achievements to give attention to God's wondrous acts and too fearful of man to fear the God of heaven.

4. God's Word is wonderful because it strengthens the weak (vs 28).

MY SOUL WEEPS BECAUSE OF GRIEF (119:28A).
This word "weep" is so heavy that translators had difficulty translating it in a way that communicates its full weight. It literally means "to drop through" or "to melt" or "pour out." Following are different translations for the same phrase.

VERSION	PSALM 119:28A
ASV	My soul melteth for heaviness
BBE	My soul is wasted with sorrow
ESV	My soul melts away for sorrow
NIV	My soul is weary with sorrow
NLV	I weep with grief
CEV	I am overcome with sorrow
YLT	My soul hath dropped from affliction

This man is crippled with sorrow. He's an ocean of tears. His face is probably painted with lines of grief. Sorrow makes people weak, limp and helpless as it sucks strength from their soul and body.

But let's look at what God's Word does for the weak:

STRENGTHEN ME ACCORDING TO YOUR WORD (119:28B).
God's Word is like protein for your muscles, or gasoline for your car. My wife

and I used to minister to an elderly lady at a church where I pastored. From a human perspective, her life was frankly miserable. Her husband was not saved and treated her terribly. Her son was addicted to drugs and married a substance-abusing stripper. They had a child but due to drugs the child was turned over to a foster home which ended in a bitter family battle permeated with lies, deceit, and hostility.

I often thought I could not endure that kind of suffering. Her suffering made our trials seem miniscule. She suffered unbearable pain, every day like another arrow in her side. But God gave her a miraculous ability to endure and still rejoice. And He did this through His Word.

Every time I saw this elderly lady, Scripture flowed from her mouth. Our conversations went like this:

"Hi Mrs.—"

"Seth, the Lord is my shepherd I shall not want..."

"How are you doing—"

"My God has supplied all my needs according to His riches and glory in Christ Jesus!"

"Has your family situation improved?"

"No, but God causes all things to work together for good to those who love God..." Though she was weighed down with almost unbearable suffering, God's Word made her strong.

5. God's Word is wonderful because it guides the lost (vss 29-30).

REMOVE THE FALSE WAY FROM ME AND
GRACIOUSLY GRANT ME YOUR LAW (119:29).

Without God's Word you are no better off than if you were dropped from a helicopter into the middle of a South American jungle with no compass, no map, and no guide. You cannot guide your own life and end up with happiness, holiness, and heaven. The moment you take the burden of holy living upon your shoulders alone, you will sink into the quicksand of your own arrogance.

This does not mean that your efforts don't count, but begin by asking God to remove the false way, the way that is not through Christ. Ask Him to help you. Ask Him to protect you. Ask Him to strengthen you. Then, go out and live for Him!

The psalmist knows that he cannot walk down two paths at the same time, so he asks God to remove the false way from him. "God! Take it away! Move it as far from me as the farthest planet in the outermost galaxy!"

In verse 29 we saw the psalmist's requests but now in verse 30 we see his resolutions.

I HAVE CHOSEN THE FAITHFUL WAY
I HAVE PLACED YOUR ORDINANCES BEFORE ME (119:30)

All throughout this psalm, the psalmist views following God's law as a journey down a road.

Psalm 119:1	*"How blessed are those whose **way** is blameless."*
Psalm 119:9	*"How can a young man keep his **way** pure?"*
Psalm 119:14	*"I have rejoiced in the **way** of Your testimonies."*
Psalm 119:27	*"Make me understand the **way** of Your precepts."*
Psalm 119:29	*"Removed the false **way** from me."*

No matter where the psalmist goes, he will not rest until he has scaled that jagged path that leads to the pearly gates. No one takes a highway to heaven; it's more like a rugged mountain trail.

You stand at a crossroads. One road leads to the pleasures of this life: exotic lusts, the applause and glory of man and delicious foods. The pleasure road may lead to wealth such that you never have to work again, wealth that will buy anything you want, including thousands of servants who meet your wishes at the tap of your scepter. And this road is wide, smoothly paved, and a breezy coast downhill.

The other road is a mountain trail. It is narrow and curving. It will take you by steep precipices, sharp crags, and dizzying heights. It winds up, up, and up on painfully steep paths. And on this road is a man from Nazareth. On His back he drags a cross to which He must be nailed. And He calls out, "You, follow Me!" Perhaps if I tell you where these two roads end it will influence which one you pick.

That wide road decked with delicacies and pleasures leads down, down, faster and faster until those who take it can no longer stop. It finally drops you into a massive hole of melting lava, screaming agony, and excruciating pain where you will wish for death but never die. And never will you be given reprieve from these unbearable tortures.

The narrow road is hard and difficult. It is painful and bloody and you will suffer on the path. You will sometimes fall hard but not without help from the Master to get you up again. This road leads you to tall gates of pearl that open to a street of gold leading on to a majestic throne, upon which sits the same One who beckoned you to follow Him while He carried His ugly tree. But this time instead of a crown of thorns He wears a diadem of gold. His home is a place of unending happiness and pure joy, a place where no tear is shed, no cry is ever heard. The only sound you hear is the thundering voice of God Himself and the thousands of saints and angels who sing His praises! Which road will you take?

The problem is not that we haven't heard God's Word. It is not that we don't know what it's about. It's that we've chosen to put God's Word beside us, behind us, or off some place where it won't convict us too deeply. Unlike the psalmist, we do not place God's ordinances before us.

Every few weeks my desk yields to the second law of thermodynamics. It looks as though it was struck by a tornado, buried under a mountain of papers, books and things to do.

Years ago I found it frustrating to work at a desk struck by entropy, so I emptied a drawer, stuck everything inside, and decided to get back to it in the next few days. A day went by. A week went by. A month went by. Finally, a year and a half later I opened that drawer by accident. Whoa! I had forgotten I owned that stuff.

That day I learned that if I want to get something done, I have to put it on my desk where it will drive me crazy until it gets done. That's exactly what you must do with the Word of God. Put it in front of you and let it bug you until you start heeding its commands.

6. God's Word is wonderful because it comforts the discouraged (vs 31).

I CLING TO YOUR TESTIMONIES (119:31A).
Instead of clinging to his past and living in the dark guilt of his own sins, the psalmist turns to the Word and clings to it for life. The word "cling" is the same word used in verse 25, "My soul cleaves to the dust." If the psalmist's soul hadn't cleaved to the dust he would never feel so urgent a need to cleave to God's testimonies.

O LORD, DO NOT PUT ME TO SHAME! (119:31B).
Few things plague a soul like shame. Nothing brings a soul lower and kills it more quickly. Guilt has rendered thousands of gifted men and women completely useless and the shame of guilt has brought suicide to the lives of millions. Shame kills courage by *discouraging* the believer. So the psalmist prays in verse 31: "O LORD, do not put me to shame!"

It is the psalmist's soul in the dust (vs 25), his lack of intimacy with God's Word (vs 27), his grievous weeping (vs 28), the temptation of the false way (vs 29), and his shame for his own sin (vs 31) that breaks him down until he can do nothing but cry out in desperation for the Word of God. But this is good.

It was Job's loss of his children, wealth and even his own health that spurred him to say, "The LORD gave and the LORD has taken away. Blessed be the name of the LORD" (Job 1:21).

It was David's adultery that moved him to pray, "Be gracious to me, O God, according to Your lovingkindness" (Ps 51:1).

It was Paul's thorn in the flesh that brought him to the conclusion, "Most gladly, therefore, I will rather boast about my weaknesses, so that the power of Christ may dwell in me" (2 Cor 12:9).

It is no wonder that A. W. Tozer said, "It is doubtful that God would use a man greatly whom He has not hurt deeply."

7. God's Word is wonderful because it frees the imprisoned (vs 32).

I SHALL RUN THE WAY OF YOUR COMMANDMENTS (119:32).
Up to this verse the psalmist has made 3 resolutions:

1. "I have chosen the faithful way" (vs 30).
2. "I have placed Your ordinances before me" (vs 30).
3. "I cling to Your testimonies" (vs 31).

He chose (vs 30), he placed (vs 30), and he clung (vs 31). But this time he runs (vs 32). This is not a walk, a stroll or even a jog. No, the psalmist puts on his sprinting shoes, finds the path of Scripture, and runs with all his might!

"Way" or "path" are very popular words in this psalm, but especially in this section. In verse 26 the psalmist has told of his ways. He has confessed his *paths* of sin to God. In verse 29 the psalmist asks God to remove the false *way* from him. Having confessed his sinful ways, He now wishes that God will remove this *path* from his sight so he can never set toe upon it again and he can "*run* the way of Your commandments."

The psalmist has moved from confessing his sinful way, to requesting that God remove the sinful way, to running God's way.

FOR YOU WILL ENLARGE MY HEART (119:32).
There has been much debate over the interpretation of this phrase, but I believe that the context gives us the answer. The word "heart" always refers to the inner person, one's soul, feelings, or will. In this context it appears to mean "affection," an affection and love for God.

The psalmist loves God but feels that his heart is too small to love Him more. He feels restrained by his own mortality. He is like a basketball player who jumps with all his might but finds that his legs are too short to get his hands over the rim.

Have you ever felt like that? Too weak to love God more? The psalmist's imprisonment to his own weakness has made him feel like a slave, but God enlarges his heart and sets him free to obey God. People today love to talk about freedom, "In Christ I am free." Sometimes people use this freedom as an excuse for justifying sin in their life. But note that this is not freedom from anything, but a freedom to obey God (Rom 6:1-2). God gives this kind of freedom in abundance.

In this chapter we have discussed seven reasons why God's Word is absolutely wonderful:

1) It revives the dead (vs 25).
2) It teaches the ignorant (vs 26).
3) It uplifts the downcast (vs 27).
4) It strengthens the weak (vs 28).
5) It guides the lost (vss 29-30).
6) It comforts the discouraged (vs 31).
7) It frees the imprisoned (vs 32).

The Scripture is the...pole-star to direct us to heaven...The Scripture is the compass by which the rudder of our will is to be steered; it is the field in which Christ, the Pearl of price, is hid; it is a rock of diamonds...it is a spiritual optic-glass in which the glory of God is resplendent, it is the panacea or "universal medicine" for the soul. The leaves of Scripture are like the leaves of the tree of life 'for the healing of the nations'...it is the sea-mark which shows us the rocks of sin to avoid; it is the antidote against error and apostasy, the two-edged sword which wounds the old serpent. It is our bulwark to with-stand the force of lust; like the Capitol of Rome, which was a place of strength and ammunition. The Scripture is the 'tower of David,' whereon the shields of our faith hang.

~ Thomas Watson ~

QUESTIONS FOR CONTEMPLATION

1. What kind of suffering is the psalmist going through as he writes this section?

2. What resolute decisions does the psalmist make (or has he already made) in these verses?

3. Taking each verse, write down what God's Word does for the believer. Then write down what kind of person needs that action of the Word. For example, in verse 25 we see that God's Word revives. What kind of person needs revival? A tired person.

4. Ask yourself which kind of person you are most like from the above and write out what you will do to apply the Word in this area.

7

Mining the Treasure House of Wisdom
Psalm 119:97-104

If you spent half your life digging into the side of a mountain in search of gold, and finally brought your loads of treasure to a dealer to discover that your findings were nothing more than fools gold, you'd be disappointed.

Imagine that an old miner sees your dilemma and says, "You come with me, and I'll show you where you can find a solid mountain of gold." This sounds too good to be true and under normal circumstances you would reject his offer, but your desperation is so great that you are willing to try anything. So you hesitantly follow this miner into the jungles. He takes you on a long trek across many rivers, over lakes, and through thick brush. This goes on for several weeks, and one day, discouraged and tired, you decide to return home. But at the brink of giving up, you lift your eyes to behold the object of your destination: a mountain of solid gold. The old miner chuckles with satisfaction and then turns to you and says, "This is the El Dorado that Sir Walter Raleigh searched for and never found. And today, it is all yours." You stand amazed, delighting in the fact that you don't have to dig through miles of sand, rock, and quartz to find your gold. It's right there for the taking. That's what you find when you mine the Word of God. God's Word is a treasure house of wisdom.

The world mines for wisdom through psychology, mysticism, sensationalism, pleasure, pragmatism, materialism, statistics, and human opinion. But no matter how hard and fast people dig, their labor will not yield gold because they are digging in the wrong mountain. Their search is as hopeless as finding water on the moon or snow in the Amazon.

Professor and commentator, George Zemek, said that wisdom comes "from the God of the Word through the Word of God to the child of God."[1] Psalm 119:97-104 is the epitome of this truth. It is remarkable that this is the first

---

[1] George J. Zemek, *The Word of God in the Child of God: Exegetical, Theological, and Homiletical Reflections from the 119th Psalm* (Self Published, n. d.), 231.

eight verse strophe without a single prayer request. Instead, the psalmist makes bold affirmations, one after another, about the wisdom he receives from feeding on God's holy Word.

From this passage, you will find two digging tools for mining wisdom from the Word of God.

Tool #1: Make sure you are digging the right mountain (vss 98-100).

No matter how hard he works, the miner will find no gold if he mines the wrong mountain. Likewise, no matter how hard someone seeks wisdom, if he is not seeking in the Holy Scriptures, his search is in vain. In the following three verses, the psalmist shows that he has greater wisdom than three groups of people: his enemies, his teachers, and the elderly. First, his enemies:

> YOUR COMMANDMENTS MAKE ME WISER THAN MY ENEMIES,
> FOR THEY ARE EVER MINE (119:98).

The psalmist is not boasting about his accomplishments but exalting God for His Word. The proud credit themselves for their achievements, but the godly credit God, for all wisdom starts with Him.

The source of the psalmist's wisdom is God's commandments which make him wise because they are from God. Like a teddy bear to a child, the psalmist holds God's Word close to his heart, treasuring it, meditating on it, and studying it, making the psalmist wiser than his opponents.

> I HAVE MORE INSIGHT THAN ALL MY TEACHERS,
> FOR YOUR TESTIMONIES ARE MY MEDITATION (119:99).

Teachers can be an intimidating group of people, yet the psalmist surpasses them all, for His teacher is the Creator of teachers and his schoolbook the Book of books. Just as the top students are developed by the best teachers, the wisest men are those who learn from the all-wise God. As Charles Spurgeon said, "The letter can make us knowing, but only the divine Spirit can make us wise."[2]

People assume that those with doctorate degrees in theology or years of teaching experience must be wise. But these men are sometimes infants in wisdom compared to the disciple who sits at Christ's feet and savors every word. The wisest believer is the believer who meditates on God's Word, making it the bloodstream of his life.

To meditate on God's Word requires great discipline of the mind. It has been said that reading increases one's vocabulary. This is only as true as the mind is disciplined. The disciplined mind thinks about and chews on those

---

2   Spurgeon, 330.

new words, but the lazy mind forgets them quickly. One of the great benefits of schooling is not that the student can learn a new trade, but that his schooling proves he has disciplined his mind over a long period of time. Watching television is enjoyable because it requires no exercise of the brain. But reading, deep discussions, thoughtful meditation, and solving of problems train a mind in discipline. And what better subject to think upon than the perfect Word of God?

I UNDERSTAND MORE THAN THE AGED, BECAUSE
I HAVE OBSERVED YOUR PRECEPTS (119:100).

Elderly men and women can be very wise after years of gaining knowledge, but the psalmist surpasses them all as he learns from the Ancient One who cannot be matched in length of years. Many years of life can give a man great wisdom if he is diligent in applying his knowledge, yet age in man is no guarantee for wisdom. Many have chosen to waste their knowledge like the prodigal son wasted his wealth. Solomon himself, the wisest man on earth said, "A poor yet wise lad is better than an old and foolish king who no longer knows how to receive instruction" (Eccl 4:13).

The key to this psalmist's wisdom is his willingness to submit to a greater source of wisdom than himself. Those on this earth who look to themselves for wisdom are the greatest fools. A child who ignores his father's warning and runs out onto the freeway will be wept over as foolish when his coffin is lowered into the earth. Likewise, only an ardent fool will despise the Word of the only wise God (Rom 16:27) and his end will be much worse than a coffin. The more man relies solely on the knowledge he gains from this world, the greater a fool he becomes, for his increased knowledge does not result in recognition of the Creator. Pride says, "If I know this much, why would I need Him?" Henry Ironside wisely stated the following in the first half of the twentieth century.

And now that science has demonstrated the possibility of conquering such dire visitations as yellow fever, cholera, and bubonic plague by proper sanitation and extermination of vermin, the majority—instead of gratefully recognizing the Creator's goodness in making known such things to physical suffering—actually deride religion and scorn the Word of the Lord, supposing that increased scientific knowledge has made the concept of an intelligent Creator and an overruling Deity unnecessary, if not altogether absurd.[3]

The psalmist possesses God's Word as his own (vs 98), making it his brain

---

3   Henry Ironside, *Unless You Repent* (West Port Colborne: Gospel Folio Press), 83.

food every day (vs 99), as he carefully observes it (vs 100). However, these three words "wiser," "insight," and "understanding" don't only mean Bible knowledge, but great discretion in applying that knowledge. Wisdom is not the ability to quote Scripture verses, state Bible themes, and explain profound doctrines. Wisdom is the competence to apply the Word to daily living. Moses instructed the house of Israel in Deuteronomy 4:5-6 with these words,

> See, I have taught you statutes and judgments just as the LORD my God commanded me, that you should do thus in the land where you are entering to possess it. So keep and do them, for that is your wisdom and your understanding in the sight of the peoples who will hear all these statutes and say, "Surely this great nation is a wise and understanding people."

Tool #2: Make sure you are mining the right gold (vss 97, 101-104).

To mine the right mountain means to dig into God's Word rather than other books. When we mine the right gold, we apply the Word. Knowledge by itself cannot create wisdom, but knowledge of God's Word applied to the trials, temptations, and joys of this life will forge wisdom far greater than the world can know. There is a lot of fool's gold out there, and to mine the right gold you need to hate sin and love what is good.

OH HOW I LOVE YOUR LAW!
IT IS MY MEDITATION ALL THE DAY (119:97).

"Oh" is an expression of wonder and marvel. The psalmist is so in love with God's Word that he cannot contain himself. He cries out to God expressing his love for His Word and then offers the proof that he loves it by putting himself through ceaseless meditation. We think about the things we love all the time. John Calvin said, "If any person boasts that he loves the Divine Law, and yet neglects the study of it, and applies his mind to other things, he betrays the grossest hypocrisy..."[4] If you love God's Word, it will saturate your thoughts. And the more you muse on it, the deeper your affections for it will grow.

Spurgeon commented, "It is said of some men that the more you know them the less you admire them; but the reverse is true of God's Word. Familiarity with the Word of God breeds affection, and affection seeks yet greater familiarity."[5]

Today we rarely hear the prayer, "Oh God, I love Your Law!" We prefer to call it "God's Word" or "God's message," or simply "the Bible." These terms are less threatening and more appealing. While they accurately depict God's

---

4   John Calvin, *Calvin's Commentaries*, electronic ed (Garland: Galaxie Software, 2000), n. p.
5   Spurgeon, 330.

revelation to man, they leave out a vital aspect. The "law" reminds us of justice. It reminds us of God's burning holiness. It reminds us that we deserve the eternal wrath of God and only by His pure mercy and grace has that flame been quenched.

So why can the psalmist praise God for His law with such fervor? Because he keeps it! The law that condemns the pagan when he breaks it is the same law that comforts the believer when he keeps it.

I HAVE RESTRAINED MY FEET FROM EVERY EVIL WAY, THAT I MAY KEEP YOUR WORD (119:101).

Here the psalmist expounds on the practical benefits of gleaning wisdom from God's precious Word, which has turned him from evil (verses 101-102) and has satisfied his soul (verse 103).

There is no keeping of God's Word without a shunning of evil. But studying God's Word does not automatically make people godly. The believer must volitionally choose to turn his feet from every evil path that presents itself. Our life path is created by many tiny decisions every hour. One sinful decision leads to another and one righteous decision leads to another righteous decision. A thought reaps a decision, decisions reap a lifetime, and lifetimes reap a legacy.

He mentions "feet" because they indicate direction. Where the feet go, the body goes. He wants the direction of his life to be turned away from sinful trails. If evil paths were not tempting, the psalmist would have no need to restrain himself. The fact that he must restrain his feet shows that he is tempted to sin. So what keeps him from sinning? His motive. The next phrase says, "that I may keep Your Word." When the great priority of one's life is to keep the Word, (vs 97), the very Word that has grown him in wisdom (vss 98-100), he will turn his feet from those sinful paths that beckon him to dishonor God.

Notice how the two go together: If one gains wisdom from God's Word then he will hate evil. As Leupold says, "One cannot be lax about evil and expect to profit in the use of the Word."[6]

I HAVE NOT TURNED ASIDE FROM YOUR ORDINANCES, FOR YOU YOURSELF HAVE TAUGHT ME (119:102).

The psalmist now states in the negative what he said positively in verse 101. In verse 101 he wrote, "He has restrained his feet" and now in verse 102 he writes, "he will not turn aside." Why will he not turn aside? Because God has taught him!

Notice the emphatic "You Yourself." The psalmist reminds God of what

---

6   Leupold Sabourin quoted by Zemek, 238..

He already knows. God Himself has taught the psalmist and it is for that reason the psalmist refuses to turn away from His Word.

Teachers, professors, and educators teach you knowledge. They can even explain to you the wisdom they have learned. But they cannot give you wisdom in the way only God can. While the teacher may impart knowledge of God's Word and His universe, it is only the God of the universe who gives divine discretion in applying it.

HOW SWEET ARE YOUR WORDS TO MY TASTE!
YES, SWEETER THAN HONEY TO MY MOUTH! (119:103).

Again the psalmist explodes in irresistible praise and love for God's Word. Honey is used throughout the Old Testament as an illustration of luxurious living (Ex 3:8, 17; 13:5) or something sweet (Proverbs 24:13). God's Word has become so precious to the psalmist that he savors it like honey from the comb. In Psalm 19, David says that God's Word is "more desirable than gold, yes, than much fine gold. Sweeter also than honey and the drippings of the honeycomb" (Ps 19:10). Every word of God tastes like a precious pocket of honey in his mouth!

My Armenian mechanic recently replaced my car battery. After some friendly chit chat I asked him, "So, what will you do when you retire?"

"What everybody else does."

"What does everybody else do?"

"Do nothing!"

"I see. And then after you die, then what will you do?"

"Sleep."

"And if you stand before God and He asks you, 'Henry, why should I let you into heaven?' What will you say?"

"Cause I tried to be a good person. But let me tell you something, Seth. Armenians don't like to talk about Christianity. We come from a Christian nation. And people talk about it so much and practice it so little that we are sick of just talking about it and just live it."

"But don't you like to talk about things you enjoy? If I love my wife, I like to talk about my wife. If I love cars, I talk about cars." And so it is with the psalmist. Discussing the Word beats every possible conversation topic.

FROM YOUR PRECEPTS I GET UNDERSTANDING;
THEREFORE I HATE EVERY FALSE WAY (119:104).

Notice how this entire passage opens with "O how I love your law!" and closes with the parallel statement, "I hate every false way." The psalmist closes this section with a final word on his love for the wisdom he gains from God's Word and his hatred for every path that leads away from God's Word.

If you love God, you will hate your sin. To leave room for sin is to join league with Satan's host of evils. The more tender your affections grow toward your Savior, the more fierce your wrath will be toward sin.

Every believer will agree that he should annihilate his sin. But what about those one or two sins which are so hard to let go? On this very question George Swinnock says,

> Universality in this is a sure sign of sincerity. Herod spits out some sins, when he rolls others as sweet morsels in his mouth. A hypocrite ever leaves the devil some nest-egg to sit upon, though he take many away. Some men will not buy some commodities, because they cannot have them at their own price, but they lay out the same money on others; so hypocrites forbear some sins, yea, are displeased at them, because they cannot have them without disgrace or disease, or some other disadvantage; but they lay out the same love upon other sins which will suit better with their designs. Some affirm that what the sea loseth in one place it gaineth in another; so what ground the corruption of the unconverted loseth one way, it gaineth another. There is in him some one lust especially which is his favourite; some king sin, like Agag, which must be spared when others are destroyed. ...But now the regenerate laboureth to cleanse himself from all pollutions, both of flesh and spirit.[7]

From Psalm 119:97-104 we have discovered two digging tools for mining wisdom from the Word of God:

Tool #1: Make sure you are digging the right mountain. Get your wisdom from God's Word (vss 98-100).
Tool #2: Make sure you are mining the right gold. Apply that knowledge to your daily life (vss 97, 101-104).

---

7   Swinnock quoted by Spurgeon, 340.

It is said that when the famous missionary, Dr. David Livingstone, started his trek across Africa, he carried 73 books in three packs weighing 180 pounds. After the party had gone 300 miles, Livingstone was obliged to throw away some of the books because of the fatigue of those carrying his baggage. As he continued on his journey his library grew smaller and smaller, until he had but one book left—his Bible, and this one he did not toss away. Livingstone knew what the real treasure was.

QUESTIONS FOR CONTEMPLATION

1. What does it mean in verse 97 when the psalmist says the law is his meditation all the day? Does he read the Bible all day?

2. Who are the three groups of men mentioned in verses 98-100? What significance do their titles play in this passage?

3. Compare verses 101 and 102. Are they saying the same thing? Are they saying something different? Explain.

4. What is the main theme of this passage? Make an outline for this passage and tell how the different parts relate to the main theme.

5. List some VERY specific ways you are going to apply what God is teaching you in this passage.

C H A P †E R

8

What God's Word Will Do to You
Psalm 119:129-136

A select few people in this world are plagued with the dreaded disease: toe fungus. If you have never seen toe fungus then get on your knees and give praise to God. Toe fungus can perform masterful artistry on your toe, doubling its size, twisting its shape, or raising the toenail so high you could hide a cigar butt underneath. I can describe it with color because my left big toe was a victim of this disease. I visited a toe doctor for help. He was a true professional toe doctor. Even his license plate said, "DR. FOOT."

After diagnosing my malady he suggested I take a special pill called "Lamisil" for six months. Before I spent a fortune on Lamisil and blood tests, I asked the doctor, "What will it do to me?"

That's a popular question when a patient must undergo an operation, take new medicine, or suffer a physical exam. And it's a fair question to ask about God's Word. What will it do to me? If I bury my mind in this Book, what will happen to my character, my mind and my life?

The psalmist answers that question in Psalm 119:129-136. The Word will do three things to you when you choose to marinate your mind in its truth.

1. If you marinate your mind with God's Word, it will produce supreme happiness (vss 129-131).

YOUR TESTIMONIES ARE WONDERFUL;
THEREFORE MY SOUL OBSERVES THEM (119:129).

The verse literally reads: "Your testimonies are wonders." This word "wonder" does not just mean great. It means extraordinary. It means beyond human comprehension.

But how could the psalmist observe something that is beyond comprehension? This appears to be a contradiction. "Because Your Word is beyond understanding, I observe it." But this proves that true understanding of God's Word is a miracle. No man or woman can truly understand the Word of God without God's miraculous help. The Holy Spirit opens the truth of God's Word to the heart of the believer and applies it to his life (1 John 2:27).

Out of all the wonderful things on this earth, the psalmist mentions the chief wonder of all: God's testimonies. Theme parks, dessert, vacation, and lemonade on a blistering hot day bring satisfaction for a brief moment, but the satisfaction goes no deeper than the body. Worldly people live for this kind of immediate gratification, and the moment it is consumed, they want something else because the satisfaction does not last.

But the psalmist observes something *unearthly*: the testimonies of God. And the psalmist does not just observe these with his eyes or his mouth, but with his soul. The devotion comes from within, not without. It is not an obligated duty or grievous burden. It is his sheer joy and pleasure to observe God's testimonies! It is not the pressure of penance or the duty of praying five times a day to spare his soul from a few million years of wrath. It is his delight! It is a sad thing when it takes a man or a woman an entire lifetime to discover that the things of this life—man-made religion, entertainment, food, wealth, and physical beauty—will never bring true happiness. But the psalmist is wise for he looks for the happiness found in God's Word. And that is supreme happiness.

THE UNFOLDING OF YOUR WORDS GIVES LIGHT; IT GIVES UNDERSTANDING TO THE SIMPLE (119:130).

Just as a student must open a book before he can read it, so God's Word must unfold itself to the reader before he can understand it. It enlightens the mind to truth. It would be better to be a blind man, reading the Bible in Braille than to see all the wonders of the world with perfectly good eyes, only to end up in hell to stare at the flames of God's wrath for all eternity.

God's Word, which is "too wonderful for comprehension" (verse 129), gives understanding even "to the simple." The most simple beggar can become wiser than the greatest rabbi through understanding God's Word. We live in the age of information. Never before have believers been able to collect so much data through the internet, media, and libraries, but all the data in the world can not compare to the mountain of wisdom that the simple-minded can mine from God's Holy Word. David testifies of this in Psalm 19:7, "The law of the LORD is perfect, restoring the soul; the testimony of the LORD is sure making wise the simple."

This word "simple" derives from a root which means to be "spacious," "wide" or "open." The picture here is not one of weak acumen, but one with humble openness to God's instruction and true dependence on His precepts

(Ps 19:8; 116:6; 119:130). And yet it is often the poor, the unknown or the uncultured person who is able to digest the Holy Scriptures because his mind is not cluttered with pride, deceit and self-worship. Christ spent most of His time with the "little" people (Matt 9:10-13), and Paul himself testifies that "there were not many wise according to the flesh, not many mighty, not many noble; but God has chosen the foolish things of the world to shame the wise, and God has chosen the weak things of the world to shame the things which are strong" (1 Cor 1:26-27). The term "open-minded" has become connected to the liberals and tolerance-promoting freethinkers, but in God's eyes open-mindedness is a great complement when one's mind is open to the Word of God.

How many books today claim that they can give supreme happiness to the reader? And for the few that do, how many can back up that claim? For every ounce of joy a man-written book may bring, the Bible will trump it with an ocean of supreme happiness.

I OPENED MY MOUTH WIDE AND PANTED,
FOR I LONGED FOR YOUR COMMANDMENTS (119:131).

Like a man craving water in Death Valley, the psalmist opens his mouth and pants after God's Word. His statement reverberates with David's in Psalm 42:1, "As the deer pants for the water brooks, so my soul pants for You O God." The parched soul of the psalmist craves God like a dessicated tongue craves water. I find it significant that he does not compare his craving with hunger. The body can go many days without food, but not water. Few can live beyond a week without water, and to stay healthy, most people need to drink six to eight glasses of water per day.

As a child I was infatuated with the early American Indians. I relived the Indian life by sewing together my own loin cloths, breeches, and moccasins out of leather. I built forts and teepees and trapped raccoons, opossums and chipmunks. But no animal intrigued me more than the white-tailed deer. Its acute senses and incredible speed thrilled me. One day I spent several hours crawling through thick trees and weeds to a frequent spot where I knew deer liked to rest. After what seemed like days of creeping at inch-worm speed, I spotted a deer coming down to the season brook. His mouth was open and he panted like a dog. Without hesitation, he shot like a bee straight to that brook and didn't move until he had drunk deeply.

That experience brought Psalm 42:1 to life! I pondered how a deer could crave a simple drink of water more than I longed for God Himself. Why do we fail to long for Him? Because we look for happiness everywhere but in God alone. The only true and lasting happiness in this life will be found in a growing and enrapturing adoration of and love for the Lord and Savior Jesus Christ. Fill the psalmist's open mouth with all the pleasures, all the temptations, and all the vices of this world and you'll find it only works like salt, leaving him thirstier for the Word of God. The psalmist longs for God's Word because he knows that it will bring him supreme happiness.

2. If you marinate your mind with God's Word it will produce dogged purpose (vss 132-135).

In his book, *Welcome to the Family*, John MacArthur tells the story of Franz Kafka:

> Franz Kafka, the gifted Czech-born writer who lived at the beginning of the 20th century, used a parable to illustrate the futility of man's search for truth. He described a bombed-out city of rubble where death and ruin were everywhere. People had been crushed under rocks, where they lay dying in agony. In the middle of this total holocaust, one solitary figure sits in a bathroom. Kafka called him the defiant fisherman. He is seated on a toilet seat with a fishing line dangling into a bathtub. There is no water in the tub, and obviously no fish, but the defiant fisherman keeps on fishing anyhow. That, said Kafka, is what the search for truth is like.[1]

Lack of truth creates a sense of purposelessness and lack of purpose creates hopelessness. If a man cannot find truth, he will not be able to explain the purpose of his existence. For him right and wrong rest on the balance scale of man's wavering opinion. People without purpose are a people without hope. But because the psalmist has God's Word, he has great hope. And not just any hope, but a dogged hope. A hope with purpose. He knows why God created him, who God is, and what God expects of him. This gives him purpose for living.

In the next four verses, the psalmist's requests of God demonstrate his undying purpose for living. The Psalmist does not make random requests spurred on by the emotion of the moment. Notice that each request carries focused purpose.

TURN TO ME AND BE GRACIOUS TO ME, AFTER YOUR MANNER
WITH THOSE WHO LOVE YOUR NAME (119:132).

The psalmist lives to gain God's forgiveness. This is one of the few verses of Psalm 119 that does not mention the Word. Nonetheless, it's just as precious.

"Turn to me! See my condition and have mercy. See my contrite heart and

---

1   John MacArthur, *Welcome to the Family* (Nashville: Thomas Nelson, 2005), 31.

grant forgiveness." He yearns for the eyes of God to turn to him in compassion and mercy. What son can be happier than the son forgiven by his father? And what could be more hopeless than a God who refuses to forgive? God is under absolutely no obligation to forgive, but He chooses to do so from the merciful kindness of His heart. Spurgeon said of God, "If he looked in stern justice his eyes would not endure us, but looking in mercy he spares and blesses us."[2]

This psalmist is one humble man. He does not ask for some great favor or wish to be granted. He does not request physical strength or monetary wealth. The psalmist asks not for the pleasures of this world, but he simply prays for mercy and grace. He always lives in full awareness of his complete unworthiness but with vivid awareness of God's delight to forgive and shower mercy. Sinful men hope God will not notice them. In their chest rests a trembling fear that God will see their sin and pour out the judgment they deserve. Godly men, however, seek the attention of His forgiving gaze.

The psalmist writes, "After your manner with those who love Your name." He knows that it is in the very nature of God to be merciful to those who belong to Him. He could not make this statement if he was not an avid student of God's acts of mercy shown throughout history. God reserves His most special and gracious acts of kindness for His own children. This is a key concept. The assurance of knowing that you belong to God creates confidence in pleading His mercy.

Peter's denial was not too great a sin for Christ to cleanse and make him the head apostle of the early church. The adulterous woman in John 8 was not so wicked that Christ could not say, "Neither do I condemn you. Go and sin no more" (John 8:11). Zaccheus's life of thievery and deception was not so unforgivable that Christ would not tell him, "I must dine with you today" (Luke 9:1-10). And your sins are not so many that Christ would not die a torturous death to redeem you from all your transgressions. There is no sin too great for God to forgive, nor too evil for Christ to die for.

ESTABLISH MY FOOTSTEPS IN YOUR WORD, AND DO NOT LET ANY INIQUITY HAVE DOMINION OVER ME (119:133).

The psalmist lives to gain God's stability. The word "establish" is in a Hebrew tense that emphasizes the causer of the action. It could be translated, "Cause my footsteps to be established in Your Word." We cannot establish ourselves any more than a tree can establish itself in mid air. Its roots must sink deep into the earth to create stability and hold it upright.

Like a plant, if our roots sink into a six inch pot with no room to grow and

---

2   Spurgeon, 379.

no sure foundation, it will only take a slight wind to blow us over. But when God plants our souls, our affections, our thoughts and our motives into the garden of His Word, we become strong and healthy with deep roots and room to grow and no wind or rain can move us. God's Word has anchored us to the Lord Himself.

While the first half of verse 133 gives the request, the second half provides the motive: *"And do not let any iniquity have dominion over me."* The psalmist seeks a solid anchor, not for his stocks and bonds, not for his business account, not even for his health, the unity of his family or the protection of his social security. He seeks a rock foundation for the purity of his own soul. He knows that if he is set like concrete in the Word of God, sin will never be his master.

I believe that the psalmist knows that God's children are free from their sin. But I believe he knows equally well that God's children are often tempted to be ruled by sin. Sin is a powerful and cruel tyrant. The Arabic word for "sultan," a ruler of a Muslim country, is derived from the same root as "dominion" in this verse. You cannot allow sin into your life without putting it on the throne. When you submit to sin you pay it obeisance as your king and the only way to dethrone its power is through repentance by the grace of God. Trying to hold your sin at bay or allowing it to enter just a few parts of your life will not restrain its power. It must be hacked to pieces just as Samuel dismembered King Agag (1 Sam 15:33). Give it an ounce of mercy and it will bind you in shackles. In the year 1666 Michael Bruce said, "I had rather be a prisoner to man all my life than be in bondage to sin [for] one day."[3]

Notice also that the psalmist recognizes God's authority even over the power of sin. This is why he says, "God, You keep iniquity from ruling over me." The psalmist appeals to the great Ruler of the universe for help against his personal sin.

There are times in my life where I am tempted so intensely it seems unbearable. The pull for wickedness grows so strong I feel as if the only way to relieve the pressure is by yielding. But when I cry out to God for help, when I tell Him I can't bear this by myself, invariably He comes to my aid. He has never once forsaken me in my hour of need and never will He forsake you if you are His child. He gladly helps those who are His (Rom 8:38-39; 2 Tim 2:19).

REDEEM ME FROM THE OPPRESSION OF MAN, THAT I MAY KEEP YOUR PRECEPTS (119:134).

The psalmist lives to gain God's redemption. To redeem means to purchase for a price, and sometimes to purchase from slavery. The psalmist is oppressed by

---

3   Michael Bruce quoted by Spurgeon, 387.

those who hate his stand for God's Word, and so he turns to God for deliverance. God is in the business of redeeming His people. He redeemed Jacob from evil (Gen 48:16), Israel from Egypt (Ex 13:14-15), David from distress (2 Sam 4:9), and the believer from his sin through the death of Jesus Christ (Mk 10:45).

Why does the psalmist seek redemption? To relieve his pain? To pacify his sufferings? No. He seeks redemption so that he can keep God's precepts. The wicked deeds of the oppressors merely serve to distract the psalmist from his commitment to God. The psalmist is not seeking his own comfort, but God's glory. The pain of not being able to obey God is much greater to him than the pain of persecution for his faith.

The more godly a man is, the more he will be persecuted for his godliness (2 Tim 3:12; John 15:20). John the Baptist preached Christ so they beheaded him. Stephen preached Christ so they stoned Him. Christ preached Himself so they crucified Him. And in every case, who did these men entrust themselves to? God alone! They cried out to Him for strength and God's grace was sufficient (Luke 22:41-44; 1 Pet 2:22-23).

MAKE YOUR FACE SHINE UPON YOUR SERVANT, AND TEACH ME YOUR STATUTES (119:135).

The psalmist lives to gain God's favor. This verse echoes the prayer Aaron was to pray for Israel (Num 6:24-26). Here the Psalmist prays for God's favor to be poured out upon him. If God seeks throughout the earth to find those that please Him, the psalmist wants to be in this group.

We must seek God's favor more than our success, for to have God's favor *is* the greatest success. The greatest blessing man can know is not a successful ministry, not a happy family, not a loving marriage, but to know that God is pleased with his life. Out of this flow all the blessings of God (James 1:17). If God is pleased with your living, He will bless you with the greatest blessing any believer can receive, that is God's favor!

The psalmist also seeks God's instruction: "Teach me your statutes." Both requests, God's favor and God's teaching, are intensely personal and intimate. The psalmist is not satisfied with a ritualistic relationship with the King of the universe. He wants a close, intimate, endearing connection with His God in heaven.

Every request of these four verses (132-135) is direct and without apology. "Lord, turn to me, establish me, redeem me, and show me your favor!" The psalmist can pray with great boldness because he knows that God delights in doing all four of these things. His knowledge of God's character gives him meaningful purpose for living.

3. If you marinate your mind with God's Word, it will produce sacred sadness (vs 136).

MY EYES SHED STREAMS OF WATER,
BECAUSE THEY DO NOT KEEP YOUR LAW (119:136).

As Solomon wisely said, "there is a time to weep" (Eccl 3:4), and the psalmist now finds that time. His misery is not sadness over his own sin or anguish fed by the guilt of his sinful conduct, but a sacred, holy sadness, caused by his love for God's glory.

Why would the psalmist shed rivers of tears just because others break God's law? Should he not say, "That's their problem, not mine?" If someone harmed your spouse or your best friend it would bring you great sorrow. If someone slandered your brother or killed your dear child, you'd rightly weep tears of grief. Why? Because you love them deeply. When someone close to you is offended, you are offended. When someone close to you is hurt, you are hurt. This psalmist is so zealous for God's holiness and God's honor that to see an unbeliever break God's law moves him to tears. He feels the pain of God being dishonored in his own chest and this causes him to weep.

This passage proves that the psalmist's hate for those who break God's law is neither vindictive nor sinful (vs 113). He is consumed by God's glory. When he sees the ungodly sneer at God's holiness, it makes him angry. When he sees the ungodly break God's law, it brings him to tears.

How often do you find a prideful Christian weeping over an unbeliever's sin? Do you ever see a believer who points out the sins of others, while blind to his own failures, crying streams of tears because an unbeliever has dishonored God? It is only the humble consumed with God's glory who suffer when God's glory is dishonored.

Barnes says rightly that "there is nothing for which we should be excited to deeper emotion in respect to our fellow-men than for the fact that they are violators of the law of God and exposed to its fearful penalty."[4] The psalmist is not an arrogant, prideful hypocrite, but a humble man consumed with God's holiness.

It is a healthy thing to weep over the sins of others and not commend ourselves like the proud Pharisee in Luke 18:11. Rather we should let others' sin warn us against our own propensity toward evil. "If we grieve not for others, their sin may become ours."[5]

---

4   Albert Barnes, quoted by Zemek, 303.
5   William Nicholson, quoted by Spurgeon, 389.

From Psalm 119:129-136 we have studied three things God's Word can do to you when you choose to marinate your mind in its truth:

1. It will produce supreme happiness (vss 129-131).
2. It will produce dogged purpose (vss 132-135).
3. It will produce sacred sadness (vs 136).

At King Edward the Sixth's royal coronation, he was presented with three swords, signifying that he was monarch of three kingdoms. But the king said that there was one sword missing.

"Which one is that?"

"The Holy Bible," replied the king "which is the sword of the Spirit, and is to be preferred before these ensigns of royalty."

QUESTIONS FOR CONTEMPLATION

1. Read through the passage and note all the ways that the Word influences the psalmist.

2. What is the psalmist struggling against in this passage?

3. Why does God's Word produce supreme happiness?

4. What is "sacred sadness?" Is there a time to be sad? What are right and wrong motives for being sad?

5. How is God's Word positively impacting your life today? How much time do you spend in it on a daily basis?

Cling to God's Word Like a Rock in a Storm
Psalm 119:81-88, 89-96, 153-160

The year was 1969 and the place was Pass Christian, Mississippi. In spite of Police Chief Jerry Peralta's warning, a group of twenty or more people gathered in their apartment complex for a "hurricane party" in the face of the threatening hurricane, Camille, which was fast approaching. Located only 250 feet from the beach, Peralta told them to leave, but reminiscent to the pagans in Noah's day, they laughed back and one man responded, "This is my land. If you want me off, you'll have to arrest me."

Unsuccessful, the police chief left, but the hurricane did not. At record-breaking winds of 205 miles per hour and waves cresting almost 30 feet high, Camille blew the little community of Pass Christian, Mississippi to smithereens. It left the only a single survivor, a five year old boy, clinging desperately to a mattress.[1]

At some point those partiers' pleasure turned to horror, but then it was too late. Unlike the residents of this city, in the middle of intense turmoil or heavy trials, the believer does not have to suffer unbearable disaster without hope. He has the Word of God, the believer's single-most trustworthy, life-giving companion in the dark jungles of this sinful world.

Few places in Scripture express the believer's utter dependence on the life-giving Word like the psalmist does in Psalm 119. In the following three sections we will look at 1) What to do when the suffering is unbearable (119:81-88), 2) Why you cannot survive without God's Word (119:89-96), and 3) How to pray when you need help from God (119:153-160).

---

1   *Christian Values Quarterly*, Spring/Summer (1994): 10.

What to Do When Suffering is Unbearable
Psalm 119:81-88

- The LA Times reports that costs related to stress, such as busy traffic, over-packed schedules and high pressure managers costs the United States a total of $300 billion annually.
- A study from the University of Michigan claims that the common cold blows away $40 billion per year.
- The Marin Institute says that alcohol-related problems give the US a $184.6 billion hangover annually.
- According to the same source, cigarette smoking has burned up $137 billion each year.
- Underage drinking last year cost the nation $53 billion, says the National Academy of Sciences.
- According to the US Chamber of Commerce, cocaine alone snorted away $47 billion from American businesses last year.
- The U.S. Department of Justice claims that $450 billion is lifted from the nation's pocket every year by crime.
- $9.3 billion worth of gambling losses were reported to the IRS in the year 2000.
- In the words of a Chicago research firm, during Super Bowl week, the average American spends 10 minutes each work day talking about football, costing employers $800 million in lost productivity.
- Headaches pound the US industry for $50 billion a year according to the National Headache Foundation.[1]

These costs illustrate the magnitude of the painful world we live in. Whether it be drug abuse, physical sickness or a deep loss, pain is very real. But a believer in Christ is quite familiar with another kind of pain: suffering in

---

1 *Readers Digest* (July 2004): 144-145.

obedience. Though the internal joy far exceeds the pain, one suffers for obeying God. A believer suffering for a righteous cause pleases God. The apostle Peter wrote the following to believers who were suffering greatly for their faith:

"For it is better, if God should will it so, that you suffer for doing what is right rather than for doing what is wrong" (1 Pet 3:17).

"For what credit is there if, when you sin and are harshly treated, you endure it with patience? But if when you do what is right and suffer for it you patiently endure it, this finds favor with God" (1 Pet 2:20).

Suffering is not only natural to the Christian life, but necessary. It has been said, "A Christian is like a tea bag—not much good until it has gone through hot water."[2] C. H. Spurgeon wrote, "I dare say that the greatest earthly blessing that God can give to any of us is health, with the exception of sickness."[3]

In Psalm 119:81-88 we read about a man whose sufferings were intense, and from these verses we find four tools for surviving suffering:

Tool #1: Face your suffering (vss 81-87).

Many believers respond to suffering by ignoring it, trying to replace it with something else, or calling it something different than what it really is. But the psalmist does none of these. He faces his suffering boldly.

MY SOUL LANGUISHES FOR YOUR SALVATION;
I WAIT FOR YOUR WORD (119:81).

The word "languish" means "to be at one's end, to be finished" or "to be spent." Notice that he does not say, "I am languishing." Or "my body is languishing." No, his suffering is too deep for those terms. His soul is suffering from deep within.

A man's whose soul is at peace with God more easily endures intense physical torture than a man with health and wealth whose emotions are crushed by the betrayal of a dear friend. Internal suffering bites deeper, holds on longer, and is a living death. More people have committed suicide to relieve themselves of emotional pain than those who have ended their lives because of physical pain.

Emotional pain can also cause physical pain. A hypochondriac becomes sick just by thinking he is sick. Doctors have repeatedly testified that more than half of the physical sicknesses of their patients are triggered by emotional

---

2   Michael P. Green, *Illustrations for Biblical Preaching: Over 1500 Sermon Illustrations* Arranged by Topic and Indexed Exhaustively, electronic edition, (Grand Rapids: Baker Book House, 1989), n. p.
3   Robert J. Morgan, *Nelson's Complete Book of Stories, Illustrations, and Quotes*, electronic edition, (Nashville: Thomas Nelson Publishers, 2000), 738.

conditions.

For a moment, consider the horrid sufferings that people everywhere face every day:

- A husband discovers his wife has been cheating on him.
- A couple finds themselves plunged into financial debt.
- A mother is informed that her son has been charged with murder.
- A child is told that his father went down in a plane wreck.
- A student suddenly learns that her best friend has been slandering her.

This pain cuts deeper into the soul than any tool of physical torture. What is the psalmist's soul languishing for? God's salvation. "My soul languishes for your salvation"(119:81). Salvation from what? From hell? Not likely since his previous testimony confirms that he knows that he is a believer. From physical pain? No, for as we discussed, it is not his body that suffers. It has to be salvation from his internal torment. The psalmist cries out for God to end his horrid emotional pain.

MY EYES FAIL WITH LONGING FOR YOUR WORD, WHILE I SAY, "WHEN WILL YOU COMFORT ME?" (119:82).

The psalmist's agony has caused him to crave God's Word intensely. When I was eleven years old, my father took me on a scouting trip with his friend to investigate the countryside where he would be deer hunting. But we made a big mistake when we left the truck—we took no water. After a full day of hiking through dry brush, over hills and under a burning sun, my tongue swelled and all I could think about was water. We finally arrived back at the truck to discover that my dad's friend had collected water in milk jugs that weren't rinsed. The water tasted like sour milk, but we were so thirsty we didn't care.

In the same way, the psalmist craves God's Word so much that his eyes feel as though they are wasting away in their longing just to see a few letters, a few words, of God's precious Book.

"When will You comfort me?" (119:82b). The psalmist also craves God's Word because he knows that God's comfort comes through His Word. His suffering brought him to the realization that only God's comfort will soothe his tortured soul (2 Cor 1:3-4).

THOUGH I HAVE BECOME LIKE A WINESKIN IN THE SMOKE... (119:83A).

In the psalmist's day, men used animal hides to hold their wine. But if left near a fire, the smoke would suck out the moisture and turn the leather brittle and unusable. Like a dried up wineskin, the psalmist feels wasted away.

HOW MANY ARE THE DAYS OF YOUR SERVANT? WHEN WILL YOU EXECUTE JUDGMENT ON THOSE WHO PERSECUTE ME? (119:84A).

By asking this question the psalmist acknowledges that God has already ordained how many days he will live (Ps 139:16). He realizes that he cannot add or subtract a single day of his life on this globe. Therefore, he cries out in wailful abjection to know how long he must live in this pain.

Notice that both questions in verse 84 are questions of time. How long must I live? And how long until you will punish my persecutors? The psalmist admits that God rules over the timing of every event—even the painful ones.

But why does the psalmist ask God to "execute judgment on those who persecute me" (vs 84)? Although it is true that we are to pray for our enemies and love those who persecute us, this request contradicts neither command.

Will God punish unrepentant sinners? Yes. Is God righteous and just to punish unrepentant sinners? Yes. The psalmist is simply asking God to act according to His character and no sin is committed.

The psalmist is not hating or despising his enemies, but praying for God's justice to shine. Notice also that instead of retaliating against his enemies, instead of returning evil for evil, he simply takes the matter to God, and asks God to be the Judge of the wicked (Rom 12:19).

THE ARROGANT HAVE DUG PITS FOR ME, MEN WHO ARE NOT IN ACCORD WITH YOUR LAW (119:85).

During the Old Testament period, before a king entered battle he calculated where the enemy was likely to flee and dug pits in that vicinity. When the king's army gained victory, the enemy would retreat into the area of covered pits which often caused more casualties than the sword.

In a similar way, the proud and haughty have tried to trap the psalmist in his own sin. Why do unbelievers despise the gospel of Jesus Christ? Why do pagans turn violent if you tell them that they are living in sin? Because nothing disturbs an unholy person more than holiness.

It is the psalmist's godliness that drives his enemies mad, and the only way they can alleviate this annoyance is by attempting to trap the psalmist in his own sin. He lives by the Word and they do all that they can to make him fall by it.

...THEY HAVE PERSECUTED ME WITH A LIE; HELP ME! (119:186B).

Has a close friend ever slandered you behind your back? Few things burn more deeply than gossip and lies (James 3:5-6). John Dryden, a seventeenth-century British dramatist and poet, once commented on man's propensity to gossip:

There is a lust in man no charm can tame,
Of loudly publishing his neighbor's shame.
Hence, on eagles' wings immortal scandals fly,
While virtuous actions are but born and die.[4]

THEY ALMOST DESTROYED ME ON EARTH... (119:87B).
The psalmist has been so battered by the hatred of his enemies he feels like he has almost died. Note that the psalmist has fully faced his suffering in its fullest reality. But he does not stop there.

Tool #2: Talk to God about your suffering (vss 81-87).

If you observe carefully, you will find that this passage (119:81-88) is full of personal pronouns. The Psalmist says **Your** salvation (81), **Your** word (81), **Your** word (82), when will **You** comfort me (82), **Your** statutes (83), **Your** servant (84), when will **You** execute judgment (84), **Your** law (85), **Your** commandments (86), **Your** precepts (87), **Your** lovingkindness (88), and **Your** mouth (88). The psalmist is talking *to God Himself* about his suffering. His mind is full of God's presence and is acutely conscious of God's listening ear.

Of all the people in your life, whom do you talk to first when you are hurting? The person you trust the most. The person you are closest to. Your response to trials is a direct reflection of your intimacy with God.

When suffering does not drive a believer to God, that believer lives like an atheist. If following the world's answer, we cope with suffering by changing our surroundings, doing things in excess, or just carrying it all by ourselves. And soon we are crushed and broken, because we did not take our trials to the only One who can help us.

John Bunyan wrote, "You can do more than pray after you have prayed but you cannot do more than pray until you have prayed."[5]

Charles Spurgeon said, "If a little bird, hunted by a hawk, flew into the bosom of a heathen, the heathen could not betray him for seeking refuge. How much less will God turn out those who seek refuge in Him?"[6]

Tool #3: View your suffering in light of the Word of God (vss 81, 83, 86, 87).

MY SOUL LANGUISHES FOR YOUR SALVATION;
I WAIT FOR YOUR WORD (119:81).
The psalmist's soul is pulverized to dust, but God's Word gives him the hope he

---

4   Green, n. p.
5   Kent and Barbara Hughes, *Liberating Ministry from the Success Syndrome* (Wheaton: Tyndale House Publishers, 1987), 72.
6   Spurgeon, 370.

needs to live on. A suicidal person often looks for one final sliver of hope before finally jumping off the bridge. And even one drop of hope has proven to keep a man or woman from ending his life. For the true believer, the Word makes life worth living. As one author put it: "When you get to the end of your rope, tie a knot and hold on."

...I DO NOT FORGET YOUR STATUTES (119:83B).

His soul has been baked dry, but remembering God's Word is like spring water to his shriveled spirit.

ALL YOUR COMMANDMENTS ARE FAITHFUL...(119:86A).

Though he is pricked with the lies of his enemies, God's Word is a rock of trustworthiness.

...BUT AS FOR ME, I DID NOT FORSAKE YOUR PRECEPTS (119:87B).

In the first part of verse 87 the psalmist writes, "They almost destroyed me on earth..." The psalmist has reached his limit. He cannot take anymore. But once again, he turns to the Word and says, "But as for me, I did not forsake Your precepts." His enemies persecute him so relentlessly that the thought of throwing God's Word overboard crosses his mind. His faithfulness to God is the very cause of his persecution, so to resign from obedience would relieve him of pain. But he refuses to give up. Why? Because he views his suffering in light of God's Word.

Tool #4: Live to keep the Word of God (vs 88).

REVIVE ME ACCORDING TO YOUR LOVINGKINDNESS, SO THAT I MAY KEEP THE TESTIMONY OF YOUR MOUTH (119:88).

Revive me so that I may be relieved from pain? No. So that I may keep the testimony of your very mouth!

The "rough riders" who fought at Theodore Roosevelt's side in the Spanish-American War of the late 1800's (some twenty years following the Civil War), were carefully selected from different races, backgrounds, and parts of the world. Some were Indians, some tennis athletes, some sharpshooters, and some mountain men. One day they drank a toast, "To the officers—may they get killed, wounded, or promoted!"[7] That should be the attitude of the true Christian believer!

It matters not how I suffer, I live to obey Him. If I cannot obey him, I have no reason for living!

---

[7]   Edmund Morris, *The Rise of Theodore Roosevelt* (New York: Coard McCann & Geoghegan, 1979), 636.

The psalmist asks God to revive him. What is it that would move God to revive the psalmist? "Revive me according to Your lovingkindness (119:88a).

God does not revive his people out of dutiful requirement. He revives His people out of the sheer delight of showering them with His comfort. This word "lovingkindness" is best translated as "faithful love." When you are afflicted there is great comfort in knowing that God's faithful lovingkindness does not change with the weather or fade with the night. Only when you grasp God's lovingkindness, His mercy and compassion, will you savor comfort in unbearable suffering.

In this chapter we uncovered four strategies for surviving suffering:

Tool #1: Face your suffering (vss 81-87).
Tool #2: Talk to God about your suffering (vss 81-87).
Tool #3: View your suffering in light of the Word of God (vss 81, 83, 86, 87).
Tool #4: Live to keep the Word of God (vs 88).

A cruel Englishman who acquired slaves from Africa and transported them like animals to be sold at auctions wrote the most popular song of English-speaking blacks in the entire world—Amazing Grace. After his conversion, John Newton became a pastor and opposed the slave trade. At age 82, weak and blind, he said these words, "My memory is nearly gone, but I remember two things: that I am a great sinner, and that Christ is a great Savior!"[8] That is the testimony of a man who understood God's great mercy!

Today the choice is yours: you can be crushed in your suffering, or you can embrace it thankfully and turn to God for help.

---

8   Randy Alcorn, *The Grace and Truth Paradox* (Sisters: Multnomah Publishers, 2003), 48-49.

QUESTIONS FOR CONTEMPLATION

1. Read through the passage again and list all the ways the psalmist is suffering.

2. Now think of suffering you experience. How do you respond to it?

3. Why is it so important to face your suffering? Why does it help to talk to God about it?

4. How does God's Word help us in our suffering (see verses 81, 83, 86, 87)?

5. How are you going to respond the next time you suffer?

The Word: Your Survival Kit for Staying Alive
Psalm 119:89-96

If your body is deprived of water for five days or food for two weeks your life will end. If your heart stops beating, your life be over in just three to five minutes. The death of a cancer patient starts with the self destruction of one cell. AIDS begins with a single virus which invades the body and destroys the immune system. Just as the body cannot survive without organs, blood, and water, so the believer cannot survive in this sin-saturated world without the Word of God. You are doomed to failure if you don't have the Word of God in your heart and mind.

The psalmist gives us two reasons why the believer needs God's Word in Psalm 119:89-91.

1. The Word is a shouting testimony to God's faithfulness (vss 89-91).

FOREVER, O LORD, YOUR WORD IS SETTLED IN HEAVEN (119:89). The Hebrew word "settled" literally means "stands firm." The tense of the verb indicates that this is an ongoing, unending condition. God's Word stands firm continually, never ending and God's Word cannot be shaken. God's Word will not fail.

God promises to give us everything we need for life and godliness (2 Pet 1:3), and the natural assumption of 2 Timothy 3:16 is that God will continue to preserve His Word so that we may fulfill its purpose. God has providentially preserved His Word on earth for thousands of years in spite of the rage of emperors and rulers.

It is true that God's people have not always possessed all of the Scriptures. In King Josiah's day, the land of Israel lived in moral debauchery for such a long time that the Israelites literally lost the book of the Law (2 Kings 22). Fortunately, the high priest Hilkiah stumbled upon it and a nationwide revival resulted. But before he found it, the people of Israel had gone so long without God's Word that they forgot what it said!

But even though Israel failed to keep track of the Scriptures, God never failed to faithfully preserve them. In verse 89, the psalmist emphasizes the unending nature of God's Word in heaven by placing the word "forever" at the beginning. He does not say, "Your word stands forever, but *Forever* your word stands in heaven." Flowers wilt and streams run dry, but God's Word will never cease to be. Liars lie and deceivers deceive but the Word of God is always true. Charlatans claim to know the future, but in time the future claims them as quacks. Palm readers, fortune-tellers, horoscopists, mediums, and false prophets will all pass away with their claims, but God's Word always does exactly what it says.

Christ promised, "For truly I say to you, until heaven and earth pass away not the smallest letter or stroke shall pass away from the law until all is accomplished" (Matt 5:18). Emperors may burn it, heretics may twist it and pagans may reject it, but they will lie in their graves while God's Word outlives them all. Every star, planet, and celestial body will some day go up in smoke (2 Pet 3:10), but God's Word will continue on. Men change their minds, revise their doctrines, and adjust their laws, but God's Word will not shift (Rom 3:4). His commands, His precepts, His rules, His laws and His testimonies will last forever and ever.

This is why Christ said, "Heaven and earth pass away but My words will not pass away" (Matt 24:35) and Isaiah wrote, "The grass withers, the flower fades, but the word of our God stands forever" (Is 40:8). You can trust His Word!

Dig down to the root of every sin and doubt, and you will find the soil of distrust for God's eternal Word. At the heart of every sin is some disbelief, and at the heart of every virtue stands the immovable conviction that, "Forever, O LORD, Your word is settled in heaven."

YOUR FAITHFULNESS CONTINUES THROUGHOUT ALL GENERATIONS;
YOU ESTABLISHED THE EARTH, AND IT STANDS.
THEY STAND THIS DAY ACCORDING TO YOUR ORDINANCES,
FOR ALL THINGS ARE YOUR SERVANTS (119:90-91).

God's faithfulness stands firm and continues "throughout all generations." God is not only faithful to one generation. Humans are born and humans die but God remains faithful throughout the eons of time. The death of a man does not change God's faithfulness. Though Abraham died long ago, God still keeps the covenant He made with him. His faithfulness far outlasts the span of human life, for it is *from and to* all eternity.

To be faithful means to be true to what one has said or promised. To spontaneously wash my neighbor's car every Saturday would be a kind act, but not necessarily a faithful act. It would be faithfulness to my own decision to do this every week, but not faithfulness to my neighbor since I promised him nothing. However, if I pledged to my neighbor to scrub his car every Saturday and did so, then I have been faithful because I have kept my word. In the same way, God's faithfulness is directly connected to His Word. You cannot know His faithfulness if you do not know His Word.

In the second half of verse 90 the psalmist writes, "You established the earth, and it stands." Men build houses, but in time termites bring them back to dust. Men erect cities, but any city left to itself will soon deteriorate. Yet God's creation constantly repairs itself, just as the death of a seed produces new life or a lightning-caused fire brings fresh new growth to a forest.

The fixed laws of creation are shouting testimonies to God's faithful Word. In verses 90b-91, he begins to illustrate this faithfulness by looking at the standing world which God created by His own "ordinances." This word "ordinances" is much like the decree of a king who makes a rule which the entire kingdom must obey, no matter the difficulty. If they obey, they are deemed faithful. In the same way, God's universe[1] operates by fixed laws. The fact that these fixed laws never change is a testimony to God's faithfulness to His Word.

In the beginning, God told the earth to spin on its invisible axis. Eight to ten thousand years later, it's still spinning. That's faithfulness. In the beginning, God told the sun to burn with tremendous heat. Eight to ten millenniums later it still burns, making life possible on earth. That's faithfulness.

The mixture of hot and cold air creates tornadoes. Weathermen base their predictions on the fixed patterns of the atmosphere. You can walk on lakes when the temperature drops below freezing. Fire makes meat edible by killing germs. Ice floats. Millions of industries depend on the fixed laws of God's universe. Scientists, chemists, doctors, contractors, firemen, engineers—every occupation in the world—depends on God's fixed laws.

Imagine for a moment that the fixed laws of nature suddenly changed just for three seconds:

- Floating ice in the north and south poles would sink and flood the ocean. The ocean would overspill, causing massive floods killing millions of humans, plants, and creatures.
- Electricity would not operate according to God's prescribed command, creating worldwide blackouts and killing billions of lives who depend on it.
- Airplanes would suddenly spin out of control as the laws of air pressure would fail to keep the planes in the sky.
- Humans, massive rocks, and water would float off to space as the laws

---

[1] "They" in verse 91 refers to the heavens and the earth.

of gravity stop.

• Worst of all, the restraint of God's own decree which keeps the protons and the neutrons in every atom pulling together could create an electrical charge reversal, causing the protons and neutrons to repel, ending in the explosion of every atom. That would be the end of the universe.

It is no wonder that Ralph Waldo Emerson wrote, "All I have seen teaches me to trust the Creator for all I have not seen." The author of Hebrews testified to the faithfulness of God through His Son who "upholds all things by the Word of His power" (Heb 1:3) or as Paul says, "In Christ all things hold together" (Col 1:17).

The next time you doubt the faithfulness of God, step outside and observe God's handiwork around you. See how it grows and is preserved. See how planets refrain from crashing into our globe; how the sun is never too close or too far from the earth; how the seasons never fail to follow their cycles. To doubt God's faithfulness, one has to boldly lie in the face of all evidence.

And if God is this faithful in His creation to unbelievers, how much more faithful will He be in His written Word toward His own people! "Thus says the Lord, 'Who gives the sun for light by day and the fixed order of the moon and the stars for light by night, Who stirs up the sea so that its waves roar; the Lord of hosts is His name: If this fixed order departs from before Me,' declares the Lord, 'Then the offspring of Israel also will cease from being a nation before Me forever'" (Jer 31:35-36).

And notice the reason all of creation submits itself to God's ordinances: "for all things are Your servants" (vs 91b). Everything in existence is faithful to God's command because God is the sovereign ruler of the universe. Whenever He wishes, God can reverse the fixed laws of nature to accomplish His purpose. The hungry lions did not eat Daniel (Dan 6:21-22), and the sun stopped for Joshua (Josh 10:12-14).

It is ironic that the unbeliever's very life depends on the faithfulness of God's Word which created this world, but he rejects His written Word which will reward him with eternal death. If the entire world is dependent upon God's laws in nature, then how much more is your soul dependent upon the laws of His written Word![2] Indeed the Word of God is a shouting testimony to God's faithfulness!

2. The Word is a nutritious feast for the believer's soul (vss 92–96).

Spurgeon wrote, "That word which has preserved the heavens and the earth also

---

2   *"God's general revelation is the guarantee of the dependability of His special revelation,"* (Zemek, 218).

preserves the people of God in their time of trial."[3] This is seen in verses 92-96.

IF YOUR LAW HAD NOT BEEN MY DELIGHT,
THEN I WOULD HAVE PERISHED IN MY AFFLICTION (119:92).

This is the third of five times that the psalmist expresses his delight in the Word of God (vss 24, 77, 92, 143, 174). In the dark tunnel of misery and despair, the only flame of hope that keeps the psalmist alive is the delight of knowing, meditating on, obeying, and cherishing the Holy Scriptures. Edmund Calamy said it well, "The word of God delighted in is the afflicted saint's antidote against ruin and destruction."[4]

I WILL NEVER FORGET YOUR PRECEPTS,
FOR BY THEM YOU HAVE REVIVED ME (119:93).

The psalmist covenants to remember God's commands because these commandments have restored him in the midst of dark hours. Those who taste the sweetness of God's Word in the middle of crushing trials will treasure it far more dearly than those who never feel their need for it.

Imagine that your plane crashes into the ocean. You swim to a deserted island, and you live there on raw clams and rain water for three years. From the day you are rescued until the end of your life you will never forget the precious amenities of flowing water and cooked food. Water tastes best in the desert, hot soup tastes best at the north pole. In the same way, God's Word tastes sweetest in the middle of dire need.

I AM YOURS, SAVE ME;
FOR I HAVE SOUGHT YOUR PRECEPTS (119:94).

As his passion builds, the psalmist can no better express his love for God than to cry out, "I am Yours! Save me!" William Cowper paraphrases verse 94 beautifully:

> *Thine by creation, I was made by thee;*
> *Thine by adoption, I was assigned over to thee;*
> *Thine by donation, I was given to thee*
> *Thine by marriage , I was espoused to thee*
> *Thine by redemption, I was purchased by thee*
> *Thine by stipulation, I have vowed myself unto thee.*[5]

The psalmist even mouths the proof that he belongs to God when he says,

---

3   Spurgeon, 316.
4   Edmund Calamy quoted by Spurgeon, 323.
5   William Cowper quoted by Spurgeon, 326.

"for I have sought your precepts." Those who keep God's Word belong to God.

In Galatians 5:24, Paul wrote that those who belong to Christ Jesus have "crucified the flesh with its passions and desires." Shortly before His death Christ told His disciples, "If anyone loves Me, he will keep My word; and My Father will love him, and We will come to him and make Our abode with him" (John 14:23).

In a world with kidnappers, a child with a father is far more secure than an orphan. He knows that he belongs to his parents and it is their duty and honor to protect their child. How much more confidence are we to have in the midst of fear, knowing that we belong to our Father who is in heaven!

THE WICKED WAIT FOR ME TO DESTROY ME;
I SHALL DILIGENTLY CONSIDER YOUR TESTIMONIES (119:95).

The psalmist shows full awareness of these wicked men. "Poised as predators,"[6] they are like wild beasts waiting to pounce and tear him apart. But just as he did numerous times in verses 81-88, instead of fretting over his enemies or lashing out in revenge, the psalmist views his dilemma through the eyes of the Word. The psalmist turns on the beacon light of God's Word and sees things the way they really are. While the wicked wait in stealth for the opportunity to jump him, the psalmist ignores their plots and finds comfort by diligently considering the testimonies of God's Word. While they wait, he works. While they plan in secret, he prays in secret.

The harder they press, the deeper he goes into the Word of God. Their wicked intentions drive the psalmist deeper and deeper into the Bible. The psalmist's testimony is living evidence that the only way to endure suffering is to take hold of the life jacket of God's Word and never let go.

I HAVE SEEN A LIMIT TO ALL PERFECTION (119:9 6A).

This Hebrew phrase literally reads: "I have seen an end to all perfection." As Spurgeon says, "There is no perfection beneath the moon."[7] From the perspective of this life, all good things do come to an end. The taste of a banquet, the smell of a rose and the joy of living itself all eventually end in death. George Swinnock said it well. "[It is] the world in a flame, and all its pomp and pride, and glory, and gallantry, and crowns and scepters, and riches, and treasures, turned into ashes."[8]

The psalmist feels the vanity of finding lasting happiness in this life. Like trying to grasp a helium balloon set loose in the sky, the believer will never find

---

6   Zemek, 226.
7   Spurgeon, 317.
8   Swinnock quoted by Spurgeon, 326.

a lasting peace for his soul on this sinful earth. He must look elsewhere. He must look to the Word.

YOUR COMMANDMENT IS EXCEEDINGLY BROAD (119:96B).
A powerful literary device used by authors of Scripture to emphasize a very strong point is to put two words of complete opposite meaning side by side. The psalmist does this with "end" and "broad." The verse reads in the Hebrew more like this in its literal order: "In all of completeness I have seen an **end**; **broad** is your commandment very much."

By "broad" the psalmist means that God's Word is infinitely sufficient to satisfy, strengthen, and protect the believer. This life is fleeting but God's Word is eternal. The pleasures of this life vaporize like steam, but in God's Word you will find eternal comforts and undying delight.

- *It brings delight to the taste (vs 92.)*
- *It brings life to the heart (vs 93).*
- *It brings peace to the soul (vss 94-95).*
- *It brings gladness to one's life (vs 96).*

From Psalm 119:89-91, we have learned two reasons why we need God's Word:

1. The Word is a shouting testimony to God's faithfulness (vss 89-91)
2. The Word is a nutritious feast for the believer's soul (vss 92-96)

We give great attention to the last speeches of friends. A parent's dying words are received as oracles. Oh, let all this provoke us to diligence in hearing. Let us think, "This may be the last time that Aaron's bell shall sound in our ears and before another day is passed we may be in a another world."
~ Thomas Watson[9] ~

---

9   Watson, 18.

QUESTIONS FOR CONTEMPLATION

1. What do verses 89-91 teach about the relationship between God's sovereignty and His Word? Does this mean God controls all things? Does this mean that man does not have free will? Does this mean that man is not accountable for his actions since God controls all things? Explain.

2. What has God's Word done for the psalmist in verses 92-93? Why was it necessary to delight in God's law to prevent the psalmist from perishing in his affliction (92)?

3. What is so incredible about 94a? Write down 3 practical examples of how a believer can live this out.

4. What is the great comfort in verse 96a?

5. How has God used this passage in your life? How has he convicted you and challenged your need to grow in Him?

What to Do When You Need Help from God
Psalm 119:153-160

Have you ever felt helpless? Perhaps the temptation to sin seemed unbearable. Perhaps getting out of debt seemed impossible. Or maybe your relationship with a loved one turned sour and your efforts to restore it went bankrupt. Maybe you've felt bitterness toward someone for weeks, and could not bring yourself to forgive them. Or maybe you know you've been coward when it comes to witnessing and you hate that you keep chickening out. Perhaps you want to love God more but you wonder why you don't desire to do so. Or your life is plagued with laziness and it's too hard to get disciplined. You want to grow in your knowledge of God's Word, but the task is nothing less than overwhelming, and you haven't the slightest notion on where to start.

Do you ever feel that you are failing as a father or mother? Your child is difficult and getting worse and you've become desperate in your efforts to curb his rebellion. Or perhaps you run to food like an addict to escape your problems, and as your body swells bigger, your despair grows deeper. Perhaps you are ostracized at work for being a Christian. You are the butt of every joke and the object of every attack because you're just too different.

Life is like this sometimes—almost unbearable. Sinful desires come from the inside and relentless trials from the outside. But there is good news. No matter what your problem is, no matter how big it is, no matter how long you've had to bear its crushing weight, you can find help from God. And God does not just give some help, He provides all the help you need.

How do we get this help? We don't pray desperate, empty prayers, remembering our problem but quickly forgetting God's promises. We start by embracing the promises of God as the psalmist does. Psalm 119:153-160 is a psalm of despair and a psalm of hope, a psalm of pain and a psalm of comfort. In this psalm, the psalmist requests God's help no fewer than six times! And yet he prays with tremendous confidence, knowing the answer to his request is more real than the pain he suffers.

There is no power in the prayers themselves, but in the God Who answers them. This is not a prayer mantra or a magic charmer that rubs the divine glass ball and wheels in the requested goods on silver platters.

From this passage, you will find three prayers that you can pray when you need help from God. These prayers are simply methods of remembering three promises God has guaranteed to every one of His children. These promises are not *chances* and not *maybes*, but guaranteed pledges sealed by the mouth of God Himself! Promises you can trust. Promises that God will fulfill even if He must deliver them on the wings of angels.

Prayer #1: Oh God, deliver me, for I am your child! (vss 153, 155, 157, 158).

God delivers His people. Even a brief sketch of God's dealings with Israel waves like a banner of God's faithfulness. And with full knowledge that Israel would spit in His face after Moses' death, He still herded them into the Promised Land (Deut 31:27-29; cf. Josh 24:19).

The God of Israel yesterday is the same God of the Christian today. He is the God who delivered Abraham from Pharaoh (Gen 12:10-20), Isaac from the Philistines (Gen 26:6-11) and Jacob from his own brother (Gen 32:9-12; 33:1-17). He is the God Who saved Jacob's twelve sons from starvation (Gen 37-50), and liberated Israel from slavery (Ex 1-14), giving her water from a rock (Ex 15:22-25) and manna from the sky (Ex 16:1-21). He is the God who crushed nations like dust before Joshua (Josh 1-12) and forgave and delivered Israel again and again during the time of the Judges. He is the God who gave Israel a king (1 Sam 9), made her strong and wealthy (1 Kings 1-10) and brought her back from exile (2 Chron 36:22-23; Ezra 1). Even when He knew she would reject the Messiah and sentence His Son to crucifixion (John 19:11), He delivered her. And He is the God who will deliver you...if you are His child.

But do you know you are His child? If you have received His gift of salvation your life will show it. How you live your life is the flag of your heart, showing where your allegiance lies.

LOOK UPON MY AFFLICTION AND RESCUE ME, FOR I DO NOT FORGET YOUR LAW (119:153).

The psalmist prays for help. Lord, look upon my affliction and rescue me! He prays with boldness. The word he uses for "rescue" means *to draw or pull out.* "God, draw me out of trouble and affliction!" he prays.

Then he adds, "For I do not forget your law?" His obedience qualifies him for God's deliverance. It is not that his obedience earns God's favor, but rather his obedience proves that he is God's child. A father does not rescue his son from certain death because his son was obedient that day, but rather because he is his son. God remembers those who remember Him, and delivers those who honor Him, for they are His children.

The psalmist's obedience is his mark of citizenship in God's kingdom. Just as countries protect their own citizens from outside invaders, so God protects His own people from the affliction of the wicked.

SALVATION IS FAR FROM THE WICKED, FOR THEY DO NOT SEEK YOUR STATUTES (119:155).

The God who saves those who do not forget His law (vs 153) is the God who will not save those who do not seek His statutes (vs 155). The absence of God's salvation is not a neutral state. If His salvation is not yours then His judgment will be. If you are not saved by God, then you are damned by God. All who live lives of nonchalant rebellion against God are not His children, and the only expectation waiting for them beyond this life are the thirsty flames of hell.

The wicked may search for God's salvation over every hill, but they will not find it unless they repent of their deeds and seek God's great mercy. Unbelievers cry out to God for help when a disaster hits. They admit He exists when their life is in danger, but their admission of His existence passes when the danger is over. They only cry for help because they love their life and the end of their life only means the end of the pursuit of their lusts.

When I was younger I listened to a pastor tell about an atheist who was in a car full of Christians. The Christians talked to her about God, but she adamantly refused to believe. Suddenly the car swerved and almost crashed. In her fear the girl cried out, "Oh God, help us!" Her facade of atheism quickly melted.

Sudden danger makes unbelievers religious until the danger passes, but sometimes it can be the catalyst for change as in the case of Jonah's fellow sailors. The moment the storm passed they, "feared the LORD greatly, and they offered a sacrifice to the LORD and made vows" (Jonah 1:16). Those were not the actions of a three hour believer. They vowed to serve God and their lives were changed. These men no longer fit the description of Psalm 119:155 for they now pursued God's statutes.

MANY ARE MY PERSECUTORS AND MY ADVERSARIES, YET I DO NOT TURN ASIDE FROM YOUR TESTIMONIES (119:157).

Just as God's mercies are many, so are the persecutors of the psalmist. Those who chase him and hate him are great in number. That's enough to discourage any believer, but this saint will not give up for he holds fast to God's testimonies.

Those who follow Christ and expect no persecution are as foolish as those who wish to fight for their country, but think it can be done without sacrifice. Christ told His disciples, "Don't call me Master and expect to somehow miss out on my suffering" (paraphrase of John 15:20). Don't expect to receive heaven without hurt, growth without growing pains, sanctification without sacrifice, maturity without misery or development without distress. This very principle goes all the way back to the enmity between Satan and Eve's seed (Gen 3:15) and we are not exempt. Suffering is a part of the package, and the believer is called to consider it a gift from God (Philipp 1:29).

In the end, the persecutors who tempted the psalmist to leave God unknowingly served as reinforcements to solidify his devotion to God. Trials do one of two things to the believer: push him away from God or draw him nearer. Trials test the heart and the believer's response is dictated by the believer's heart condition.

Trials invite the believer to choose sincere love for God. They will expose the person who has merely believed out of convenience instead of conviction. If living for God were easy and trial-free, millions of unsaved people would profess to believe in Christ. But as soon as their life is at risk for believing in Christ, suddenly the convictions they once held dear are despised.

Remember Gollum fighting Frodo for the ring in the very last book of the Lord of the Rings trilogy? As the ring flew off the precipice, Gollum had to make a decision: follow the ring into the lava or give it up and preserve his own life. The choice was simple. He loved the ring so much that even his own life was no longer precious to him as he fell off the cliff into the lake of fire. Is your affection for Christ so great that you would give up your own life before letting go of Him? The hot zeal of many followers of Christ has all too often melted to water when they realized that the road they are traveling will take them to a cross before it will take them to heaven.

But bring in all the Christian-hating, Christ-blaspheming sinners of this world and let them tear the psalmist to pieces, and even in the gray face of death itself, he will not forsake God's testimonies! For to die with Christ is more precious than to live without Him.

I BEHOLD THE TREACHEROUS AND LOATHE THEM, BECAUSE THEY DO NOT KEEP YOUR WORD (119:158).

These treacherous are the faithless, deceitful, and the wicked. The psalmist looks at them with detest. They despise God's Word, and for this the psalmist despises them.

His hatred is not motivated by love for himself. He does not hate them for making him suffer. The psalmist loathes them for loathing God's Word. He is so devoted to God's glory that even the slightest attempt to steal that glory angers the psalmist. He feels a jealousy for God's glory similar to what a husband feels for his wife's purity. It is impossible to love one thing and its arch enemy equally for the second love will cancel the love for the first.

Would he who loves to drink water love also to drown in it? Would he who loves fire to cook his food and keep him warm also cherish that fire when it destroys his body and turns him to ashes? What would you think if you saw a woman marching in a pro-choice parade and later picketing against an abortion clinic? Neither party would respect her support, for one side invalidates her actions on the other.

Spurgeon's comment shows how the psalmist's hate was driven by his passion for God's glory: "My grief was occasioned more by their sin against God than by their enmity against myself. I could bear their evil treatment of my words, but not their neglect of thy word...That they should have no love for me is a trifle; but to despise the teaching of the Lord is abominable."[1]

Prayer #2: Oh God, deliver me, for Your Word promises deliverance! (vss 154, 156, 160).

PLEAD MY CAUSE AND REDEEM ME;
REVIVE ME ACCORDING TO YOUR WORD (119:154).

Just as a defense lawyer will plead the case of his client, so God will plead the case of His child. But God is both the final judge *and* the lawyer, the jury *and* the defense attorney. The psalmist's deliverance does not depend on any other entity. The One who pleads his case is the One who will finally judge his case.

Satan delights in bringing accusations against God's people (Rev 12:10), pointing out their sins and parading their failures. But with Christ by his side, the Christian has nothing to fear. Every bit of God's wrath against your sin has been poured out upon Christ on the cross (2 Cor 5:21), leaving not a scrap of sin unpunished.

When Joshua stood drenched in the filthy rags of his own sin, Satan showed up to accuse him before God. But instead of rebuking Joshua, God turned and rebuked Satan saying, "Is this not a brand plucked from the fire?" (Zech 3:2). And then God removed Joshua's filthy garments and dressed him in clean robes of festivity. When you stand in the righteousness of God, none can bring accusation against you. Even though your sins once were as murderous as a weapon, God has washed you, making you whiter than snow (Is 1:18). It is the question of Paul, "Who will bring a charge against God's elect?" (Rom 8:33), and the obvious answer is, "No one! For Christ has taken every charge

---

1   Spurgeon, 415.

both great and small upon Himself!"

One day a father and daughter walked together through a prairie when the father suddenly spotted a grass fire moving quickly towards them. In moments the father realized that they were in deep trouble for they could never outrun the speed of this wall of fire.

"Quick!" he said. "Let's make a fire to combat the one coming towards us!" They lit the grass on fire and fanned the flames.

As the other grass fire neared, the girl screamed in terror, but the father calmed her, "Do not fear. We are now standing on burnt ground, ground where the flames have already been, and therefore we are safe." When you stand in Christ, you stand safely where the flames of God's wrath have already been. So accept His infinite forgiveness.

The psalmist prays, "Redeem me" (vs 154). The psalmist prays for the very redemption that finds its roots in the law God gave to Moses. If an Israelite was so indebted to a foreigner that he had to sell himself to that foreigner, the Israelite's relative could buy his freedom back (Lev 25:47-49). Just as Boaz redeemed Ruth to preserve the line of Naomi's husband, Elimelech, and just as Christ redeemed us from the bondage of sin, so the psalmist begs God to redeem him from the afflictions of his enemies.

But the psalmist not only requests the pleading of his case and redemption from his affliction, but revival from despair: "Revive me according to Your Word" (vs 154). Persecutions have driven him to deep sadness and he asks that God would give him new life, a revival of joy and delight just as the Word promises.

GREAT ARE YOUR MERCIES, O LORD; REVIVE ME ACCORDING TO YOUR ORDINANCES (119:156).

Before one entertains the thought that perhaps God is cruel or harsh because He didn't save the wicked in verse 155, let him consider God's great mercies in verse 156. As sure as the wicked will be damned forever, so the believer will be saved forever by the great mercy of God. Satan despises both of these characteristics of God's person, always softening God's wrath and hardening His mercy. But both are abundantly true.

The text says that God's mercies are great. This word "great" could be translated as "much" or "many." Satan will do all he can to make you doubt God's mercy, portraying Him as an angry father always looking over your shoulder with a beating stick in his hand. Satan knows that to convince a believer that God is not merciful would drive the believer into utter despair and into more sin and disbelief.

But this is not the picture the psalmist draws. The psalmist boldly prays for the revival that God's Word has promised because he knows that God is merciful. To give mercy means to withhold the punishment that one deserves. The psalmist knows that he deserves judgment for he is a sinner, yet he boldly prays for God's revival, knowing that God is ready to cast his sin as far as the east is from the west.

God will not shun the broken and humble-hearted. A man once told me, "We can always expect God's judgment, but not always His mercy." This man held a very perverted view of God's character. We sin every day! If his statement was true, every sinner who ever lived would be agonizing in hell at this very moment.

If God is merciful to the sparrow (Matt 10:29-31) and if He shows mercy to the wicked by giving them sun and rain (Matt 5:45), by temporarily withholding their judgment and giving all an opportunity to repent and believe (2 Pet 3:9), why would you ever doubt his mercy toward you, a child of God? If God would not obliterate the wicked cities of Sodom and Gomorrah with just ten righteous people (Gen 18:23-33), why would you hesitate to embrace His mercy today? His mercies are more numerous than the grains of sand on all the beaches. Were the oceans made of ink, the pen used to record His mercies would drain the oceans dry. Were all the planets and all the stars made of lead, His mercies would weigh more still. Fill the universe from end to end with all His abundant compassions and you will only scratched the surface of His infinite compassions.

A few days ago my wife was not feeling well, so I asked my five year old daughter to wash the dishes and be careful to not spill water on the floor. Ten minutes later she came into my office with lips turned down and said, "Papa, I tried and tried but I got water on the floor." I followed her into the kitchen to find five hand towels in a stack used to sop up the liquid. It suddenly hit me how good she was to come to me for mercy instead of hiding or lying about her mistake. I knelt down beside her and said, "Audrey, I am very glad that you tried your best and then came for help. And you can do the same with God. When you fail again and again, just go to Him, tell Him you want to do what is right, but that it is very difficult and ask Him to help you. He will never turn you out."

The Christian who hides or ignores his sin, lies about his sin, or is broken with discouragement over his continued blunders fails to understand that God is infinitely merciful, gladly forgives, and will help him to obey. God would much rather see you on your knees pleading tears of help, then walking strong in your own strength with a proud heart.

David knew mercy when he wrote, "The righteous cry, and the LORD hears and delivers them out of all their troubles. The LORD is near to the brokenhearted and saves those who are crushed in spirit" (Ps 34:17-18).

THE SUM OF YOUR WORD IS TRUTH, AND EVERY ONE OF YOUR RIGHTEOUS ORDINANCES IS EVERLASTING (119:160).

A summary of all of God's Word is only *truth* and nothing more. Like a piece of gold, no matter from what angle you view it, how you test it, or what light it sits under, it will always come out the same way: as pure gold.

The psalmist moves from the totality of God's Word to the individuality of each ordinance. We see him twice repeating the phrase: "every one." Each of these ordinances, each decree of God, every single word of the divine breath is perfectly righteous and lasts forever.

Every syllable of God's Word in every chapter of His Holy Book can suffer the fiercest storms, the deadliest attacks and the cruelest twistings, yet in the end it still comes forth, not faded or weakened. It remains true, righteous, and everlasting.

Under violent persecution and grievous pain, the psalmist can speak this whole verse without mentioning his own dilemmas. How can he do this?

The psalmist takes a reprieve from his earnest pleas for he finds comfort in something far more relieving than his own words: God's Word. In the truth, righteousness, and eternality of God's Word he finds more hope than in all the remedies this world offers.

A man dying of cancer who trusts Christ suffers with a smile in his eyes for he knows that he is passing into a much better place and that the joy of being in his Savior's arms will outmatch the most extreme suffering possible in this present life. But how can he have such assurance? Because he clings to the truth, the righteousness and the eternality of God's Word!

Prayer #3: Oh God, deliver me, for You delight in delivering! (vs 159).

CONSIDER HOW I LOVE YOUR PRECEPTS; REVIVE ME, O LORD, ACCORDING TO YOUR LOVINGKINDNESS (119:159).

It is God's very nature to deliver. The psalmist calls upon God's own character as a reminder to God that he has promised deliverance. "God, consider how merciful you are! Remember that you are a God of merciful compassion!" The psalmist again asks for revival as he did in verse 156. But this time, instead of calling upon God's ordinances he calls upon God's lovingkindness as a reason for God to revive him.

When you are living in sin and testing God's patience, it's hard to be bold when you request help. The guilt of your conscience questions your own commitment and you may even question your own salvation. But after you repent and seek God's forgiveness, you come boldly and without hesitance, pleading the throne of heaven for help, for you know by your repentance that you are His, and it is by God's character that He will come to your need.

If I snuck up behind my two year old son and said, "Boo!" he'd fall on the floor giggling uncontrollably. But if I approached a thief decoding a bank safe and said, "Boo!" he'd run like a hound or pull a gun on me. Notice that in both cases I did exactly the same thing and yet an adult man is terrified while the two year old is delighted. Why? Because one is guilty, the other is innocent. Nothing encourages boldness in prayer like a clean conscience who knows a gracious God.

God's mercy would not be revealed were his servants not sinful. Thus the psalmist does not call upon his own faithfulness here as a reason for God's deliverance. He claims that God is gracious. In Spurgeon's words, "This is the great gun which he (the psalmist) brings up last to the conflict: it is his ultimate argument, if this succeed not he must fail. He has long been knocking at mercy's gate, and with this plea he strikes his heaviest blow."[2]

In Psalm 119:153-160 we have looked at three prayer requests that you can pray when you need help from God:

Prayer #1: Oh God, deliver me, for I am your child!
        (vss 153, 155, 157, 158).
Prayer #2: Oh God, deliver me, for Your Word promises deliverance!
        (vss 154, 156, 160).
Prayer #3: Oh God, deliver me, for You delight in delivering!
        (vs 159).

---

2   Ibid.

In the ancient legend of King Arthur, the holy knight Sir Galahad, son of Lancelot, rode his horse through the country until he came upon the Maiden's Castle. It was a strong castle surrounded by deep ditches and a furious river. Seeing an old English peasant passing by, he asked what men called this castle.

"Fair sir," replied the churn, "it is the Maiden's Castle."

"It is a cursed place," said Galahad, "and all its masters are but felons, full of mischief and hardness and shame."

"For that good reason," said the old man, "thou art well advised to turn back."

"For that same reason," replied Sir Galahad, "will I more certainly ride on."[3] Sir Galahad rode on toward the castle with boldness, because his dedication to righteousness towered high above his fear of evil. But why can the Christian ride on? Why can he have unflinching confidence in the face of danger and opposition? Because he knows three things:

1) *That God delivers His children,*
2) *That God promises deliverance,*
3) *And that God delights in doing it!*

---

3   Sir James Knowles, *King Arthur and His Knights*, p. 291.

QUESTIONS FOR CONTEMPLATION

1. Why does the psalmist need God's help?

2. How often does the believer need God's help? What is wrong if the believer only cries out to God when things go bad?

3. How does the psalmist contrast himself with his enemies?

4. What assurance do you have that God will deliver you in time of need? Do you live like this or do you resort to worry? Do you try to fix things in your power and trust man's help or do you trust in the Lord's power instead?

STRATEGY 4

Follow God's Word as a Guide in Prayer
Psalm 119:33-40, 73-80, 145-152

Make it your rule to rise so early that you will never see the face of man in business until you have first visited the face of God on your knees.

This is one of my life mottos. Though I have failed it many times, I want this to be my morning pattern to the end of my days. Are you convicted when asked, "How is your prayer life?"

I am convinced that one of the chief causes for the lack of fervent, ceaseless prayer is a sickly diet of God's Word. When I meet someone new and he asks questions about my life, interests, family or my church, I naturally want to engage in extended conversation. In the same way, when God speaks to us through His Word, we naturally speak back to Him through prayer.

Another reason for weak prayer is a perverted view of God's sovereignty. Because God is the ultimate Ruler, He has the power to answer our prayers. The Bible clearly teaches that God responds to prayer (James 5:16; 1 Sam 1:20; Is 37:21) without interfering with His ultimate will over all things (Is 46:9-10; 1 Sam 2:6-7). If you believe that your prayer has no impact on the God Who rules the world, I can assure you that your prayer life will be feeble and sickly. The prayers of one who does not believe God will respond lack passion, intensity, and earnestness. There are no sweating blood drops like those of Christ in the Garden (Luke 22:44). There are no moving, voiceless lips like those of Hannah in the temple (1 Sam 1:13), painful fasting like that of Daniel (Dan 9:3), crying out like that of Samuel (1 Sam 15:11), or falling upon the ground like that of David (2 Sam 12:16).

God listened to Abraham who prayed for the restoration of Abimelech's people from barrenness (Gen 20:17). He delivered Israel from Egypt (Ex 2:23-25; 14:10-31), Jacob from Esau (Gen 32:9-12; 33:1-17), His people from foreign oppression (Judg 3:9; Ne 9:27), the Jews from the Philistines (1 Sa 7:8–11),

David from distress (Ps 118:5), Hezekiah from the Assyrians (2 Kings 20:6), Jehoshaphat from the Arameans (2 Chron 18:31), and Manasseh from captivity (2 Chron 33:13, 19), and all because men prayed. Was it not prayer that moved God to deliver Nehemiah from harm (Neh 2:4, 11), Jonah from drowning (Jonah 1:17; 2:1–2, 10), Peter from the waves (Matt 14:30–31) and Paul and Silas from jail (Acts 16:25–26)? Yes, it is true that God performed these wonders because He had decreed them, but the Bible also makes it blatantly clear that God responded to these men's prayers. Was it not God who listened to the voice of Moses (Ex 32:11-14), Joshua (Josh 10:12-14), Elijah (1 Kings 18:36-38) and the thief on the cross (Luke 23:42-43)?

He is the God who saved Miriam from leprosy (Num 12:13-15) and Hezekiah from death (2 Kings 20:1-3, 5) in answer to prayer. He is the God who gave the sign of the fleece to Gideon (Judg 6:36–40), strength to Samson (Judg 16:28–30), a son to Hannah (1 Sam 1:27), wisdom to Solomon (1 Kings 3:9-13), life to the widow's son (1 Kings 17:22), rain to Elijah (1 Kings 17:1; 18:1, 41-45) and blessings to Jabez (1 Chron 4:10), all in response to prayer. It was after prayer that God gave a safe journey to Ezra (Ezra 8:21–23), a son to Zacharias (Luke 1:7–17, 57), life to Tabitha (Acts 9:40), and direction to Cornelius (Acts 10:31–33).

He is the God who forgave Israel because Moses prayed (Num 14:13-20), convicted the returnees because Ezra prayed (Ezra 10:1-4) and gave healing because the lepers prayed (Luke 18:13–14). Did He not move the sun for Isaiah (2 Kings 20:11) and stop the sun for Joshua (Josh 10:12-14)? When His people pray, the Bible teaches that God will grant them justice (Luke 18:7–8), confidence (Acts 4:29) and deliverance (Acts 12:5-17).

The men that prayed have a nature like ours and (James 5:17) struggle against the same passions of the flesh that we battle. It was imperfect men who prayed when God gave wisdom to Daniel (Dan 2:17-23), a child to Isaac (Gen 25:21) and blindness to the Arameans (2 Kings 6:18). It was men, through whom God chose to be glorified by answering their prayers.

In this section we will discover how to follow God's Word as a guide in prayer. This fourth strategy looks at 1) How God can help you keep His Word (119:33-40), 2) How to pray about God's Word (119:73-80), and 3) Divine instant messaging (119:145-152).

How God Can Help You Keep His Word
Psalm 119:33-40

Lau Yat-fai, a 23 year old delivery worker in Hong Kong, had dreams of becoming an American basketball star. He sued two beauty centers because their treatments did not make him taller. He was five feet, nine inches! The beauty centers agreed to give him twenty more treatments including electrical currents and drugs for free. He said, "This is my future career, after all. I won't give up my dream of becoming a basketball star."[1]

Many people deny reality and embrace illusions. The illusion that you can be godly by your own effort, that you can obey God's Word by your own strength, is a deadly diagnosis for dissapointment. Many hang on to the ill-conceived dream that if you just try hard enough, pray long enough, read enough of the Bible and do more witnessing, you can become a super-Christian. It is a humanistic spirit that says, "I can please God on my own."

At the heart of this reasoning lies an atheistic attitude. It is the attitude of a fool, the fool who says in his heart, "I can be godly without God." This oxymoron would make as much sense to say, "I can be a football player without a football," or "I will be a real estate agent without houses to sell."

We don't sit back in the LaZboy and wait for God to make us godly. We cannot take one step toward God unless He gives us the strength and grace to do it. Yet we are to volitionally and willfully obey God.

The author of Psalm 119 understood what it meant to rely upon God in order to keep His Word. And that is why from verses 33-40 we find the prayer of a man laid out before God, extremely conscious of his dependence on God's strength for his obedience. You not only need the Word of God to become holy, you need the God of the Word to keep you holy. The God who saved you while you were an enemy is the same One who will keep you while you are His friend.

---

1   *World Magazine* (October 23, 2004): 11.

From Psalm 119:33-40 we will find six crucial requests that you can ask from God every time you need help obeying His Word:

1. Ask that you will learn the Word with a motive of obedience (vss 33-34).

TEACH ME, O LORD, THE WAY OF YOUR STATUTES, AND I SHALL OBSERVE IT TO THE END. GIVE ME UNDERSTANDING, THAT I MAY OBSERVE YOUR LAW AND KEEP IT WITH ALL MY HEART (119:33-34). Notice that the psalmist is resolved to keep God's Word. He has carved his resolutions in cement. Compare this to most new year resolutions:

• *New year resolutions are temporary. But the psalmist's resolution is eternal: "and I shall observe it to the end" (vs 33).*
• *Most New Year's resolutions are self-motivated. They're all about what one would like to do for himself. But the psalmist's resolutions are about what God would like him to do. He is committed to God's will instead of his own: "your statutes" (vs 33) and "Your law" (vs 34).*

If you observe verses 33 and 34 very carefully, you will see how the psalmist has gone from learning to understanding. He prays, "Teach me O Lord" in verse 33 and then "give me understanding" in verse 34. He has gone from "head knowledge" to "heart experience." The psalmist understands that knowing is not enough. He wants to experience God's Word.

The psalmist refused to place undue attention on external appearances. How often do we vainly wonder: How did my teaching sound? Did I pray well? Am I singing on tune? Did someone notice my new tie? What kind of impression will this make on others? But Christ warned against this, "When you pray, you are not to be like the hypocrites; for they love to stand and pray in the synagogues and on the street corners so that they may be seen by men. Truly I say to you, they have their reward in full" (Matt 6:5).

He then gives the alternative: "But you, when you pray, go into your inner room, close your door and pray to your Father who is in secret, and your Father who sees what is done in secret will reward you" (Matt 6:6). The psalmist is concerned about only one thing: his heart. If your heart is in the right place, your external appearance will be as well.

Why does he want to learn and understand God's Word? So that he may "observe it to the end" (33b) and "keep it with all my heart" (34b). The first motive is a time commitment: to keep it forever. The second is a degree commitment: to keep it whole-heartedly. The first is a sacrifice of time. The second is a sacrifice of devotion. When you ask God to help you learn His

Word so that you may obey it, remember that obedience will always require a sacrifice of time and devotion.

2. Ask that you will obey the Word with a heart of delight (vs 35).

MAKE ME WALK IN THE PATH OF YOUR COMMANDMENTS, FOR I DELIGHT IN IT (119:35).

The psalmist does not just need God's help to learn. He needs God's help to obey. He prays, "Make me walk." Notice that God is doing the causing here. This does not mean that Christian living is being God's puppet or laying like a lifeless dummy. It means that though you still choose to obey, you need God's help for strength to do it.

When your alarm clock rings in the morning, does it make you get up? Not at all. The alarm simply tells you it's 5 a.m. but it's your choice whether or not you will get out of bed. However, you can still ignore your alarm clock and go back to sleep, you could not have risen at the right time without its help. Praying Psalm 199:35 is like setting your alarm before you go to sleep. It is your responsibility to obey, but just as you need your alarm to wake you, you need God's strength to obey Him. Paul understood this principle:

> For I am confident of this very thing, that He who began a good work in you will perfect it until the day of Christ Jesus. (Philippians 1:6) Faithful is He who calls you, and He also will bring it to pass. (1 Thessalonians 5:24) So then, my beloved, just as you have always obeyed, not as in my presence only, but now much more in my absence, work out your salvation with fear and trembling; for it is God who is at work in you, both to will and to work for His good pleasure. (Philippians 2:12-13)

Beloved, you can no more obey God by yourself than a sailor can row his canoe through the sand on the beach. But when you pray for the tide of God's strength, the ocean's waters flow in, and rowing is a breeze.

3. Ask that you will love the Word with abhorrence for sin (vss 36-37).

His first request was to understand God's Word. His second was to obey God's Word. And now it is to love God's Word.

INCLINE MY HEART TO YOUR TESTIMONIES AND NOT TO DISHONEST GAIN. TURN AWAY MY EYES FROM LOOKING AT VANITY, AND REVIVE ME IN YOUR WAYS (119:36-37).

Notice that there are two sides to this request: to hate sin and to love God's Word. You cannot love God's Word and love sin at the same time. A love for sin will squelch all love for God's Word as quickly as a drop of poison will destroy a glass of drinking water.

The psalmist asks God to "incline my heart to your testimonies," in other words, to "make me desire Your Word." This word "incline" is a command. It is not the command of a disrespectful subordinate, but an urgent and holy command. His great confidence to command God comes from his knowledge that his request is God's will.

The psalmist asks God to turn his heart away from gaining profit at another's expense or to accrue revenue by sinful methods. God's testimonies and dishonest gain are antithetical—at extreme odds with each other. And here the psalmist lays them side by side to clarify which one he wants, and which one he detests.

In verse 36 the psalmist's concern is his heart, but in verse 37, his eyes. The eyes are the gate to one's heart and if he can protect his eyes, he can protect his heart. By saying, "turn away my eyes from looking at vanity," the psalmist admits that his flesh sometimes craves vain things, which is a common temptation to every human (1 Cor 10:13).

But why does the psalmist pray, "revive me"? Because vanity always produces death. Pornography, adultery, infatuation with your looks, a life consumed with selfish ambition, a craving for earthly riches—all these things will kill the human soul little by little.

This world is full of evil distractions. Instead, it's time we get distracted by the Word. Let it catch your attention and earn your devotion!

4. Ask that you will be grounded in the Word with an attitude of reverence (vs 38).

ESTABLISH YOUR WORD TO YOUR SERVANT,
AS THAT WHICH PRODUCES REVERENCE FOR YOU" (119:38).
This should be the prayer of every believer who finds himself doubting God. What if God really didn't send Jesus Christ? What if Jesus really wasn't God? What if the Bible is full of error? What if this whole thing is a big joke and there's no such thing as God at all?

I have met a number of Christians who are frightfully susceptible to this kind of thinking. They are not grounded in God's Word. When I was twelve years old, my brother and I built our own log cabin using hatchets and axes. To lay the foundation we needed four stout pressure bearing posts. I will never forget digging the holes for the posts. Being seven years my senior, my brother was wise enough to know that the deeper the posts, the more stable our cabin. We went deep. And let me tell you, that was one solid foundation.

Show me a believer who doubts God's Word and I will show you a believer with no reverence for God in his heart. Doubting the Word of God kills reverence for God like salt destroys snails. It obliterates your spiritual foundation, but when the Word grows deep roots into your heart, it produces a flower of adoration for God's person.

Notice how the psalmist focuses all of his attention on God. "Teach me *Your* statutes" (33), "That I may observe *Your* law" (34), "Make me walk in *Your* commandments" (35), "Incline my heart to *Your* testimonies" (36), "Revive me in *Your* Ways" (37), "Establish *Your* word" (38), "As that which produces reverence for *You*" (38), "*Your* ordinances are good" (39), "I long for *Your* precepts" (40) and "Revive me through *Your* righteousness" (40). This wealth of personal pronouns emphasizes the psalmist's utter dependence on God. If the church needs to regain anything today, it is utter reverence for God.

Though they quickly replaced worship of God with adulation of relics, the early Roman Catholic Church understood this reverence. That is why they erected massive cathedrals. Just stepping inside one makes you feel small and suddenly you find yourself whispering. If this is true of the Roman Catholic Church who rejects salvation by faith alone, how much truer should it be of the Protestant church! John Murray was right when he wrote, "The fear of God is the soul of godliness."[2]

5. Ask that you will take in the Word with a clear conscience (vs 39).

TURN AWAY MY REPROACH WHICH I DREAD,
FOR YOUR ORDINANCES ARE GOOD (119:39).

In this context I do not believe the reproach is the reproach of the psalmist's sin but the reproach of the psalmist's enemies who scoff at him. For some men, the ridicule of others is more painful than a sword in their ribs. Spurgeon writes, "Many would sooner bear burning at the stake than the trial of cruel mockings."[3]

But note the reason the psalmist hates the reproach of his enemies: "for *Your* ordinances are good." The psalmist is not concerned about his reputation but the Lord's. If the psalmist claims to live by God's Word, and his enemies mock and ridicule his holy living, then they are really mocking the Word of God. Thus he prays (paraphrased), "God, please take away the vicious attacks of my enemies, because Your ordinances are good, and they deserve no such shame."

---

2   John Murray quoted by Zemek, 142.
3   Spurgeon, 211.

6. Ask that you will hunger for the Word with a craving appetite (vs 40).

BEHOLD, I LONG FOR YOUR PRECEPTS;
REVIVE ME THROUGH YOUR RIGHTEOUSNESS (119:40).

The psalmist longs for God's Word. He loves it and cannot bear to be without it. Like a wife longs for her husband who has been abroad on the battle lines for years, so the psalmist craves to be with, think about, study, and apply God's precepts.

The psalmist is also drained. With little life left in him, he feels too stale and cold to enjoy this Word that he loves, so he prays, "Revive me! Make me alive again!" His hunger for the Holy Scriptures reminds me of the true story of a man from Kansas City who survived a horrible explosion that took away his sight and his fingers. Devastated that he could no longer read the Bible, even in Braille, he heard of a lady in England who developed a special system for reading Braille with the lips. The man sent for the program, but when it arrived he was shocked to realize that the explosion had not only taken his sight and demolished his fingers, but also destroyed the nerve endings of his lips so that he could not feel the special letters. Despairing, the man planned to send the program back, but gave the Book one last kiss before he let it go. As he kissed it, his tongue accidentally touched the letters and he suddenly realized that his tongue could feel them. In no time at all he had read the Bible from cover to cover four times over with his tongue!

From Psalm 119:33-40 we have looked at six crucial requests that you can ask from God every time you need help obeying His Word:

1. Ask that you will learn the Word with a motive of obedience (vss 33- 34).
2. Ask that you will obey the Word with a heart of delight (vs 35).
3. Ask that you will love the Word with an abhorrence for sin (vss 36-37).
4. Ask that you will be grounded in the Word with an attitude of reverence (vs 38).
5. Ask that you will take in the Word with a clear conscience (vs 39).
6. Ask that you will hunger for the Word with a craving appetite (vs 40).

Frank Sinatra sang: "I did it my way," and he's still doing it his way. And so will you if you don't cast your whole self upon God in complete dependence on Him to sanctify you. If Christ had to trust the Holy Spirit of God for strength to obey His Father (Matt 4:1; Luke 4:1), then how much more do we! If He needed angels to minister to Him (Matt 4:11; Luke 22:43), and if He needed to cry out for God's will from the Garden of Gethsemane, then only a fool would think he could obey God's Word without the help of the God who wrote it.

Today would you be humble enough to admit your utter dependence upon God to keep His Word? Would you be bold enough to pray right now, "God, I've been trying too hard in my power. I've been trying to be holy without help from the Holy One of Israel. Please help me God so that I may keep your Word."

QUESTIONS FOR CONTEMPLATION

1. How does verse 33 compare to most New Year resolutions?

2. What does the psalmist desperately desire in verses 33 and 34?

3. This is the first section of Psalm 119 that includes a request in every single verse. Write down the psalmist's request of God in each verse. What does this teach you about the relationship between obeying God and asking for His help? What other lessons does this teach you?

4. Looking at each request in this section, what does each request teach you about our own weakness without God's help?

5. Take your notes and talk to someone about them. You might even want to teach a lesson based on this. Make sure you relate to him/her how God has used this passage to convict and grow you.

13

How to Pray Using God's Word
Psalm 119:73-80

There are two kinds of people in this world: those who love Scrabble and those who do not. Scrabble is my wife's favorite board game, and she can always test my love for her by asking me to play it with her.

If you have played much Scrabble, you know that the person with the best vocabulary and creativity always wins. Sometimes I will make up a really cool word like "gizongo" or "plunkeedong" and then look in the dictionary in hopes it is a real word. Not finding it, I turn to my wife and say, "Honey, they forgot to list it here."

We do the same with prayer. We pray for something we really want, hoping it is God's will, even though we know it probably is not. How do you know if your prayers are pleasing to God? The psalmist answers this question in Psalm 119:73-80.

Notice the unique structure of this passage. The first and last verse, second and second to the last, third and third to the last, and the two middle verses share the same subject. This unique structure unfolds the four main themes of this passage with God's compassion as the centerpiece.

VERSE

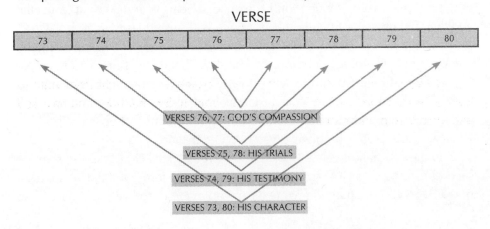

| 73 | 74 | 75 | 76 | 77 | 78 | 79 | 80 |

VERSES 76, 77: GOD'S COMPASSION

VERSES 75, 78: HIS TRIALS

VERSES 74, 79: HIS TESTIMONY

VERSES 73, 80: HIS CHARACTER

In Psalm 119:73-80, there are four prayers that will solidify your prayer life and shape your mind to pray in a way that pleases God.

#1 Pray for: The ingenuity of God's Word to cultivate your character (verses 73, 80).

In verse 73 the psalmist prays for understanding and in verse 80 he prays to be blameless.

> YOUR HANDS MADE ME AND FASHIONED ME;
> GIVE ME UNDERSTANDING, THAT I MAY LEARN
> YOUR COMMANDMENTS (119:73).

God created and fashioned the psalmist personally with His own "hands." His words echo David in Psalm 139:13, "For You formed my inward parts; You wove me in my mother's womb." The one made by his master naturally wants to learn from his master so he prays, "Give me understanding that I may learn Your commandments."

The psalmist needs a mind of understanding before he can learn God's commandments. Only God can enable true understanding of His Word. In the Spring of 2005, my wife and I held a massive moving sale at our apartment complex. An elderly man approached me with a video entitled. *"The Homeland of Jesus."*

"How much do you want for this?" he asked.

"One buck."

"Alright, I'll buy it."

"I was wondering," I asked, "why are you interested in Jesus' homeland?"

"I've been studying it all my life," the man responded.

"So you must believe that Jesus lived."

"Yes, I do. I love archaeology and geography that reflects His time."

He then waxed eloquent on his extended years of research on Jesus' life and the land of Israel. I finally asked, "Have you trusted Jesus as your Savior?" He chuckled nervously and walked away. People like Jesus as a historical figure, an object of archaeology or as a part of history. That's safe. But if you ask them to trust Him as their Lord and Savior, they will often scorn you. This man knew many historical and archaeological facts about Jesus. But his mind was still darkened by sin and his soul still a servant of Jesus' greatest enemy (Eph 2:2). Why? Because God had not yet given him understanding.

In the first half of verse 73 the psalmist recognizes God as Creator. In the second half, he sees God as Teacher. The God who fashioned the vessel must now fill the vessel. Spurgeon wrote, "He who made us to live must make us to learn; he who gave us power to stand must give us grace to understand."[1]

God knows you infinitely better than you know yourself, for He framed you. He delicately wired every nerve in your brain. He weaved together every organ, every artery, every muscle, every cell in your body.

If you want to understand your car, you don't seek the advice of a restaurant chef. Ask your car dealer, and of course he'll tell you that it's fast, runs like butter, and lasts forever, but most likely he doesn't understand its working mechanical parts. The factory worker in Delaware can't help you, for he's only an expert at the part he made. Not even the CEO of the car company would be much help. If you really want to know your car, you go to the man who designed that car.

Your Creator has not only designed you, He has designed the entire universe, every star, every planet, every frog, every leaf, every molecule and every cell. He decrees all things, rules over all things, and knows all things that have happened, that are happening, and will ever happen. You cannot find a better Teacher!

The psalmist is simply asking God to finish the work that He already started. God crafted the psalmist's entire being, but his being is not perfect. It is stained with sin, broken in guilt, and clouded by an evil sin nature. The psalmist prays that God will now complete His work by giving him understanding of God's commandments.

MAY MY HEART BE BLAMELESS IN YOUR STATUTES,
SO THAT I WILL NOT BE ASHAMED (119:80).

The psalmist does not just desire *understanding of* God's Word, but a heart *cleansed by* God's Word. A blameless heart will produce a blameless life. The psalmist is wise. He knows that a clean life is not good enough. Many men have clean lives, yet their hearts are full of wickedness, walking as a dead man's body covered with fresh flowers. And notice the motive: "so that I will not be ashamed." The psalmist knows that a sinful heart produces a shameful life.

#2 Pray for: The competence of God's Word to strengthen your influence (vss 74, 79).

In this next section we find a tremendous love for others. His personal growth in love for God and His Word ignites a passion to see others grow also.

MAY THOSE WHO FEAR YOU SEE ME AND BE GLAD,
BECAUSE I WAIT FOR YOUR WORD (119:74).

The psalmist prays for believers with the words, "those who fear You," and

---

1   Spurgeon, 288..

his request is quite simple, "May other believers see me. "He knows it brings great joy and encouragement for believers to see the psalmist waiting for God's command like a soldier ready to act at a split-second call to action.

The psalmist's motivation is the happiness of other believers! He wants his testimony to be so strong that every believer who sees him will be filled with joy. In Psalm 34:2, David writes, "My soul will make its boast in the LORD; the humble will hear it and rejoice." Just to hear a man boasting in God's goodness floods the humble heart with joy!

Men who fear God want their lives to be an open testimony to others, while men with secret sin addictions live in fear that they may be discovered. They don't want to be exposed (Eph 5:8-13). But a godly man loves the light, because it exposes their Christ-likeness and in turn helps others.

A Christ-honoring reputation is an invaluable asset. And it only takes seconds to lose it. Not long ago a lady stole $4.52 worth of gasoline and the court ordered her to walk around in the public with a sandwich-board sign that says, "I was caught stealing gas."[2] Imagine the shame she suffered. It only takes five seconds of sin to destroy five years of good testimony.

MAY THOSE WHO FEAR YOU TURN TO ME, EVEN THOSE WHO KNOW YOUR TESTIMONIES (119:79).

In verse 74 the psalmist requested a good testimony ("let them see me"), but now in verse 79 he requests good leadership ("let them turn to me"). At first glance this verse makes the psalmist appear prideful. Who would dare to tell others to follow him? Is this arrogant? Not at all. The man of God has every right to tell others to follow him if he is following God. That's the definition of true spiritual leadership: leading others to follow Christ. For the same reason Paul commanded the Corinthians, "Be imitators of me, just as I also am of Christ" (1 Cor 11:1).

Some believers live under the cloud of deception that it is prideful to want others to see your good works. That belief is as deceptive as it is false. In His sermon on the mount, Christ commands the people to, "Let your light shine before men in such a way that they may see your good works and glorify your Father who is in heaven" (Matt 5:16). The motives that drove Christ's statement can be found in the last words of the verse, "and glorify your Father in heaven." God's glory drove every decision, thought, and word He spoke. Likewise, the psalmist longs to be a tool by which other men may love God more and bring Him glory.

A believer seeking Christ is a magnet for others seeking Christ. People who

---

2   *Time Magazine* (August 14, 2004): 9.

love Christ are attracted to men who preach Christ. Charles Spurgeon wrote, "Despondent spirits spread the infection of depression, and hence few are glad to see them, while those whose hopes are grounded upon God's word carry sunshine in their faces, and are welcomed by their fellows."[3]

#3 Pray for: The vigor of God's Word to endure your trials (vss 75, 78).

I KNOW, O LORD, THAT YOUR JUDGMENTS ARE RIGHTEOUS, AND
THAT IN FAITHFULNESS YOU HAVE AFFLICTED ME (119:75).

In the Hebrew language this text literally reads, "I know, O Lord, that Your judgments are righteousness itself." In the original text, the word "righteousness" is not an adjective but a noun. God's commandments are not just righteous in character, but they are righteousness itself.

The psalmist knows that not a molecule of mud could tarnish the purity of God's judgments. And because he knows this, he can say in all sincerity, "In faithfulness You have afflicted me."

The man who knows that all of God's judgments are perfectly righteous will not worry in the face of even the fiercest trials. He knows that God does all things perfectly, and hidden in every trial is a lesson from God. But the man who forgets that God's judgments are righteous will suffer unbearable anger, bitterness, and despair.

If your father beat you as a child for the pleasure of watching you suffer, then his beatings would bring you great grief and despair. But if you knew that every whack of the stick to your backside was because he loved you dearly and was rescuing your soul from Sheol, how gladly you could tell him afterwards: "In faithfulness you have afflicted me!" Likewise, the author of the book of Hebrews told his readers, "For those whom the Lord loves He disciplines and He scourges every son whom He receives" (Heb 12:6). God's afflictions are not only perfectly good, but they always serve a purpose. The author of Hebrews continues,

It is for discipline that you endure; God deals with you as with sons; for what son is there whom his father does not discipline? But if you are without discipline, of which all have become partakers, then you are illegitimate children and not sons. Furthermore, we had earthly fathers to discipline us, and we respected them; shall we not much rather be subject to the Father of spirits, and live? For they disciplined us for a short time as seemed best to them, but He disciplines us for our good, so that we may share His holiness. All discipline for the moment seems not to be joyful, but sorrowful; yet to those who have been trained by

---

3   Spurgeon, 288.

it, afterwards it yields the peaceful fruit of righteousness
(Hebrews 12:7-11).

MAY THE ARROGANT BE ASHAMED, FOR THEY SUBVERT ME WITH A LIE; BUT I SHALL MEDITATE ON YOUR PRECEPTS (119:78).

"They subvert me with a lie" literally means "they bend me with a lie." The psalmist prays that the arrogant will "be ashamed" when they scorn and mock him. This is not unkind. It is actually a very merciful prayer. No man comes to God for forgiveness until he first feels the hideous shame of his own sin. Notice his response when he is slandered: first he prays, and then he turns to the Word: "But I shall meditate on Your precepts." In sheer contrast to the minds of the arrogant, poisoned with slander, he will set his mind on God's commands. The best response to persecution is always to pray and then turn to the Word of God.

The psalmist has been afflicted in two ways: in verse 75, God afflicts him and in verse 78, his enemies afflict him. Yet in both cases, he prays to God! In verse 75, the psalmist accepts God's affliction gladly and in verse 78, he prays for his enemies to be ashamed of their sin and then turns to meditation on God's Word. No matter what the trial, the psalmist turns to God!

It is noteworthy that not once does the psalmist ask for reprieve from his suffering. Instead he accepts it with a desire to learn from it. This attitude is incredible. To whom do you turn when you suffer trials? Your parents? Siblings? Your spouse or children? Novels, TV, alcohol? More good works? More ministry? Or maybe you turn to secular sources like Oprah, Dr. Phil, or Dr. Laura. Perhaps you try to work it out in your head until you're more afflicted than you were in the first place. There is only one proper response: when you suffer affliction, turn to God and He will help you!

#4 Pray for: The pledge of God's Word to receive God's compassion (vss 76, 77).

O MAY YOUR LOVINGKINDNESS COMFORT ME, ACCORDING TO YOUR WORD TO YOUR SERVANT. MAY YOUR COMPASSION COME TO ME THAT I MAY LIVE, FOR YOUR LAW IS MY DELIGHT (119:176-177).

Everyone on this earth wants compassion and love. But notice how boldly and earnestly the psalmist cries out to God for these things. "O" is a Hebrew word communicating burning desire and heartfelt need as if he to say, "I pray!" or "Please!"

The psalmist asks that God's compassion will come to him. If the psalmist were able to go and "get" God's compassion it would no longer be compassion. True compassion is no longer compassion the moment it is obligated. It must come by its own free will, and this God gladly gives for His very nature is compassionate.

But why can the psalmist pray with such passion and confidence? Because the psalmist knows that God's compassion brings comfort (vs 76) and His lovingkindness brings life (vs 77). In Matthew Henry's words: "In God's favour is life and in God's frown is death."

Charles Spurgeon tells the story of two or three boys approaching one of their comrades. "Let us go and get some cherries out of your father's garden!" they scheme.

"No," the faithful boy replies, "I cannot steal and my father does not wish those cherries to be picked."

"Oh! But your father is so kind and he never beats you."

"Ah!" the boy answers. "I know that is true, and that is the very reason why I would not steal his cherries."[4] May the mercy of your perfect Father in heaven move you to obedience!

From Psalm 119:73-80, we have looked at four prayer requests that you can pray to solidify a biblical prayer life:

1. Pray for the ingenuity of God's Word to cultivate your character (vss 73, 80).
2. Pray for the competence of God's Word to shape your testimony (vss 74, 79).
3. Pray for the vigor of God's Word to endure your trials (vss 75, 78).
4. Pray for the pledge of God's Word to receive God's compassion (vss 76, 77).

When we pray, genuinely pray, the real condition of our heart is revealed.
This is as it should be. This is when God truly begins to work with us.
The adventure is just beginning.
~ Richard J. Foster ~

---

4   Spurgeon, *Lectures*, 388.

QUESTIONS FOR CONTEMPLATION

1. Why is verse 73a the foundation of verse 73b?

2. Why would those who fear God be glad when they see the psalmist (verse 74)? Why would they turn to the psalmist (verse 79)?

3. Record all of the psalmist's prayer requests in this passage. Now turn those requests into points for a lesson and share them with someone.

14

Divine Instant Messaging
Psalm 119:145-152

Ten to fifteen years ago instant messaging was beyond mankind's dreams. Having a virtual conversation was as unheard of as cell phones were in the 1950's. The first time I used instant messaging I thought it was a blast. But after a few months, I looked back to realize that I had wasted hours of time talking about nothing. So I gave it up.

There is another kind of instant messaging that is never a waste of time. It's called "divine" instant messaging, or *prayer*. In Psalm 119:145-152, we find one of the most personal and devotionally rich prayers ever prayed. I want to pray like this psalmist prayed. His prayer bleeds with tender intimacy and familiarity, yet never so familiar that he loses reverence for God.

Prayer has always been highly respected. Rotary clubs begin with prayer; millions observe the National Day of Prayer and even Congress still opens with prayer. I think most believers' struggle is not how to respect prayer, but how to do it. How do we talk to the Almighty Creator of the universe, the God of heaven and earth, the God at whose very breath we could be swept away in an instant?

From Psalm 119:145-152, the psalmist exemplifies three patterns for prayer:

Pattern #1: Pray in dependence (vss 145-147).

> I CRIED WITH ALL MY HEART; ANSWER ME, O LORD!
> I WILL OBSERVE YOUR STATUTES (119:145).

The psalmist's attitude of dependence flows from his heart. Spurgeon says, "Heart-cries are the essence of prayer."[1] All Bible knowledge will do nothing for the man who prays without a heart of sincerity. Did the psalmist cry out loud or in silence? We do not know and nor does it matter, for a silent mouth with a

---

1   Spurgeon, *Treasury*, 401.

clean heart is far more precious than an eloquent tongue with a dead heart.

And this cry is not a dead, passionless, half-hearted prayer. He holds nothing back. It is a suffering soul consumed with God's power to save. Thomas Brooks rightly said, "If the heart be dumb, God will certainly be deaf."[2]

God is not tickled by the length of your prayers, how long they are; the color of your prayers, how eloquent they are; the chant of your prayers, how repetitive they are; the music of your prayers, how beautiful they are; or the noise of your prayers, how loud they are. God seeks for the holiness of your prayers, how pure they are.[3]

Richard Wurmbrand who suffered years of persecution for helping the underground church in Romania tells the story of how he explained the gospel to someone who wanted to become a Christian.

"Let us pray," Wurmbrand said.

But not knowing the Christianese we become so coldly familiar with, the new convert fell to his knees and said, "Oh God, what a fine chap you are. If I were You and You were me I would never forgive you of your sins. But you are really a very nice chap. I love you with all of my heart."[4] There is more to be said for that man's prayer than many of the prayers of seasoned saints, for his prayer was real. The new believer felt true dependence on God.

At first it seems odd in Psalm 119:145 that the psalmist's only request is a vocal answer from God. When we cry out, we normally request an action. We plead God to change our situation, to remove our trial, or to relieve us of sickness. But here the psalmist is content to simply cry out for the comfort of God's simple response. The simple and sweet reply of God and to know that He is listening to the psalmist's cry comforts his soul.

One of the most painful tools of revenge in a relationship is "the silent treatment." When your dearest friend or lifemate spouse refuses to talk to you, it hurts. It is shaming and disgracing for one's existence to not be recognized. The sick feeling a Jr. Higher feels in his stomach when he stands in a circle of classmates and not a single student even looks at him is the same agony the psalmist does not wish for.

What could be more agonizing than to be ignored by God Almighty? What could be more disheartening than to not even know if He is listening?

I CRIED TO YOU; SAVE ME AND
I SHALL KEEP YOUR TESTIMONIES (119:146).

Again the psalmist cries for God. But this time he requests not an answer but

2   Ibid., 405.
3   This statement was inspired by Thomas Brooks quoted by Spurgeon, 405.
4   Richard Wurmbrand, *Tortured for Christ* (Bartlesville: Living Sacrifice Book Company), 18.

an action. Not confirmation that God is listening but confirmation that God will act for him. The wicked draw near (vs 150) and he needs help. Their numbers are greater, their strategies more cunning, and the psalmist will not survive their persecution unless the Lord delivers him.

The simplicity of this prayer is astounding, "Save me." When the believer is under great pressure and close to danger, he does not waste time with elaborate words but drives to the central need: "Save me!"

Some of the best prayers are the most simple. As Peter sank into the ferocious sea he cried out, "Lord, save me!" (Matt 14:30). When the Persian king, Artaxerxes, questioned Nehemiah's sadness which could result in Nehemiah's decapitation (for a sad composure in the presence of the Persian king was an offense punishable by death) Nehemiah writes, "So I prayed to the God of heaven" (Neh 2:4). Neither of these men had time for eloquent quotations of Scripture or theological pontification. But this didn't keep them from prayer.

Even Christ's prayer in the Garden of Gethsemane was nothing more than a fervent request for God's will to be done (Luke 22:42). John Welch's prayer, night after night, was nothing more than "Lord, grant me Scotland!" It was Bobby Richardson, the former New York Yankees' second baseman, at a Fellowship of Christian Athletes who prayed, "Dear God, Your will—nothing more, nothing less, nothing else. Amen."[5] That's real dependence.

I RISE BEFORE DAWN AND CRY FOR HELP;
I WAIT FOR YOUR WORDS (119:147).

For a third time, the psalmist cries to God, and this time he begs for help. He rises before the sun rises, showing the urgency of his request and his continual awareness of God's existence. It matters not if it's morning, noon, or night. God is always ready to hear the prayer of His servant.

Would you get up early to buy tickets to the next Dodgers game? Do you rise early so that you don't have to stand in line at the bank or to get an early start on your next vacation? We are good at rising early for our convenience, but how often do we rise early to commune with God? (Dan 6:10).

Pattern #2: Pray with resolve (vss 145-147).

This second pattern covers the same verses as the first pattern, but in them we find something else. Notice that in all three verses the psalmist asserts his commitment to obedience. He says, "I will observe your statutes" (vs 145), "I shall keep Your testimonies" (vs 146), and "I wait for Your words" (vs 147). In these three verses we see the balance of dependence and obedience. We

---

5   Olford, 219.

are utterly dependent on God for help, and yet we must choose to obey Him with all our resolve. Resolve without dependence is desperate but dependence without resolve is feeble. The believer must strive for both.

You are so dependent on God you will die without Him, and yet your dependence is not real trust if you do nothing about it.

Pattern #3: Pray with understanding (vss 148-152).

Watch how the psalmist receives his understanding of the Word through meditation on the Word.[6]

MY EYES ANTICIPATE THE NIGHT WATCHES, THAT I MAY MEDITATE ON YOUR WORD (119:148).

Night watches were periods of time during the night when guards would take turns watching for enemies who may attack the city.[7] The psalmist "anticipates" these night watches; he is already awake when these men come on duty, because for him this is an ideal time to meditate on God's Word.[8] The NIV states, "My eyes stay open through the watches of the night, that I may meditate on your promises."

Why would the psalmist meditate at this time of the day? I believe it is because he is so hungry for communion with God that he looks for the most peaceful and undistracted time. His holy fervor is so intense that sleep is a threat to his communion with God! He will not let his eyelids close lest he drift off into unconscious slumber and break off this blessed fellowship with God in heaven.

We find David doing the same thing in Psalm 63:6, "When I remember You on my bed, I meditate on You in the night watches." As Thomas Watson said, "Meditation necessitates a Christian's retiring of himself, a locking himself up from the world. Meditation is a work which cannot be done in a crowd."[9]

There are numerous ways a believer today can meditate on God's Word in solitary peace. Do you ever go on walks with God? Sometimes after a hard day or tedious study I will go for a run through our neighborhood. After I've run myself to exhaustion I will walk, making this a time of conversation with my Maker. These moments are unforgettable.

Would you do this with a friend? Then do it with God! Find a time of the

---

6   He knows the Word and therefore he knows the Lord of the Word. Millions of unbelievers claim to know God, but their knowledge of Him has been created by their own imagination, experiences, and opinions of others. Until their knowledge is shaped by God's Word, their knowledge is biased and inaccurate.

7   In Hebrew culture there was a beginning watch (Lam 2:19), a middle watch (Judges 17:19), and a morning watch (Ex 14:24; 1 Sam 11:11). These watches lasted from approximately sunset to 10pm, 10pm-2am, and 2am-6am. Even the temple had its own watch guards who stayed up all night and opened its doors in the morning (1 Chron 9:26-27).

8   This word "anticipate" means "to come before" in the original Hebrew.

9   Watson, 23.

day or a special place where you and God can be alone and just enjoy Him! Perhaps it's after school, in the quite hours of the morning, or before you go to bed. Maybe the best time is at midnight or in a quiet chapel. Use these moments to tell God about your day. Tell him about your temptations. Talk to Him about your worries. Speak to Him as Moses did with God on Mt. Sinai. "Thus the Lord used to speak to Moses face to face just as a man speaks to his friend" (Ex 33:11).

But see again the psalmist's motive: "That I may meditate on Your word." If study is the "eating of truth," then meditation is the "digestion of truth." You cannot own a principle of God's Word until it has soaked and baked in the heart of your soul and entered your bloodstream. In Spurgeon's words, meditation is the fuel which sustains the flame of prayer.[10]

HEAR MY VOICE ACCORDING TO
YOUR LOVINGKINDNESS; REVIVE ME, O LORD,
ACCORDING TO YOUR ORDINANCES (119:149).

Meditation makes him intimately familiar with God's person and the psalmist makes two requests: hear my voice and revive me. These requests are beached upon two very important truths: God's lovingkindness and God's ordinances. He cries out, "God, because I know that you are full of lovingkindness, please hear my voice. And God, because your ordinances have promised me protection, please revive me!" Prayer would be hopeless if we did not know the character of the One to whom we pray.

Your knowledge of others influences how you speak to them. If your manager at work promised you a $1000 bonus to beat the deadline on completing your project, you'd have no problem requesting that bonus when you beat the deadline. But if he never promised this bonus, you wouldn't be very confident asking, "May I have $1000 bonus today for doing my job so quickly?" The believer who meditates on and revels in God's Word can pray with boldness and confidence because he knows God's promise, "Ask, and it will be given to you; seek, and you will find; knock, and it will be opened to you" (Matt 7:7).

Try reading this verse minus the references to God's character, "Hear my voice, revive me, O Lord." It's dead. There is no impetus for praying. Why is the psalmist confident that God will hear his voice? Because he knows that God is full of lovingkindness. And why is he sure that God will revive him? Because he knows God's ordinances which promise this.

---

10   Spurgeon, 402.

THOSE WHO FOLLOW AFTER WICKEDNESS DRAW NEAR;
THEY ARE FAR FROM YOUR LAW (119:150).

The psalmist possesses a tremendous sense of God's holiness. It distresses him that the wicked are near to him but far from God. Godly men do not desire the camaraderie of the ungodly. They do not shun evangelism opportunities or refuse to serve the lost, but they are careful when men so far from God come so near that they might tempt them.

YOU ARE NEAR, O LORD, AND ALL
YOUR COMMANDMENTS ARE TRUTH (119:151).

In the middle of his despair that the wicked are drawing close, he remembers that Someone else is also near. He is like a terrified child standing within striking distance of a rattlesnake, who at the moment of despair looks up to see his father standing by his side. Because God is near and His commandments are true, the psalmist is comforted. This time he reveals tremendous understanding of God's presence.

OF OLD I HAVE KNOWN FROM YOUR TESTIMONIES,
THAT YOU HAVE FOUNDED THEM FOREVER (119:152).

For the psalmist, the Word of God is fresh but not new, inspiring but not unplanned. For countless hours the psalmist has fed upon God's breathtaking testimonies which God has held forever. There is no beginning and no end to these testimonies. They are fixed for all eternity; they will no more change than God will change. This alone should bring great confidence to the believer's prayer. As Spurgeon wrote, "A man cannot have much expectation from a changing friend, but he may well have confidence in a God who cannot change."[11] Meditate on God's Word and you will find it to be more fixed than the seasons and more stable than the mountains.

Following are three practical ways for applying these three patterns of prayer that we have looked at:

- *Next time you are faced with a tough decision, before you even start to reason with yourself on how you will respond, go to God in prayer.*
- *Next time you find yourself hesitant to obey the Lord, write down three resolves that you intend to follow through on.*
- *Next time your prayer feels dead and lifeless, spend five minutes meditating on God's attributes and praising Him for those.*

---

11   Spurgeon, 404.

From Psalm 119:145-152 we have studied three patterns for prayer:

Pattern #1: Pray in dependence (vss 145-147).
Pattern #2: Pray with resolve (vss 145-147).
Pattern #3: Pray with understanding (vss 148-152).

On August 12, 1860, Charles Spurgeon told this amazing story:

Constantine, the Emperor of Rome, saw that on the coins of the other Emperors, their images were in an erect posture—triumphing. Instead, thereof, he ordered that his image should be struck kneeling, for said he, "That is the way in which I have triumphed."

You cannot triumph, until you are on your knees before your Maker praying in dependence, with resolve, and full of understanding.

QUESTIONS FOR CONTEMPLATION

1. What has this passage taught you about praying?

2. What areas in you prayer life need to grow?

3. Why does the psalmist cry to God? What is the attitude in which he pleads?

4. Write down three principles that you learned from this passage that you can apply this week in your prayer life.

STRATEGY 5

Shine God's Word on Your Heart and Life
Psalm 119:65-72, 105-112, 161-168, 169 -176

It has been said, "Men do not reject the Bible because it contradicts itself, but because it contradicts them." Were the hearts of Bible-rejecting authors peeled back until you could see the real motive underneath, you would find a heart deeply offended by a Book that speaks the truth. Yet some men have not failed to see its priceless value:

> Andrew Jackson wrote, "That Book, Sir, is the rock on which our republic rests." Charles Dickens said, "The New Testament is the very best book that was or ever will be known in the world." "It is impossible," said George Washington, "to righteously govern the world without God and the Bible." Ronald Reagan wrote, "Within the covers of one single book, the Bible, are all the answers to all the problems that face us today—if only we would read and believe."

But admiring the Word is not enough. The Word is a double-edged sword made for judging the thoughts and intentions of the human soul (Heb 4:12). The Word is a flame made for burning out the sin of wickedness (Jer 23:29). The Word is a hammer, forged to smash the pride of self righteousness (Jer 23:29). The Word is a mirror, made to reflect the shambled condition of man's heart (Jam 1:23-25), so that he may see his wretchedness, repent and obey God.

The psalmist is a living example of this. He is not content to log an arsenal of truths in his head. He takes the Word eighteen inches—the greatest distance in the world—from his head to his heart. The psalmist shines the Word on his life like a lighthouse beam, illuminating the dark places of sin and neglect. He is not the man in the book of James who after looking at his sinful condition flees like a jackrabbit. He stays to get things right.

Perhaps the greatest spiritual epidemic ever to strike the church today is a fear of confessing sin (James 5:16). Lone Ranger Christians fear being exposed, so instead of humbly confessing their sin and getting help from other believers, they let their sins fester in private until they have weaved a web so monstrous that it enslaves them. But the psalmist does not do this. In the next four passages, Psalm 119:65-72, 105-112, 161-168, and 169-176, we will look at how God's Word can illuminate our hearts and lives.

Enter the College of Christian Living
Psalm 119:65-72

Every student preparing for college will fill out several college applications if he wants to get into a prestigious school. I have yet to meet one person who actually enjoyed filling out college applications. It's painful and wearisome.

Yet in spite of the long hours of filling out forms followed by months of waiting, college applications are essential because they test the candidate to see if he will succeed. If the applicant is accepted, the school has a pretty good idea that the student is qualified and will keep up with the rigorous demands of the school.

As a believer you are in a college too. It's not a liberal arts college, a private college or even a Bible college. It's the "College of Christian Living." God is the Professor and you are the student. Just as college applications test a student's readiness for a school, so Psalm 119:65-72 tests the believer's readiness for spiritual growth. From these verses you will find four tests for entering the "College of Christian Living."

1. Accept God's loving discipline (vss 65, 67, 71).

YOU HAVE DEALT WELL WITH YOUR SERVANT,
O LORD ACCORDING TO YOUR WORD (119:65).

Notice how the psalmist begins with an attitude of complete acceptance of God's actions. He does not complain, gripe, or grumble, but receives God's afflictions with a humble smile. God's dealings with His people are not always a guarantee of rewards, prizes, raises, and tranquility. Sometimes God's blessings come in the form of pain, trials, and even the loss of loved ones.

No matter how joyful or painful God's dealings have been, the psalmist writes, "You have dealt *well* with your servant." God's dealings are always good, and never will He do something that is not perfectly right for His children.

Why can the psalmist maintain such a positive attitude about suffering?

Because he knows it is for his good and because he expects it. He writes, "according to Your Word" (vs 65) because he knows God's afflictions are no surprise. His heart is saturated with the Word of God. A believer surprised by trials and heartache is oblivious to the Word's clear teaching that trials are necessary for the believer's growth (1 Pet 3:17; 4:1). God promises to allow suffering, temptation, and trials in our life to grow us. Be ready!

BEFORE I WAS AFFLICTED I WENT ASTRAY, BUT NOW I KEEP YOUR WORD (119:67).

Before affliction hit, before the ceiling caved in, the psamist strayed from God. So God used affliction to lovingly discipline His servant into a right walk. Next time you find yourself tempted to complain about trials, remember that trials are God's sheep dogs to bring us back into the fold of Christ's flock.

But where did this affliction come from? From God! Whether directly or indirectly—we do not know—the psalmist recognizes that God is the ultimate one responsible for suffering, and this is a good thing! God's discipline of the psalmist has made the psalmist wise. We would be wise to learn from the psalmist by seeking God before the affliction and not only after. Turning to sin only increases the amount of necessary affliction it will take to bring you back to God.

IT IS GOOD FOR ME THAT I WAS AFFLICTED, THAT I MAY LEARN YOUR STATUTES! (119:71).

Here the psalmist says it plainly: affliction is good. A good, righteous, gracious, merciful, and kind God afflicts His own people because He loves them. "He who withholds his rod hates his son, But he who loves him disciplines him diligently" (Prov 13:24). As this is true for a child, so it is true for the child of God! The author of Hebrews expounds,

> ...and you have forgotten the exhortation which is addressed to you as sons, "My son, do not regard lightly the discipline of the Lord, nor faint when you are reproved by Him, for those whom the Lord loves He disciplines, and He scourges every son whom He receives (Heb 12:5-6).

The psalmist calls the affliction good for a very specific reason: "That I may learn your statutes!" (vs 71b). The only time a believer will see affliction as a bad thing is when he fails to see the purpose behind the affliction. Jerry Bridges writes, "God never wastes pain. He always uses it to accomplish His purpose. And His purpose is for His glory and our good."

Going to Bible studies, reading Scripture and listening to sermons are very good practices. But learning does not begin until you apply the Word to your daily living.

The book of Job is not about a man who suffers the consequences of alcohol addiction. It is not about a man writhing in the anguish of his own sexual immorality. Job is about a man who suffers...because he is righteous.

In chapter one, Job loses his oxen and donkeys (1:15), sheep (1:16), camels (1:17), all his servants (1:15, 16, 17), and finally his ten children (1:18-19) all in one day. In chapter two the suffering moves from Job's possessions to his own body. The boils that cover his body are so painful that he scrapes his body with a piece of broken pottery (2:7-8) and his own friends cannot even recognize him (2:12). And to top it off, Job's wife offers a very discouraging solution, "Curse God and die!" (2:9).

But Job responds: "You speak as one of the foolish women speaks. Shall we indeed accept good from God and not accept adversity?" (2:10). We gladly accept good from God, but do we accept adversity? A. W. Tozer wrote, "It is doubtful that God would ever use a man greatly whom He has not hurt deeply." And Scripture affirms this:

- *Moses was humbled as a fugitive in the wilderness before he led 2½ million people to the Promised Land.*
- *Peter denied Christ before he preached Christ.*
- *David was hunted like a rabbit in the woods before he assumed the throne.*
- *Joseph suffered the false accusation of sexual assault and incarceration before God made him 2nd ruler of all Egypt.*
- *John the Baptist grew up in no-man's land on a diet of hoppers and honey before he preached as the forerunner of the King of Kings and Lord of Lords.*

When God brings affliction to you, the question is not "why does God bring the affliction?" but rather "how will you respond to it?" Aldous Huxley said, "Experience is not what happens to you. It is what you do with what happens to you."

Affliction may be a mother enduring a hectic day in the home with dishes, laundry, and screaming kids. Affliction may be a cruel boss at work or a financial crisis. It could be sickness or the mockery you suffer for faithfully telling people about Christ. Whatever the affliction, you can say with confidence: "It is good for me that I was afflicted!"

2. Realize your need to learn from God (vss 66, 68).

People generally attend college to learn. The student must recognize his ignorance before he is ready to grow in knowledge. And look at who the psalmist asks to teach him: the Lord!

TEACH ME GOOD DISCERNMENT
AND KNOWLEDGE... (119:66A).

There is no greater teacher in heaven than God, and there was no greater teacher on earth than Christ. Notice the psalmist wants to learn "good discernment and knowledge."

Knowledge is to learning as protein is to growth. You cannot learn without it. But the psalmist doesn't just want knowledge. He's looking for "good discernment," good judgment and wisdom for making difficult choices. He desires to have knowledge so that he can know and wisdom so that he can apply what he knows.

...FOR I BELIEVE IN YOUR COMMANDMENTS (119:66B).

In order to learn, the psalmist must also have faith. The psalmist believes that God's commandments are true, trustworthy, righteous, pure and perfect. It is impossible to succeed in the "College of Christian Living" if you do not hold a high view of God's Word. Do you uphold it with the same honor that David did?

> The law of the Lord is perfect, restoring the soul; the testimony of the Lord is sure, making wise the simple. The precepts of the Lord are right, rejoicing the heart; the commandment of the Lord is pure, enlightening the eyes. The fear of the Lord is clean, enduring forever; the judgments of the Lord are true; they are righteous altogether. They are more desirable than gold, yes, than much fine gold; sweeter also than honey and the drippings of the honeycomb. (Psalm 19:7-10).

YOU ARE GOOD AND DO GOOD;
TEACH ME YOUR STATUTES (119:68).

No matter how excellent the school is, how grand the subject, or how well the textbooks are written, the quality of a student's education will be heavily influenced by the moral character of the teacher. And before the psalmist says, "teach me Your statutes" he says, "You are good and do good."

3. Respond to persecution by running to the Word (vss 69, 70).

Do you hunger to learn God's Word? Christians in Russia today are so hungry for the Word they pack out the church two hours before the pastor arrives.

THE ARROGANT HAVE FORGED A LIE AGAINST ME... (119:69A).
Arrogant men have created lies to blemish the psalmist's character. But look at his response:

...WITH ALL MY HEART I WILL OBSERVE YOUR PRECEPTS (119:69B).
Instead of deflecting their attacks or fighting back, the psalmist turns to the Word. He says, "with all my heart." He knows that if he is going to seek God while suffering persecution, he must give his whole heart to the Lord. If he gives God only 90%, the remaining 10% will think and muse over the lies of his enemies until it slowly spreads and gains control of his whole heart and he is a prisoner of another's opinions. The beauty of pain is that it forces the decision: "I will give my whole heart to God, or I will not seek Him at all." Peter the Apostle wrote,

> For you have been called for this purpose, since Christ also suffered for you, leaving you an example for you to follow in His steps, who committed no sin, nor was any deceit found in His mouth; and while being reviled, He did not revile in return; while suffering, He uttered no threats, but kept entrusting Himself to Him who judges righteously (1 Pet 2:21-23).

THEIR HEART IS COVERED WITH FAT... (119:70A).
In contrast to the psalmist's aggressive consumption of God's Word, the wicked have a heart covered with fat. In the Hebrew text, the verse literally says "gross like fat." This means their hearts are impenetrable. Their heart is so diseased with sin that it cannot receive a single precept of truth.

...BUT I DELIGHT IN YOUR LAW (119:70B).
The wicked will not understand it, but the psalmist delights in it. Persecution is one of God's most effective instruments of instruction for His students.

Richard Wurmbrand, a believer who suffered tremendous torture for serving the underground church in Romania, tells the story of how communists tried to make a Christian girl miserable. After learning that she was a Christian, the communist guards waited until the day she was to be married. Just before she was wedded to her love, the guards marched in and handcuffed the young woman. As the guards dragged her off to the torture chambers, she kissed her handcuffs and said, "I thank my heavenly bridegroom for this jewel He has presented to me on my marriage day. I thank Him that I am worthy to suffer for him."[1] Speaking of his and other Christians' sufferings in jail, Wurmbrand wrote, "One great lesson arose from all the beatings, tortures, and butchery of the communists, that the spirit is master of the body. We felt the torture but it often seemed as something distant and far removed from the spirit which is lost in the glory of Christ in His presence with us."[2]

4. Prize God's Word above all earthly treasures (vs 72).

THE LAW OF YOUR MOUTH IS BETTER TO ME THAN
THOUSANDS OF GOLD AND SILVER PIECES (119:72).

Trials may crush you. Ignorance may discourage you. Persecution may exhaust you. But as long as God's Word is more precious to you than thousands of gold and silver pieces, you need not despair!

Imagine a room full of sparkling gold pieces and glistening silver coins. Picture thousands upon thousands stacked in great piles, then add to that all of the richest men's estates—the most expensive property, the biggest mansions, and the fastest cars—and what do they add up to? A few copper coins in comparison to the eternal value of God's Word!

Things were going well for Dr. Martyn Lloyd-Jones. He received his doctorate in medical school. He was making good money. His medical career put him in association with some of the most prestigious doctors in the world. And then God called him to preach the gospel. Lloyd-Jones left his medical profession and became a pastor on a small salary for a little church in the middle of a rundown, depressed community.

People admired his sacrifice and complimented him for it. But he always repudiated their words of praise and at one point made this statement, "I gave up nothing. I received everything. I count it the highest honour that God can confer on any man to call him to be a herald of the gospel."[3] Those are the words of a man who treasured the Word of God.

A man will risk even his own life in pursuit of something of great value. Miners risk their lives for gold. Soldiers stake their lives for their country. Firemen endanger their health for citizens. And the psalmist will endure all persecution because God's Word is precious to Him. He loves what he learns!

---

1   Wurmbrand, 37-38.
2   Ibid., 42-43.
3   Ian H. Murray, 150.

In Psalm 119:65-72, we looked at four tests for true spiritual growth:

1. Accept God's loving discipline (vss 65, 67, 71).
2. Realize your need to learn from God (vss 66, 68).
3. Respond to persecution by running to the Word (vss 69, 70).
4. Prize God's Word above all earthly treasures (vs 72).

After preaching the gospel for 40 years and after printing the sermons I have preached for more than six-and-thirty years, reaching now to the number of 2,200 in weekly succession, I am fairly entitled to speak about the fullness and richness of the Bible, as a preacher's book. Brethren, it is inexhaustible. No questions about freshness will arise if we keep closely to the text of the sacred volume. There can be no difficulty as to finding themes totally distinct from those we have handled before; the variety is as infinite as the fullness...In the forty years of my own ministry I have only touched the hem of the garment of divine truth; but what virtue has flowed out of it! The Word is like its Author, infinite, immeasurable, without end.
~ Charles Spurgeon ~

QUESTIONS FOR CONTEMPLATION

1. What do these verses teach you about being a humble and hungry student of God and His Word?

2. What is the psalmist's attitude under persecution (vss 60-70) and affliction (vs 71)?

3. How does the psalmist illustrate the value of God's Word? Why is this much more powerful than saying, "It's very precious"?

4. To what does the psalmist turn when he is under persecution?

5. Think of a trial or persecution God is putting you through right now to teach you His Word. Why is knowing the Word not enough? Why must you experience affliction and persecution as well?

CHAPTER

16

How to be Dominated by the Word of God
Psalm 119:105-112

When I was twelve years old my father found a fawn abandoned by its mother. We fed it milk from a bottle and cared for it for several months. We held it, loved it, named it, and played with it like a dog. But one day, we found it lying on the ground afflicted with convulsions and diarrhea. It died a few hours later. Heartbroken, we asked a veterinarian why it died, to which he responded: "It was getting the wrong kind of milk." He said that cow's milk is too rich for a baby deer. A fawn needs its own mother's milk.

The church today is suffering a similar diet of the wrong food. Believers' souls are being fed with everything but the one food God designed for them: His Word. It's a deadly plague. If your life is not permeated—thoroughly saturated— with the Word of God, you will be a struggling, discontented and guilt-ridden believer. The Word of God must dominate your life.

From Psalm 119:105-112, we see four areas of our lives that God's Word should dominate.

1. The Word is to dominate your choices (vss 105, 106, 112).

YOUR WORD IS A LAMP TO MY FEET AND
A LIGHT TO MY PATH (119:105).

When I first started in seminary, I worked at a company which places construction workers at various locations for framing. On my first day, I was assigned to a project an hour away in normal traffic, but because I lived in the Los Angeles area, I set aside two hours of driving time. I left at five in the morning and it only took me twenty minutes to become thoroughly lost. After a frustrating search, I stopped to ask for directions. But following those instructions got me more lost than I was before. I finally humbled myself, phoned the construction office and said, "I'm lost."

The secretary's response was classic, "Do you have a Thomas Guide?"

My answer was, "No, I do not have a Thomas Guide."

"Well, that's your problem. You get a Thomas Guide and you won't be getting lost anymore." He was right.

Many believers today are running around in circles, lost in a sea of confusion and opinions because they have not studied God's map for holy living. They have not opened God's Word to seek His guidance. A believer without the Bible is more lost than a sailor at Cape Horn without his compass or an astronaut on the moon without a radar tracking station.

The psalmist says that God's Word is two things: a lamp and a light. Both are essentially the same. He's making his point in two different ways. If you've been hiking at night when the moon is black, you must shine the light on the path in front of you. You need to know where you are stepping, because if your feet slip, your whole body slips. He says, "Your word is a lamp to my feet." God's Word shows you the way so that you will not stumble into a sewer of sin.

The psalmist continues, "Your word is a...light to my path." The word "light" is sometimes translated as the "dawn" or "sunlight." Imagine how the earth would shrivel and freeze in seconds were the sun to disappear. Imagine how much worse it is for the believer who does not have the light of the Word under his arm and in his heart!

The pilgrims were mocked for "being so heavenly minded they were of no earthly use." But the opposite is true. The divine wisdom of God's Book gives the believer more practical guidance for daily living than a library of "How To" manuals could give in a lifetime. Through God's Word, the believer has all he needs for "life and godliness" (2 Pet 1:3).[1]

John, the apostle, called Jesus "The true Light which coming into the world, enlightens every man" (John 1:9). Just as Christ gives unbelievers salvation from the darkness of eternal death, so the Word gives God's child guidance for daily living. God's Word will guide you if you seek it. You'll never be distraught with the frustration of not knowing which path to take because God's Word is your lamp on dark paths and your light in murky caves.

I HAVE SWORN AND I WILL CONFIRM IT, THAT I WILL KEEP YOUR RIGHTEOUS ORDINANCES (119:106).

The psalmist is not afraid to swear utter obedience to God's Word. He is making a covenant of compliance. He is bold because he knows these ordinances are righteous. It would be painful for a soldier to fight for a country whose cause he does not believe in and whose values he does not respect. But this is not the case when seeking God because all of His ordinances and judgments are

---

[1] If your life is guided with the light of God's Word, then without the Word of God, you walk in darkness.

perfectly righteous—just in practice and purer than new snow.

Many believers refuse to swear obedience because they fear breaking that promise. But examples of God-fearing people swearing allegiance to God cover the pages of Scripture. After his dream in Bethel, Jacob swore allegiance to Yahweh as his God (Gen 28:20-22). The people of Israel made a covenant of obedience to God's laws at Mt. Sinai (Ex 19:8). The returnees from exile under Nehemiah signed a document stating complete surrender to God's Word and a tithe of all their produce (Neh 10:1-39). Story after story in Scripture testifies to the value of promising loyalty to the Lord and His Word.

Christ did not eradicate the validity of promises and pledges, but He did discourage rash oaths (Matt 5:34-37). The Jews had deceived themselves into thinking that by making an oath or elaborate promise they were somehow held more accountable than if they simply said "yes" or "no." So Christ taught them that even the simple promise of "yes" or "no" must be kept. "But your yes is to be yes and your no, no so that you may not fall under judgment" (James 5:12).

The psalmist does not take a rash oath. He says what he means and he means what he says. He understands both the promise and the importance of keeping his promise.

You can swear a life of allegiance to God without fear. Don't let the fear of failing or the terror of breaking your promise tempt you to lower the flag of your spiritual conviction. Raise it high for all to see and blow the trumpet of victory loud! As Stephen Charnock put it: "A soldier unresolved to fight may easily be defeated. ...Resolution in a weak man will perform more than strength in a coward."[2] Give Him your all, even when you know you will fall from time to time. The psalmist sinned. He blew it. Why else would he close this entire psalm with "I have gone astray like a lost sheep" (vs 176)? He still pledged radical obedience. God's grace is deep enough, wide enough, and enduring enough to cover your sin, wash it away, and make you clean again. Do not forget God's sovereign ability to help you, nor underestimate His grace to forgive you.

Christ said, "But I tell you that every careless word that people speak, they shall give an accounting for it in the day of judgment" (Matt 12:36). Does this mean that we should no longer promise to serve God, but only prove our commitment through action? Not at all! You already promised obedience to Him and to His Word. When you were saved, your actions of repentance from sin and faith in Jesus Christ alone were shouting declarations of a choice to obey God and live for Him. Your continued promise of allegiance is simply a re-affirmation of what you already did on your spiritual birthday.

The psalmist has not only "sworn" to keep God's ordinances but he states

---

2   Stephen Charnock quoted by Spurgeon, 347.

he will confirm this oath. He reasserts it with boldness, as if to say, "I have sworn, and I will guarantee that this promise is true!" I like the New Living Translation, "I've promised it once and I'll promise again."

The psalmist has made up his mind that God's Word comes first in all of his decision making. There will be times in your life when your sinful nature will tug you away from God's Word. You will desire to make decisions that displease the Creator. You will be tempted to do things that you know are not right because they make you feel good. This is the testing of your character.

When a bridge is constructed it must be tested. A bridge's strength is not tested by a cat walking on it, but when the two hundred thousand pound train crosses its tracks. The man who thinks his character is revealed when things are going well is as foolish as the shoe buyer who does not walk in shoes before he buys them. You are defined by how you respond under the pressure of great temptation and suffering.

Countless persecutors of Christians have turned to Christ after witnessing the valiant suffering of those they tortured. Would you like to see who Christ is and the fiber of His true character? Then look at Him in the wilderness for 40 days of starvation, tempted by the master of all temptation (Luke 4:1-13). See him sweat blood in the Garden of Gethsemane (Luke 22:44) and pray, "Not My will but Yours be done" (Luke 22:42). That's character.

Your entire life is made up of thousands of small decisions. The fruit of choices is a lifetime and the fruit of a lifetime is a legacy. If you are guided by God's Word (vs 105) and sworn in allegiance to His Word (verse 106), then you will reap a lifetime that will not only greatly encourage those who follow after you, but will result in heavenly rewards too great to be counted (1 Cor 3:12-15; 2 Cor 5:10).

I HAVE INCLINED MY HEART TO PERFORM YOUR STATUTES FOREVER, EVEN TO THE END (119:112).

"Inclined" means to stretch out or extend. The psalmist has stretched out his heart in passion to obey God's Word. He is not just obeying out of dutiful obligation. He is not begrudgingly seeking God simply because his pastor told him to, or because it's what the Sunday School teacher said to do. He's doing it because he loves to do it!

This commitment to obedience is not a tentative contract. There are no exceptions or back door escapes. The psalmist's commitment to obedience is to the end of his life ("even to the end") and for all eternity ("forever"). His decision is not like giving a three to five year work commitment to a company with the ever present back door option to resign early. We are afraid to give lifelong commitments to many institutions because they are not trustworthy.

Stock investors advise you not to put all your money into one company in case it goes bankrupt and you become the victim of financial destruction.

But God's Word is different. It will never fail. It outlived Methuselah who almost lived for a millennium (1 Peter 1:24-25). It outlived Noah, Abraham, and Moses. It outlived Isaiah, Daniel, Ezekiel and John the Baptist. The bones of the apostles have long ago turned to dust but God's Word still stands as alive as it ever was. That's a good investment!

2. The Word is to dominate your suffering (vss 107, 109, 110).

I AM EXCEEDINGLY AFFLICTED; REVIVE ME, O LORD,
ACCORDING TO YOUR WORD (119:107).

The psalmist suffers bitter turmoil. He uses two words in the Hebrew language to describe the magnitude of his suffering which is almost unbearable: "exceedingly afflicted."

The 21st century American cannot fully appreciate these passages on suffering and persecution. Our persecution is miniscule compared to believers who suffer in other parts of the world. However, the day will come once again when these passages will apply much more to believers.

"Revive" means to make alive. His soul is crushed under the weight of his enemies' taunts, but the psalmist is not without hope. He knows God's Word has promised him salvation so he cries out for deliverance; he cries out to God on the foundation of His promises to deliver him from this persecution.

Notice that the psalmist does not call upon his own virtue, his own merit or his own godliness as a reason for God to revive him, but instead he calls upon something far more trustworthy: God's faithfulness.

When a father's promise to play ball with his son is continually postponed because of his work, the child quickly learns that his father's words cannot be trusted. The father's promise means nothing to the child because his actions speak differently. But when you suffer affliction, you can have great confidence in calling upon your Father's faithfulness for He never fails to do what He promises.

MY LIFE IS CONTINUALLY IN MY HAND,
YET I DO NOT FORGET YOUR LAW (119:109).

The phrase "my life is continually in my hand" is an idiom for "great danger." The psalmist's own life has driven him to great distress. When afraid, the average unbeliever is tempted to look to himself, or even to search for some sort of solace in sin. But not the man of God. The law the psalmist calls upon in verse 107, he refuses to forget in verse 109. Spurgeon remarks, "While he carried his life in his hand, he also carried the law in his heart."[3]

THE WICKED HAVE LAID A SNARE FOR ME, YET I HAVE NOT GONE ASTRAY FROM YOUR PRECEPTS (119:110).

It is interesting that if the wicked are going to get the psalmist to stumble, they must do it by stealth (vss 85, 95). The psalmist is too bold about his commitments to God to willingly and blatantly compromise his testimony and give his enemies grounds for accusation. So they move in secretly and lay a trap to entice him to turn away from God.

But the psalmist does not take the bait for he has "not gone astray from Your precepts." Two things keep this psalmist on the straight and narrow road: he knows his enemy and he knows the Word.

It is an honor to be so godly that the wicked resort to traps and snares to try to make you fall. It is the honor Daniel enjoyed, "Then the commissioners and satraps began trying to find a ground of accusation against Daniel in regard to government affairs; but they could find no ground of accusation or evidence of corruption, inasmuch as he was faithful, and no negligence or corruption was to be found in him" (Dan 6:4). Daniel's reputation was so irreproachable that the only thing they could accuse him of was doing the right thing (Dan 6:5).

The Word of God aids the psalmist in his sufferings. In summary, the psalmist calls upon God's deliverance as promised in His Word (vs 107), he refuses to forget the Word (vs 109), and he holds fast to the path of God's Word (vs 110).

3. The Word is to dominate your worship (verse 108).

O ACCEPT THE FREEWILL OFFERINGS OF MY MOUTH, O LORD... (119:108A).

This verse shows pure worship in several ways:

It is freely given. In the Old Testament sacrificial system, two kinds of offerings were made: required offerings and freewill offerings. A required offering was mandatory, but a freewill offering was of one's own free will, just like the psalmist's worship here. God delights in that. The psalmist does not give it out of dutiful obligation, but rather He gives purely out of worship and love for His Father in heaven!

Remember the story when Christ sat down across from the treasury of the temple and watched the rich throw in their stashes of surplus money? Then along came a frail widow who dropped in two small copper coins, equal to about a penny today. And what did Christ say? "Truly I say to you, this poor

---

3   Spurgeon, 344.

widow put in more than all the contributors to the treasury; for they all put in out of their surplus, but she, out of her poverty, put in all she owned, all she had to live on" (Mark 12:41-44). That's freely given worship. God takes more pleasure in a simple word of sincere worship than the sacrifice of your house, car, or your entire savings account given out of obligation.

The psalmist's worship is also worship through his mouth. An "offering" typically refers to the sacrificing of an animal to God or the tithing of money or valuable metals to the treasury of the temple. But this is the one case in the entire Old Testament where it refers to the offering of one's mouth: *his words*. The psalmist's offering of praise, prayer and speaking the Word of God is by his own tongue.

He wants his worship to be acceptable. "O accept the freewill offerings of my mouth." The true worshipper desires to please the One being worshipped. He is most concerned about pleasing his Creator and delighting in God's glory.

In this modern day we have developed many substitutes for worship: church songs that focus redundantly on the singer over the Creator. Tithing from pressure instead of from a heart of thanksgiving (2 Cor 9:7). Fluffy motivational talks that titillate the flesh instead of expository sermons that feed the soul.

...AND TEACH ME YOUR ORDINANCES (119:108B).

The psalmist knows that the better he understands God's law, the more acceptable and biblical his worship will be. He does not instruct God. He learns from God.

4. The Word is to dominate your attitude (vs 111).

I HAVE INHERITED YOUR TESTIMONIES FOREVER, FOR THEY ARE THE JOY OF MY HEART (119:111).

Inheritance was integral to every part of Jewish life. The very formation of the nation of Israel, when God instituted a covenant with Abraham, depended on Israel's inheritance of the Promised Land (Gen 12:1-3; 15:18-21). God made this covenant with Isaac and Jacob, partially fulfilled it through Moses and Joshua, but will complete its fulfillment in the future kingdom of Christ on earth.

Yet, the Promised Land is not mentioned in verse 111. The disobedience of the people of Israel caused them to temporarily forfeit their right to this land and they were dragged into exile. And if we are accurate in assuming that the author of this Psalm is Daniel, then at the time of this chapter's writing, the Israelites are still exiled and spread out in Babylon, far from the land of their fathers. But the psalmist talks about a better inheritance: the inheritance of God's testimonies. When the psalmist wrote this, Israel had no physical land to claim as their inheritance, but they could rejoice in the inheritance of God's testimonies which testify of a far better land in heaven (Heb 11:9-10, 13-16). How much more joy and pleasure can be created from things above than from things on earth!

When the psalmist speaks of these testimonies he says, "They are the joy of my heart!" He revels and delights in God's testimonies. They are his zenith of happiness, his fervent ecstasy and his infinite bliss. If you view God's Word as an inheritance, as a gift and as a precious treasure, it will give you inexpressible joy.

From Psalm 119:105-112, we have observed four areas of your life that God's Word should be dominating:

1. The Word is to dominate your choices (vss 105, 106, 112).
2. The Word is to dominate your suffering (vss 107, 109, 110).
3. The Word is to dominate your worship (vs 108).
4. The Word is to dominate your attitude (vs 111).

Years ago, the great German reformer, Martin Luther, made this observation about the importance of the Word being in the believer's life:

> In truth you cannot read the Scriptures too much; and what you read, you cannot read too well; and what you read well, you cannot too well understand; and what you understand well, you cannot too well teach; and what you teach well, you cannot too well live.

The psalmist needed God's Word when he made decisions. He needed God's Word when he suffered. He needed God's Word when he worshipped. He needed God's Word when he chose his attitude. He needed God's Word all the time. Why were his decisions so godly, his suffering so well received, his worship so pure, and his attitude so good? Because his life was permeated with the Word of God.

QUESTIONS FOR CONTEMPLATION

1. What does it mean that God's Word is a lamp to the psalmist's feet and a light to his path? Why does he say "feet" and "path"?

2. In verse 106, why would the psalmist swear to keep God's righteous ordinances when he knows that he is a sinner and will fall? Is this an honest promise? Is it presumptuous?

3. In verse 108, what are the freewill offerings of the psalmist's mouth?

4. In verse 109, "in my hand" means to be in danger. How does remembering God's law help the psalmist?

5. Why is it significant that the psalmist says "I have inclined my heart to perform Your statues" in verse 112? Why didn't he simply say, "I have chosen to perform Your statutes"?

6. Give this passage a title. Make sure the title encapsulates its theme. Now write down three ways you can apply this theme in your daily life.

17

Dead Orthodoxy or Living Truth:
The Importance of the Affections
Psalm 119:161-168

Airports, hospitals, and graveyards are the three most emotional places on earth. They signify departure, sickness, birth, or death. How would you feel if, as you placed your first newborn baby into the arms of your husband, he sighed and said, "Oh boy, here come the bills?" What would you think if, at your father's death, your mother didn't shed a single tear? What would you say if, after a three month military leave, your spouse did not want to touch you when you arrived at the airport?

Though emotions vacillate, they are powerful signals. Like radar, they project what someone values and what he detests. Anger, love, sorrow, hate, joy, and fear—all of these are buds that grow from the deeper roots of a human's values.

God created us as emotional creatures. Emotions are to be received as blessings, not as something to be ashamed of. In the psalms, you find the heart and emotions of men passionate for God. As John Calvin said, "The Psalter gives voice to the emotion of every Christian experience."

I was once asked by a fellow believer, "Christ is our perfect example, is He not?"

"Why, of course," I answered.

"Then what about Him? Did he carry great affection for others and for God? Was *He* emotional?"

It's a great question and the apostle John gives us a special glimpse into the emotions of Christ. In John 11:35 we read, "Jesus wept."[1] Why did Christ weep? Some like to say, "Christ was weeping for the sinfulness of mankind. He was troubled by the consequences of sin." Though this answer sounds very doctrinal,

---

1   This verse has received the label as "the Bible's shortest verse" but actually 1 Thessalonians 5:16 which says, "Rejoice always" is the shortest because "Jesus wept," is really three words in the Greek.

it does injustice to the context. John 11:33 says that, "When Jesus therefore saw her [Mary] weeping, and the Jews who came with her also weeping, He was deeply moved in spirit and was troubled." He saw Mary weeping. He saw the Jews sobbing in sorrow over their good friend's death. And this moved Christ. His emotions were stirred.

For some reason we fear talking too much about Christ's tenderness and compassion. It makes us uncomfortable. The more we realize how tender and sensitive Christ was, the more we feel our own lack lack of sensitivity. It's convicting, so we try to present a more cold, analytical, distant Christ. In Psalm 119:161-168, we find the tears of a man who did not just choose affection, but felt affection!

Consider another question: What if a believer told you he never felt any emotion for God? The believer with no emotion or affection for God is the believer who does not know God. We were not just saved *from* divine wrath, but *to* a divine God. You were not just turned away *from* affection for sin, but *to* affection for Christ. The believer buried under the dirt of dead formalism will find it very hard to breathe. I'm not supporting a hyperventilating lunatic, but rather a man or woman whose affections are so wrapped up in God's Word that to rip away the Word would be to rip out his heart. That is the emotion you find in this passage.

Psalm 119:161-168 is unique for it contains not a single prayer request. Instead of appeals, it is packed with expressions of affection for God's Word. And from these verses we find seven traits of affection that you should have for God's Word:

1. The believer who loves God's Word is struck with awe (vs 161).

PRINCES PERSECUTE ME WITHOUT CAUSE,
BUT MY HEART STANDS IN AWE OF YOUR WORDS (119:161).

In the early part of 2006, the professional figure skater, Michelle Kwan, trained fiercely for the Olympics until she suddenly had to pull out due to a groin injury. After all her hard work, she had to retire with little reward after thousand of hours of laborious training.

The worst kind of suffering is that which has no purpose. An Olympic trainer will suffer long and hard in training when he sees the end goal: to win a gold medal. But few people put themselves through the pain of running furiously several hours every day without some goal in mind.

That is what makes the psalmist's suffering so painful. Princes persecute him without cause. He did nothing to deserve their hate or warrant their attacks. The ungodly have no logical reason for cruelty to the godly. In the early church,

Christians held love feasts and called each other "brother and sister" (terms which mean "husband and wife" in Egypt), so the world accused them of incest and pedophilia. They partook of the body of Christ in the Lord's Supper and unbelievers charged them with cannibalism. They were obedient, law-abiding, and peaceful citizens, but because they refused to worship the Roman emperor and his pagan deities, they were burned alive as insurrectionists. But had any of their enemies observed these Christians worshipping together, they would have quickly discovered that these celebrations were not immoral feasts or cannibalistic celebrations, but times of selfless worship and praise.

When one wants something to be true, his mind has tremendous ability to convince itself that the rumor is reality. The ungodly hate the psalmist's zeal for holiness because this is something they do not have. Therefore, with no legitimate reason for hounding the saint, they make up causes to justify their wicked thoughts.

Of all people, you would expect the princes, the judges of right and wrong, the men responsible for preserving justice, to be fair with the psalmist. But they are not. Yet the psalmist holds to a law higher and more noble than theirs: the law of God's Word. No matter how just human judges may be, believers will always be an object of attack, for Satan rules this world, and he vents his hatred for God by persecuting God's people (Eph 2:1-2).

But this is not the end of hope for the psalmist. Notice his response to their maltreatment: "But my heart stands in awe of Your words." His sufferings are great, but God's words are greater. This word "awe" means "dread." The psalmist stands in dread of God's Almighty Word. The greater fear of God's Word has driven out the lesser fear of wicked princes. "How little do crowns and scepters become in the judgment of that man who perceives a more majestic royalty in the commands of his God."[2] As my good friend Lee Craven comments, fleas do not bother a man when he stands in the presence of a lion. Instead of complaining about unjust treatment, he marvels at God's Word. The breathtaking wonder of God's Word acts like an antidote to his suffering.

Suffering is most unbearable for those so consumed with their sufferings that they can think of nothing but their suffering. Have you ever met a hypochondriac who filled your ears with his daily body pains, sicknesses, and surgeries? We should show compassion to those who suffer, but people who live each day so that they can complain to others about their pain are the most miserable people in the world and consequently make others around them miserable. But those who turn to God's Word and discover in it a greater power, deeper wonder, and a far more worthy topic than their own pain, find that they can endure all sorts

---

2   Spurgeon, 423.

of discomfort. They even edure it with joy, for they now do it with purpose: to glorify God. Paul's words were never truer: "Blessed be the God and Father of our Lord Jesus Christ, the Father of mercies and God of all comfort, who comforts us in all our affliction so that we will be able to comfort those who are in any affliction with the comfort with which we ourselves are comforted by God" (2 Cor 1:3-4).

Although the psalmist's enemies persecute him without cause, he does not suffer pointlessly, for he knows they hate him for his holiness and despise him for his devoutness. If his suffering is on behalf of his love for God, the cause is worthy, and with God's Word in his heart, he will endure.

2. The believer who loves God's Word is filled with joy (vs 162).

I REJOICE AT YOUR WORD,
AS ONE WHO FINDS GREAT SPOIL (119:162).

In the psalmist's day, when a king overpowered his enemies, he'd return home with goods, livestock, valuables, and even people that he plundered after the battle was over. His "spoil" was his reward for fighting bravely in battle. War means possible death, but to live through the battle and also return home with a bevy of gifts for the kingdom was cause for loud rejoicing and celebration.

But here the psalmist's spoil is not precious metals, a new set of clothes, or a herd of fat sheep. It is immortal instead of perishable, divine instead of human. What greater spoil can the believer hold in his hands than God's precious Word? What greater cause for rejoicing can the Christian have than to meditate on the great Book of all ages whose words do not lie, and whose promises will not disappoint?

Do you find yourself rejoicing at God's Word? Do you find your heart enthralled with delight when you read it? Are you so enthused with this Book that you cannot help but share it with others, and cannot let a day go by without pouring your heart into its mold?

It is amazing that right after expressing great suffering from princes (vs 161), the psalmist can shout, "I rejoice at Your word, as one who finds great spoil!" He finds God's Word far more satisfying than his sufferings are painful. The joy of God's Word outmatches the pain of persecution. The Word he trembled at in verse 161 is the Word in which he rejoices in verse 162.

This is very close to Paul's words in Romans 8:18, "For I consider that the sufferings of this present time are not worthy to be compared with the glory that is to be revealed to us." And he writes in 2 Corinthians 4:17, "For momentary, light affliction is producing for us an eternal weight of glory far beyond all comparison." To Paul, the sufferings of this life don't compare to the glory of the afterlife. It is far from an equal trade.

Put the intensity of your sufferings in a race with the rewards of God's Word, and the rewards will win every time! Imagine living a life with a heart-diseased, diabetic, or cancerous body. Imagine suffering the sorrow of all your friends and family passing away, seeing your own financial ruin and dying a torturous death. It would be better to have all these things and experience the glory that will be revealed than to live like a king with all the pleasures in perfect health and with the best of friends, yet die and end up in hell.

3. The believer who loves God's Word is roused with hate (vs 163a).

I HATE AND DESPISE FALSEHOOD... (119:163A).
This man of God who stands in awe at God's Word (161), who rejoices in God's Word (162) and who loves God's Word (163b) is the same man who detests ungodliness (163a). One can conclude that this psalmist is an emotional man. Indeed he is, but not the emotion of a wind-blown storm, constantly vacillating, rather he has emotions that are well grounded and biblically guided. His emotions are not reflexes to a sudden change of situation, but emotion etched in the granite of God's Word. All of his responses have been trained by God's Word.

One may frequently find himself in awe of the world's celebrities, rejoicing at vain things, hating those who tell him the painful truth or loving his own sin. But the man or woman of God who finds his own mind and soul intoxicated with God's Word will soon find that he fears God, not man; that he rejoices in truth, not vanity; that he hates wickedness, not purity; and that he loves truth, not sin.

The psalmist's statements make it clear that no one can love God's Word and love sin at the same time. The two can no more pair up than a tiger and goat can frolic. Just as fire cannot burn ice so the man who loves sin cannot love God's Word. Notice how he uses two verbs to describe his distaste for sin: "hate" and "despise." Spurgeon calls this a "double expression for an inexpressible loathing."[3] His hatred and detestation for wickedness is as strong as his love for God's law. And the more he loves God's Word, the stronger his hate for sin grows. This is the only kind of hatred that pleases God. Most people identify hate with sin, but it is the object and motive of one's hatred that determines whether his hatred is sanctified or sinful.

---

3   Spurgeon, 423.

4. The believer who loves God's Word is captivated with love (vs 163b).

...BUT I LOVE YOUR LAW (119:163B).

As the psalmist hates sin, he loves God's Word with equal intensity. It is impossible to devote yourself to these two enemies without hypocrisy. If you sing praises in church but blaspheme with indifference throughout the week, your mouth has pretended somewhere along the way. You are like the man who gargles mouthwash when he wakes up and then drinks sewer water for breakfast.

If you sketch sermon notes on Sunday but type in pornographic websites on Monday, your hands claim faithfulness while committing treason. To encourage a believer in a Bible study on Tuesday but then to laugh at dirty jokes in the break room on Wednesday is to tell the world that your Christianity is nothing more than a stage play.

In The Return of the King, the third movie of the Lord of the Rings trilogy, Frodo must join the white ships (a euphemism for death) and leave his good friend, Samwise, behind. It's an emotional moment of sadness. Now pretend that you bumped into Elijah Wood (the real life actor for Frodo) and had lunch with him. Would you seriously feel bad that he died in the movie? Not at all! He was only acting. Likewise, when the world and other believers see that you are only "acting" Christianity, your testimony loses all power. It turns all of the Christian faith into a mask and is actually worse than not claiming Christianity at all.

You cannot love Christ and love the world at the same time. "If anyone loves the world, the love of the Father is not in him. For all that is in the world, the lust of the flesh and the lust of the eyes and the boastful pride of life, is not from the Father but is from the world" (1 John 2:15a-16).

5. The believer who loves God's Word is flooded with praise (vs 164).

SEVEN TIMES A DAY I PRAISE YOU,
BECAUSE OF YOUR RIGHTEOUS ORDINANCES (119:164).

The psalmist has gone from awe, to joy, to hate, to love, to praise. He is so full of God's Word that he cries out to Him seven times a day! He is not prescribing a mandatory prayer schedule like the Koran prescribes for Muslims facing the Mecca five times a day. Nor is he stipulating a prayer calendar to reflect devout Hebrews' prayer lives or to justify Roman papists' canonical hours of intercession.[4] He simply sees God's Word as so righteous that he explodes in unstoppable praise!

A fire will only grow if you feed it more logs, and the more the psalmist

---

4   Spurgeon, 429.

feeds his soul with the righteous ordinances of God, the more he responds in shouting praise! That all of God's decrees and judgments are performed in perfect righteousness fills the psalmist with inexpressible joy that he cannot contain.

Don't fall prey to the idea that worship is only meant for once a week on Sundays. Do you praise Him seven times a day or more like once in seven days?[5] How often do we come home from the Sunday service feeling that we have somehow paid our worship dues that will last us for the week until the next Sunday? That is not worship. We cannot attend church to "make up" for the transgressions of the week, setting ourselves free for another six days of rebellion. Worship is to continue day in and day out.

You can always tell if someone enjoys doing something, because if he does, he will do it repeatedly. How many people stop after eating one single Frito? You may find that favorite camping spot you always take your family to, or that special vacation spot on an island. Think about your top TV show, most delectable dishe, or favorite sport. If you don't do these things again and again, it is doubtful that they are very important to you. Frequency proves loyalty, and we are loyal to that which we love.

Have you ever wondered why we sing "Hallelujah" over and over again? Hallelujah comes from two Hebrew words. The first is *hallel*, meaning "praise," and the second, *jah,* is an abbreviated version of Yahweh, also known as Jehovah, or LORD. So to shout, "Hallelujah!" is to shout, "Praise the LORD!"

Are you full of praise for God's righteous ordinances? There's an easy way to know. How often do you think, talk of, and pray about them?

6. The believer who loves God's Word is wrapped in peace (vs 165).

> THOSE WHO LOVE YOUR LAW HAVE GREAT PEACE,
> AND NOTHING CAUSES THEM TO STUMBLE (119:165).

This word "peace" is the same word for "shalom." People who love God's Word are not just calm, but have great peace. Real peace starts with being right with God. In the mid 1800's, when American Indians and White Pioneers realized the fruitless purpose of fighting, they signed a "peace treaty." This treaty guaranteed that they would be friends and never point a muzzle or draw an arrow against each other again. God has made a "peace treaty" with every human who has put his faith in Jesus Christ. This means that you are no longer at war with God. God, who was your enemy (Rom 5:10), is now your Friend (Jam 2:23). God, who was your fierce Judge, is now your gracious Redeemer.

But being right with God is not only a state of being, but an experiential

---

5   See Spurgeon, 424.

feeling. In spite of princes' persecution (vs 161), the psalmist possesses a calm and content soul. Put him in a ship tossing in peril or a life-threatening battle, yet on the inside he will be at perfect peace, for the sovereignty of God is greater than the turmoil of trials and the comfort of God is stronger than the threat of one's own life.

He who knows God's Word knows that God rules the world and is sovereign even over the world's prince, who is Satan (Eph 2:2). And he who knows that God rules, knows peace, for God is in control. What trial, what tragedy, what affliction can happen to God's people that God does not permit? None of your trials or temptations surprise God. He knows perfectly well what you are going through and He allows it only because of His immeasurable love.

Foxe's Book of Martyrs is packed with stories of men and women who sang hymns while their skin was charred with flames of fire. What gave their mind such serene peace in the face of this gruesome agony? Nothing but the Word of God. Do you find your mind more consumed with the latest NBA scores or a new recipe than with God's holy Word?

Loving God's law not only gives the believer peace, but keeps him from stumbling (vs 165b). If your highest commitment is to God's Word, no temptation, calamity, or attack from unbelievers well be so heavy that you are not able to stand strong. God promises this in 1 Corinthians 10:13, "No temptation has overtaken you but such as is common to man; and God is faithful, who will not allow you to be tempted beyond what you are able, but with the temptation will provide the way of escape also, so that you will be able to endure it." The walls of your fortress are always stronger than the attacks of your enemies. If you have chosen the path of God's Word, then He will never let it be so riddled with potholes and steep cliffs that you will stumble. Cling to His Word, and though the entire world around you fall apart, God will keep your foot stable.

The reverse is also true. A lack of love for God's Word will result in stumbling. When you yield to sin or give yourself to wanton pleasure, you choose to embrace something that stands against God's Word. There is always grace so that the believer can repent and turn back, but as Paul says, "Are we to continue in sin so that grace may increase? May it never be!" (Rom 6:1).

Some people keep God's law so that others will think highly of them. Pride is their motivation. Others keep God's law out of gloomy obligation. The motive for this is legalism. Still others keep God's law because it is momentarily convenient. The motive for this is laziness. But then there are people like the psalmist who keep God's law because they cherish its words. They are motivated by love for the One who wrote it!

But just in case the reader thinks that the psalmist's emotion is nothing more than a vapor—an experience-driven, fluctuating feeling that comes and goes like the beetles in June—look again. In the final verses of this stanza (166-168), the psalmist turns his feelings into action. He says, "I hope and do! I keep and love!" To the psalmist, godly actions cannot be void of fervent emotions.

7. The believer who loves God's Word is committed to obedience (vss 166-168).

I HOPE FOR YOUR SALVATION, O LORD,
AND DO YOUR COMMANDMENTS (119:166).

The psalmist hopes. By loving and studying the Word, the psalmist reads of God's salvation and yearns for it. He hopes and trusts in God's coming salvation that will rescue his body from enemies and his soul from hell.

You may praise the tightrope walker who pushes the wheelbarrow on a single rope strung between two skyscraper buildings, but when he tells you to "get in," you now must decide if you really have faith in his ability. The psalmist continues the second half of the verse with, "and do Your commandments." The God he hopes in is the God he obeys. It is one thing to admire God's Word from a distance. It's easy to admire Christ. Even the Pharisees were impressed with His learning (Mark 12:17; Luke 20:26). Who wouldn't respect the Bible for its high standards and morals? Who wouldn't praise it as a masterpiece of literary excellence? But when a man must entrust the eternal destiny of his soul to the person of Jesus Christ, you're asking him to remove all trust from himself. You're asking him to turn his praise into action. Adoring God from a distance won't save a single soul from God's eternal wrath. You must trust Him personally! That means you hand Him the reins.

It's like the story about the mountain climber who fell from the cliff but was saved from death by the rope still attached. He hung there in mid-air, but because it was pitch black, he could not see the ground below. So he cried out to God,

"God help me!"

And God said, "Just untie the rope and let go."

And he cried again, "But God, I can't see the ground! I'll fall to certain death!"

But God responded, "Trust me and let go." But no matter how hard he tried, the man could not remove his faith from the rope and place it in God. The next morning, hikers found the mountain climber dangling from a rope, frozen to death, hanging eighteen inches from the ground.

MY SOUL KEEPS YOUR TESTIMONIES, AND I LOVE THEM EXCEEDINGLY. I KEEP YOUR PRECEPTS AND YOUR TESTIMONIES, FOR ALL MY WAYS ARE BEFORE YOU (119:167-168).

Again he states that he will keep God's Word. In these last three verses he says it three times! "I...do your commandments...my soul keeps your testimonies... I keep Your precepts and Your testimonies." This emotion now proves to be grounded on solid steel. Emotion without commitment is like the man who shouts curses against the enemy, but turns and runs at the first sight of their guns. And commitment without emotion is as dry as desert sand, with no life and no breath. It is cold legalism and dead orthodoxy.

In Christ you find the epitome of emotion and commitment. He wept for Israel when He foresaw her coming destruction (Luke 19:41). He was moved to tears when He saw the Jews weeping over Lazarus (John 11:35). And yet the same God-Man drove swindlers from the temple with a whip (John 2:14-15), and endured 40 days of relentless temptation from Satan (Luke 4:1-13).

The psalmist's affection for the Word is inseparable from his commitment to it. In the same breath he says, "My soul keeps Your testimonies, and I love them exceedingly." As The Bible In Basic English says, "Great is my love for it."

No matter how much a mother weeps for her son who is deathly ill, her tears are drops of hypocrisy if she does not care for his needs and will not take him to the hospital. And yet a mother not moved by affection for her son's health while she coldly administers him medicine, cannot be said to love her son either.

The psalmist possess devoted obedience to God. How can he say with such confidence, "I keep your testimonies and your precepts" in verse 168? The answer is found in the last stanza of this second to last strophe of Psalm 119: "For all my ways are before you."

Because he evaluates his entire life in light of God's presence, his life is filled with obedience. This does not mean he is sinless, but godly. Confessing your sin helps you face its ugliness, diagnose its wickedness, and turn from its enslavement. He who does not confess his sin cannot possibly be free from it. A slave must first admit his condition before he will ever be free.

To open all his ways and thoughts to God, the psalmist admits that God knows all things and is present everywhere. There is no thought too deep or place too distant for God to know perfectly. Before the believer can practice confession, he must believe in the omnipresence of God. He confesses sin of which he is aware and sin of which he is not.

The psalmist must also embrace the mercy of God, for what son wants to confess his sin to a father who instead of extending him mercy will beat him with a stick? When a child is bold enough to confess a sin to his parents, he proves that those parents exemplify mercy when they discipline their son. He boldly tells them his sin because he knows that though they do not approve of his sin, they will show him mercy because he humbled himself.

A prisoner during the revolutionary war was locked in a cell for many days. Day and night a guard stared at him through a tiny slit in the cell. Whether he ate, drank, or slept, he could not escape that lidless eye. It almost drove him mad and his very breathing became a misery for the soldier's glassy gaze was inescapable.[6] So it is with every sinner who believes in God's omnipresence but forgets His mercy. To him, God is nothing more than a warrior of judgment who will level every human who breaks His commands. How hopeless we would be if God were not merciful!

From Psalm 119:161-168, we have discussed seven traits of affection for God's Word that you can develop:

1. The believer who loves God's Word is *struck* with awe (vs 161).
2. The believer who loves God's Word is *filled* with joy (vs 162).
3. The believer who loves God's Word is *roused* with hate (vs 163a).
4. The believer who loves God's Word is *captivated* with love (vs 163b).
5. The believer who loves God's Word is *flooded* with praise (vs 164).
6. The believer who loves God's Word is *wrapped* in peace (vs 165).
7. The believer who loves God's Word is *committed* to obedience (vss 166-168).

Someone saw Mr. Welch, a Suffolk minister, weeping at a table, and asked him why he was doing that. Mr. Welch responded, "Because I can love Christ no more."[7] *If you must be moved to hate, anger, love, sorrow, fear, or joy, let it be the Word of God that moves you!*

---

6   Spurgeon, *Lectures*, 403-404.
7   Ibid., p. 366.

QUESTIONS FOR CONTEMPLATION

1. Why is it so important to develop affection for God's Word?

2. What does the psalmist love and what does he hate? Why is there such a stark contrast in his feelings toward these two things?

3. Why does God's law give His people peace?

4. When you think about God's Word, what comes to mind? Burdens? Obligations? An ancient book that's hard to understand? Love? Affection? Honor?

CHAPTER

C H A P T E R

18

How to Worship a Holy God in an Unholy World
Psalm 119:169-176

The month was February and the year 2005. I drove my lovely wife to the oldest city in the USA: St. Augustine. Nestled just south of Jacksonville, Florida along the coast, this city boasted brick mansions dating back to the 1500's. As we walked through this emblem of history, an ancient but gallant church caught our attention. At the top hung a large bell. Suddenly, this bell began to ring the famous hymn, "Rejoice the Lord is King." An ironic feeling swept over me. Here came this song right into the secular public! The music filled our hearts with great gladness as we walked around rejoicing that Christ is our King, yet at the same time looking out on a sinful and dying world.

The greatest irony of all was that we were worshipping God in the midst of a Satan-ruled world. And that's precisely what the psalmist does in Psalm 119:169-176. In this passage, the psalmist writes as if his heart has flown far from this earth, traveling up to heaven to rest before the presence of God Himself. A boy's mind can race to the battlefield of guns and war, while he is playing on a concrete slab in the middle of downtown New York, where every light pole becomes a tree and every wall a dirt embankment. So real is his fantasy that he plays as if he has been time warped 150 years into the past.

This is not far from how the psalmist thinks and lives. Although he does not ignore earthly realities, heaven and God's throne are so real to him that he lives as if he were constantly before God's presence. His entire day, morning to evening, is influenced by heavenly thoughts.

Should this not be the longing of every believer? Should we not hunger to see God, to know Him in all His perfection, glory, strength and power? Should we not look daily to the clouds for the return of our Savior that we may be home forever? It's hard to look up when your head is perpetually buried in earthly things.

Your greatest priority throughout your life and into all eternity should be to worship God. The process of sanctification may not be complete, but the chief end of man, which is to glorify God and enjoy Him forever, will never alter. And you can fulfill this high calling even in the midst of a sinister world, if you live by three criteria. From Psalm 119:169-176, we find three criteria for worshipping a holy God in an unholy world.

1. Worship God by turning to His grace (vss 169a, 170a, 171a, 172a).

Notice all the occurrences of the request "let"
"Let my cry come before You" (169)
"Let my supplication come before You" (170)
"Let my lips utter praise" (171)
"Let my tongue sing of Your word" (172)
"Let Your hand be ready to help me" (173)
"Let my soul live that it may praise You" (175)

Why does he says "let, let, let, let, let and let"? Because he knows that he cannot worship God based on any goodness of his own. The psalmist knows that he does not float into God's presence on the boat of his morality but on the ship of God's grace. He knows that God could justly reject his prayer, but delights in listening because He is merciful. He needs God to reach down in mercy, pick him up and set him before the very throne. That's grace and it's the first stepping stone of true worship.

True worship starts with the realization that the worshipper is not worthy but by the grace of God who makes him worthy. To please God in worship, you must admit that you are unworthy to stand before the Almighty Creator. Without this admission you cannot embrace His grace. This passage is saturated with no fewer than ten requests that God would help the psalmist to worship in a way that pleases the Lord.

Notice also that the psalmist is not reserved about his worship. He boldly uses his cries (vs 169), his supplications (vs 170), his lips (vs 171), and his tongue (vs 172) to worship the Lord. He is not interested in the cold worship of the introvert. He wants to praise God with sound! He reminds me of the one leper who returned to thank Christ for healing him. Luke says that he "turned back, glorifying God with a *loud voice*[1]" (Luke 17:15).

LET MY CRY COME BEFORE YOU, O LORD... (119:169A).

This phrase "come before" means to "come near." The psalmist does not only desire for God to hear his cry but for his cry to come close to the ears of God and find acceptance. He cries out for help. He cries out in praise. He cries out

---

[1]   Author's emphasis

in hunger for God's acceptance. Just as King Ahasuerus extended his golden scepter to Queen Esther (Esther 5:1-2), so the psalmist desires for God to give him a hearing. This hearing is not like the artificial hearing that a judge might give to a man in court, but the hearing a good father will give to his child who comes to speak close in his ear. First he prayed for help; now he prays for his own prayer.

Dave Hintz, college and evangelism pastor of Calvary Bible Church in Burbank, CA, once said that good listening skills require not only listening to the words being said, but to the feelings and emotions wrapped up in how they are said. The same is true with the psalmist. He is not just asking God to hear the sentences he wants to say, for he knows that God knows all things and even the quietest whispers cannot sneak by His ears. But he asks that God hear his "cry." The psalmist wants God to hear his heart, his soul and his deepest feelings (Acts 15:8).

LET MY SUPPLICATION COME BEFORE YOU... (119:170A).

Many believers rush into God's presence making their needs and wants very clear. But this psalmist is a humble man. First he asks that God would hear his voice (verse 169) and then he asks God to listen to his prayer. He fully recognizes his unworthiness to enter God's presence, that he is a sinner and that God is not. Nothing can separate humans further from God than sin and that separation is infinite in time and length. But the God who is just is also merciful.

LET MY LIPS UTTER PRAISE... (119:171A).

The psalmist has gone from crying, to praying, to vocal praise! The word "utter" means to "bubble up" like a spring. The psalmist has moved from prayer requests to bubbling praise.

And see how he once again requests acceptance before God's throne. He requests that God would let his lips praise Him. This is a key principle of worship. The worshipper's greatest concern should not be the sound of the music, nor the feeling of the mood; it should not be his appearance to others, or if he gets to hear his favorite preacher. His greatest concern should be that his worship is acceptable before the throne of God. Before the worship service on Sunday is your greatest desire to have a right heart before the Lord? True worship always begins with acknowledgement of God's perfect holiness and the desire to be acceptable before Him.

We often forget Whom we are worshipping. Remove God and you remove all motive for worship. If you were presenting a gift to a king, would you be concerned about what the jesters think of you? Would you dress for the couriers or bow for the maids? What a ridiculous thought. Yet this is what we do every time we go to church to please others instead of God. George Zemek comments, "The heart's intention of the child of God was that his lips might become a gushing vehicle for praise, adoration, and thanksgiving to God."[2]

LET MY TONGUE SING OF YOUR WORD... (119:172A).

The psalmist's expression of worship grows stronger and louder in each succeeding verse. He has moved from a cry for God's attention, to a prayer for God to answer, to bubbling praise for God's teaching, to a singing tongue for God's righteousness. Notice how he becomes more specific. In verse 171 he uttered praise, but here he sings "of Your Word." In Colossians 3:16, Paul tells the Colossians to "let the Word of Christ richly dwell within you, with all wisdom, teaching and admonishing one another with psalms and hymns and spiritual songs, singing with thankfulness in your hearts to God." The indwelling Word produces vocal praise. When God's Word rests in your heart, it cannot help but break forth in singing praise through your mouth.

A steam engine fed with burning coal energizes a moving train. If the energy did not reach the wheels, they would halt and the energy would find another outlet. And so it is with the Word. Do not let the Word remain bottled inside you. Sing it out and let it enter your decision making, your thoughts, your conversation and your career planning, lest you become spiritually constipated.

A. W. Tozer wrote, "There is more healing joy in five minutes of worship than in five nights of revelry. Nobody ever worshipped God and went out and committed suicide as a hangover."[3]

Many believers today know exhaustive statistics on sports, the latest TV shows or the top twenty songs of their favorite music style. You may be one of them. But when was the last time you sat and talked with someone about Christ? When was the last moment you paused to pray with another Christian? It is a sad thing when a believer shares with other Christians what he has learned in the Word, and suddenly the whole room grows stiff and people groan in discomfort. Talking freely of Christ, prayer and the praises of God have become taboo in many circles because it's not popular in the eyes of the world. Yet this is nothing less than shame for God and fear of man. "For whoever is ashamed of Me and My words, the Son of Man will be ashamed of him when He comes in His glory, and the glory of the Father and of the holy angels" (Luke 9:26).

---

2   Zemek, 374-375.
3   A. W. Tozer, *Ten Messages on the Holy Spirit in the Tozer Pulpit*, vol. 1, compiled by Gerald B. Smith (Camp Hill: Christian Publications), 18-19.

2. Worship God by submitting to His teaching (vss 169b, 171b, 172b, 174b).

You must not worship God apart from His instruction. You cannot worship the God of the Word without using the Word of God. The Word tells you how to worship, Whom you are worshipping and what you need to do in order to worship Him.

Trying to worship God without His Word is more hopeless than trying to steer a ship without a compass. In every verse of this passage, the psalmist refers to the Word in light of his worship. If you remove all his references to the Word, you are left with a pile of meaningless phrases and ignorant attempts at praising God.

The psalmist's first request regarding the Word of God appears in the second half of verse 169:

...GIVE ME UNDERSTANDING
ACCORDING TO YOUR WORD (119:169B).

This understanding is not worldly. It is not the knowledge of scientists, the comprehension of pilots, or the mathematical analysis of engineers. It is the knowledge of God's Word. It is the kind of true knowledge that men of God crave.

The Christian who spends his whole life studying to be a good manager without spending time learning God's Word will suffer great loss at the judgment seat of Christ (1 Cor 3:12-15; 2 Cor 5:10). Though he will not be punished for a single sin, he will see how much time he wasted learning to manage people instead of learning how to please God. Of course, there is a time and place for growing one's skill to perform well, but when the believer lets this priority grow so huge that it squeezes out time for in-depth study of God's Word, he has traded eternal rewards for temporary promotions. He has traded the sun for a lamp, gold for sand.

See how the psalmist singularly seeks God's assistance in understanding the Word. Whoever aids you in the understanding of God's Word, whether it be a teacher, preacher, parent, or friend, does it only by the Holy Spirit of God who reveals His Word (1 John 2:27). God alone can give the believer true understanding of the Word and for this reason, His Word is dead to the unbeliever.

This verse cautions some higher critics. Those who spend hours at their desks, reassigning new dates to the texts of Scriptures, denying traditional authorship, and postponing dates of prophetic passages so that they no longer appear to be supernatural have, in the end, turned the Bible into a compilation of confusion which is nothing short of butchery. They have put the Scriptures on trial and made themselves its judge. Whether they be literary critics, source critics, historical critics, radical critics, form critics, tradition critics, redaction critics, rhetorical critics, canonical critics or structural critics, any time the foundation of their conclusions is speculative and elevates the critic above the text, man above God, they threaten the doctrine of inspiration. In spite of all their training, research expertise and extended doctorates, Scripture testifies that they cannot comprehend one syllable apart from the supernatural help of God's Holy Spirit (1 John 2:27). True understanding of Scripture starts with submission, not criticism.

Spurgeon wrote, "Many a man who is accounted wise after the manner of this world is a fool according to the word of the Lord."[4] They must confess with Job's friend, Elihu, "I thought age should speak, and increased years should teach wisdom. But it is a spirit in man, and the breath of the Almighty gives them understanding" (Job 32:7-8). Gleason L. Archer drove to the heart when he said, "Every man must settle for one of two alternatives: the inerrancy of Holy Scripture, or the inerrancy of his own personal judgment."[5] The psalmist chose the former.

...FOR YOU TEACH ME YOUR STATUTES (119:171B).

This man who requested God's teaching in verse 169 is now God's personal student in 171. What greater privilege can there be than to learn at the foot of God Himself!

The deeper the psalmist's Bible knowledge grows, the higher his praise reaches. Would you like to see the most vibrant and happy worshippers on earth? Find those who are most full of God's Word and you have met them! Proper love of God's Word will always produce a heart of praise. The believer who finds it boring, burdensome or wearisome should search his heart for sin. Sin hates the Word like murderers hate honest judges. It will fight to the bone and tear at the flesh sparing no shedding of blood and holding back no extent of monstrosity to silence the Word.

...FOR ALL YOUR COMMANDMENTS
ARE RIGHTEOUSNESS (119:172B).

The psalmist can sing of God's Word because God's Word is righteousness. Verse 138 described God's commandments as righteous, but here he says that they are righteousness itself. The righteousness of God cannot be known if His commandments are not known. His righteousness is not just an aspect of His character, but obligates the human and directs his life. A righteous fact is abstract

---

4   Spurgeon, 433.
5   Gleason L. Archer, *A Survey of Old Testament Introduction* (Chicago: Moody, 1994), 31.

and distant. But a righteous command gives the hearer something he must do in order to reflect the righteousness of the One who gave it. God's righteousness obligates all men to holy living.

If your employer announces that he is going to implement better customer service, you may agree with this new policy. But it's an irrelevant concept until he trains a customer greeter and performs follow up care calls for each client.

The eternal righteousness of God can only be truly known by those who hear and obey His commandments because then their lives become the living expressions of that righteousness.

...AND YOUR LAW IS MY DELIGHT (119:174B).

The psalmist delights in the Word that he longs to understand (169b), the Word that promises to deliver him (170b), the Word he longs to be taught (171b), the Word that is the essence of God's righteousness (172b) and the Word that he has chosen (173b). At some point, every student experiences the heavy burden of studying a book he does not enjoy. But the true Christian delights in God's Word, for to him it is life itself, a treasure house of wisdom, a refuge in trouble and the very words of God.

Delighting in God's Word does not mean delighting in the binding, the paper or the ink of the Bible. It means delighting in the message, in what it says, what it means and what it promises.

Menelik II, one of the greatest rulers in African history and creator of modern Ethiopia, was captured during an enemy raid and held prisoner for ten years. Finally escaping, Menelik II declared himself head of the province of Shewa. After conquering neighboring kingdoms, he developed them into modern Ethiopia and crowned himself their emperor. Italy's effort to overrun Ethiopia ended in defeat when Menelik's army decimated them at the Battle of Aduwa. His battlefield victories and his modernizing of Ethiopia through building schools, telephones and railroads made him world-famous. But he was known for one eccentricity. Every time he felt sick, he ate a few pages of the Bible, convinced that this always restored his health.

One day in December of 1913, recovering from a stroke and feeling extremely ill, he tore every page from an Egyptian edition of the book of Kings, ate them...and died. Would the believer treasure God's Word (not the paper and ink!) with the same fervency, he would find victory over even the most Herculean temptations.

3. Worship God by relying on His strength (vss 170b, 173, 174, 175, 176).

We must admit that we are too weak to worship God apart from His help.

DELIVER ME ACCORDING TO YOUR WORD (119:170B).

The psalmist prays for deliverance for two reasons: because he needs it and because the Word promises it. Without this biblical knowledge his prayer would be limp and pathetic, lacking confidence. Godly prayer is fueled by God's Word. Just as the tourist feels safe in the African jungles next to a guard who has killed a thousand lions with his spear, so the psalmist's prayers grow bolder the more the Word teaches him about God's ability to deliver.

The believer is called to give complete surrender to God's sovereignty and to admit that God alone can save. That's a good place to be! When the believer puts full responsibility for his deliverance on God's shoulders, he has no cause for fear.

LET YOUR HAND BE READY TO HELP ME,
FOR I HAVE CHOSEN YOUR PRECEPTS (119:173).

The psalmist is no longer asking for God's acceptance, but is now requesting God's help. He yearns for God's ready hand. The psalmist admits that he is not strong enough to help himself. He cannot be faithful to God unless the God of help comes to his aid.

But why would God help the psalmist? Because the psalmist has "chosen Your precepts" (173b). The psalmist has made it his life mission to serve God. His mind is not wavering between the pulls of the world and the worship of God. He knows Whom he must serve and he does it with gladness. Because he chooses God's Word, the Lord will choose him to be delivered. "A man may fitly ask help from God's hand when he has dedicated his own hand entirely to the obedience of the faith."[6]

Does a child boldly request a favor from his parents right after disobeying their commands? No. The obedient child makes his request fearlessly, for his conscience does not condemn him. "Beloved, if our heart does not condemn us, we have confidence before God; and whatever we ask we receive from Him, because we keep His commandments and do the things that are pleasing in His sight" (1 John 3:21-22).

I LONG FOR YOUR SALVATION, O LORD,
AND YOUR LAW IS MY DELIGHT (119:174).

The psalmist realizes his need for salvation. This salvation is not salvation from his enemies, but salvation from his own sins. He admits he has gone astray like

---

6   Spurgeon, 434.

a lost sheep in verse 176, needs God's help in verse 173 and desires that his soul continues to live in verse 175.

LET MY SOUL LIVE THAT IT MAY PRAISE YOU, AND LET YOUR ORDINANCES HELP ME (119:175).

Most men and women want to live. A man is often willing to give all he has to save his own life. Some live for others. A wife lives for her sickly husband; a father lives to raise his motherless kids. Some even live to help the good of all mankind. As lofty as these motives may be, none of them come a light year close to the most lofty purpose for living: to worship God. Here the psalmist wishes to live not for his own pleasure or to postpone the pain of death, but so that he may praise God! He lives to worship! And his greatest concern lies not with the life of his body but the life of his soul, for he knows this matters most to God. It would be better to be imprisoned in the body of a sickly, feeble man whose soul is saved by the blood of Christ, than to be the healthiest, strongest, and most attractive person on the planet whose last breath will usher him through the gates of hell.

The psalmist's soul is plagued with the beastly sin nature of Adam, and no matter how hard he fights against it, his soul thinks thoughts and desires deeds that ensure death. So what does he do? Does he try to purify his life with external good deeds such as giving money to the poor, food to the hungry, or service to his community? Does he vote for more conservative legislature? These may be good, but not good enough. As Randy Alcorn observes, "Behavior modification that's not empowered by God's heart-changing grace is self-righteous, as repugnant to God as the worst sins people gossip about."[7] Instead, the psalmist turns to God for life, knowing that in Him is life. John the Apostle says of the Son of God, "In Him was life and the life was the Light of men, and the Light shines in the darkness, and the darkness did not comprehend [overpower] it" (1 John 1:4-5). The psalmist seeks life from the only One who can remove the very sin that will send his soul to hell. He is consumed with a single passion: to worship and praise God.

He seeks life that he may worship God and then prays, "Let Your ordinances help me." He knows that God's Word can help him just as it promised to deliver him (170b). Instead of trusting his morality to make his soul more ethical, he trusts the grace of God to wash away his sin. With the grace of God's salvation and the power of the life-transforming Word, no demon from hell—no matter how dark—can prey upon his soul and destroy his salvation.

---

7   Alcorn, 37.

I HAVE GONE ASTRAY LIKE A LOST SHEEP; SEEK YOUR SERVANT, FOR I DO NOT FORGET YOUR COMMANDMENTS (119:176).

One would think that after 175 verses of solid praise for God's Word that the psalmist would have no propensity for straying. Yet we are reminded in the great hymn, "Come Thou Fount of Every Blessing" written by Robert Robinson, that we are "Prone to wander—Lord, I feel it—prone to leave the God I love; here's my heart—O take and seal it, seal it for Thy courts above!"

Believers who gain recognitions for godliness are often so afraid of losing their reputation that they never reveal their vulnerabilities. They tightly close their hearts. Over the years, this type of believer slowly becomes more concerned about preserving his facade of godliness than being real with other believers, asking prayer for his weaknesses and praying for others. Broken hearts and openly confessed sin is not only mandated by Scripture (James 5:16), but exemplified by godly men (Romans 7:14-25). This does not mean that every Christian should spill his guts with everyone, hanging out his dirty laundry for the world to see. But when pastors, fathers, teachers, mothers, elders and spritual leaders admit that they struggle with sin and even use themselves as examples of what not to do from time to time, it puts great relief on their followers, reminding them that they do not stand alone in their struggle against the flesh (1 Cor 10:13). A Christian leader who does not share his weakness teaches his followers to do the same. Instead of hiding behind a mask of piety, the psalmist opens his heart to God and admits his sin. Will you be a self-congratulating Pharisee who stands on a mountain of self-righteousness or the unworthy publican who goes home justified by the grace of God?

The psalmist says "I have gone astray like a lost sheep." Why does he compare himself to sheep? Numerous other Scriptures call humans "sheep" (Ps 23:1-4; 44:22; Is 53:6; Micah 2:12; Zech 10:2; 13:7; Matt 9:36; Rom 8:36; Heb 13:20). Sheep are wayward creatures who stray easily. So it is with us. We stray regularily. At one moment we swear devotion to the Lord, and the next hour finds us breaking that vow.

Sheep are also helpless. They will quickly die without a shepherd, either from the cold in the winter or hungry wolves from the forest. Temptations from Satan, the influence of unbelievers, and the sin nature of the believer's own heart stack great odds against him. Without the Shepherd, he is lunch meat for the devil.

May this last verse bring deep comfort to every believer who reads this psalm. Even the godliest of men will stray at times, but godly men do not stay astray, for then they pray, "seek Your servant, for I do not forget Your commandments" (vs 176b).

The psalmist admits that he was so lost in the forest of his own rebellion that he could not lead himself back to God! The road to the Kingdom of Heaven is often riddled with rocks and cliffs while Satan paints his paths with flowers and meadows. This means that the believer needs divine assistance to get back on the right track. But the ungodly man actually can not "go astray." He is already astray. He never comes back to God because he never was with Him in the first place. You cannot return to a place you have never been. This godly psalmist strays not like a dog who has no home, but as a lamb, whom the Shepherd must find and carry home in his arms. Even though he has strayed, even though he has committed sin and turned from God many times, he says with confidence "Seek Your servant!" and the Great Shepherd will come to find him again.

"But why would God seek you, psalmist?"

"Because I do not forget His commandments!" In spite of his weakness and failures, he will not let go of the commandments of God. Stab him with swords, burn him with torches, beat him with sticks, but his hand will not lose grip of God's precious Word!

From Psalm 119:169-176, we have found three criteria for worshipping a holy God in an unholy world:

1. Worship God by turning to His grace (vss 169a, 170a, 171a, 172a).
2. Worship God by submitting to His teaching (vss 169b, 171b, 172b, (174b).
3. Worship God by relying on His strength (vss 170b, 173, 174, 175, 176).

A story is told that one evening a large number of people attended a christening party for a baby. As the guests filed in, they dropped their coats on the bed and the party began. With laughter, snacking and joke-telling, the night went on with joy until someone asked, "Where's the baby?" Suddenly, the mother remembered that she had left the baby on the bed. Racing to the bedroom she threw back a mountain of coats to find her newborn child dead. The heavy coats of the guests had suffocated the poor infant.

These people sacrificed the important for the temporary. Distracted with social fun, they forgot the point of the party. May we not do the same in worship, sacrificing Christ for the amenities. May we never forget that worship is not the songs, programs, services or the meeting times, but first it is Christ, because through Him alone, God's grace, teaching, and strength become yours.

QUESTIONS FOR CONTEMPLATION

1. What has this passage taught you about worshipping God?

2. Why must grace precede worship? What kind of attitude should this produce in every believer?

3. Why can the believer not worship God properly without proper instruction from God?

4. Why do you need the Lord's strength to worship Him?

5. How can your worship life improve in light of this passage?

Flee to God's Word as a Refuge from Persecution
Psalm 119:17-24, 49-56, 121-128

A measure of a man's success is not what he achieves,
but what he overcomes.
~ Booker T. Washington[1] ~

In the second century A.D., realizing that he could no longer hide from his persecutors, Polycarp allowed himself to be arrested. This faithful disciple of Ignatius, who suffered martyrdom before him, was brought into the arena to stand before a group of Roman authorities and a crowd of jeering citizens who thirsted for the entertainment of another tortured Christian. The proconsul pressed him hard and said, "Swear, and I will release you. Revile Christ."

Polycarp replied, "For eighty-six years I have served him, and he has done me no evil. How could I curse my king, who saved me?" As they bound him to the post in the pyre, he looked to the sky and said his last prayer, "Lord Sovereign God...I thank you that you have deemed me worthy of this moment, so that, jointly with your martyrs, I may have a share in the cup of Christ...for this...I bless and glorify you. Amen.[2]"

We can't help but admire Polycarp's resolute courage. And perhaps you wonder, *Could I show the same bravery in the face of death?* Although you may never have to choose between death and rejecting Christ, if you are faithful to live for God's glory, you will be persecuted. Living a holy life and proclaiming God's holiness to others will cause some to hate you. Have you ever felt ostracized simply because people knew that you didn't party on the weekends? Have you ever been laughed at for being a Jesus fanatic? Have you tasted the embarrassment of being rejected after giving someone the gospel? Though milquetoast in comparison to Polycarp's suffering, these examples are true incidents of persecution.

Persecution is to be expected. John told his flock, "Do not be surprised,

---

1   Green, n. p.
2   Justo L. Gonzalez, *The Story of Christianity*, vol. 1 (San Francisco: HarperSanFrancisco, 1984), 44.

brethren, if the world hates you" (1 John 3:13). Paul wrote to Timothy, "Indeed, all who desire to live godly in Christ Jesus will be persecuted" (2 Tim 3:12). As painful as it may be, persecution has a purpose. God uses it to mold and shape you into Christ-likeness (2 Cor 1:5; Jam 1:2-4). This is why the apostle Peter said that suffering for Christ "finds favor with God" (1 Pet 2:20).

So the question is not, "Will I suffer persecution?" If you are faithful, God says that you will. If you follow Christ you will suffer as He suffered (John 15:18). The real question is: "What do I do when the persecution is unbearable?" Has your suffering for Christ ever been so bitter that you wondered how much longer you had to endure it?

The psalmist suffered like this. And in this sixth strategy of cherishing God's Word, we will look at how to flee to God's Word as a refuge in the storm of persecution. We find the answer to this key in three strophes of Psalm 119: "God's Word: A Refuge to the Broken-hearted (17-24)," "How to Remember God's Word When You Suffer the Attacks of Your Enemies (49-56)," and "How to Know if You Are Qualified for Divine Deliverance (121-128)."

CHAPTER

19

God's Word: a Refuge for the Broken-hearted
Psalm 119:17-24

Richard Wurmbrand was a devoted atheist. He visited church after church in his home country of Romania but still refused to believe in God.

One day he felt an irresistible desire to visit one of Romania's villages. Out of 12,000 that existed, he felt compelled to visit a particular one—why, he did not know. But God did. In this village, high up in the mountains, lived a carpenter who had been praying, "Dear God, I have served you faithfully on earth and I know that my reward is in heaven. But I would also like to have a reward here on earth. So please let me bring a Jew to Christ, because Jesus was from the Jewish people. I am old and sick, too tired to go out and witness. So please bring a Jew to me."

God brought Richard. When the carpenter met Richard, he gave him a Bible. Richard read this Bible and wept and wept over it until he repented and turned to Christ. His wife soon followed. Soon, Wurmbrand became a pastor and evangelist to the Russian atheists who infiltrated the country.

Because the Russians conquered Romania with communism, preaching and evangelizing became illegal, but Wurmbrand feared God more than he feared man. He continued preaching and evangelizing until he was thrown into jail and brutally tortured, physically and mentally, for fourteen years.

In 1967, years after Wurmbrand was released from prison, a battered and beaten man, he wrote a book entitled *Tortured for Christ* to recount those long dark days in prison.

In this book, Wurmbrand tells how his wife ended up in a different prison very shortly after he was incarcerated. Women and girls were raped, beaten, and mocked. They were forced to build a canal and each day complete the same workload as men. Some guards threw the women into the Danube River for fun and then fished them out, only to throw them back in again. The food was so scarce that Richard's wife ate grass to stay alive and other women survived on rats and snakes.

Richard had a son who was left to wander the streets. A lady was arrested for helping the boy, and the guards beat her so badly they knocked out all her teeth and she remained a cripple for life. The shocking truth to most believers today in the cozy United States is that more Christians have been martyred for their faith in the last 100 years than in any other age since Christ's resurrection.

No matter the degree of religious freedom in a country, every Christian suffers. It is natural for the Christian and has been since the early church. The apostles were whipped, shipwrecked, scorned, mocked, incarcerated, boiled in oil, stoned and crucified.

The irony is what these apostles said about suffering. They called suffering a *blessing*, a *gift*, your *calling* and a *reason to glorify God*. Paul told the Philippian Christians, "For to you it has been granted for Christ's sake, not only to believe in Him, but also to suffer for His sake" (Philipp 1;29).

After listing of all his sufferings—beatings, imprisonments, shipwrecks and stonings—Paul calls God "He who is blessed forever" (2 Cor 11:31). Peter felt the same way:

> But if when you do what is right and suffer for it you patiently endure it, this finds favor with God. For you have been called for this purpose, since Christ also suffered for you, leaving you an example for you to follow in His steps (1 Pet 2:20-21).
>
> But even if you should suffer for the sake of righteousness, you are blessed (1 Pet 3:14).
>
> ...but if anyone suffers as a Christian, he is not to be ashamed, but is to glorify God in this name (1 Pet 4:16).

We know that Christians are called to suffer for Christ. We know that it is good to suffer for Him. But how does God want you to react when you suffer?

Psalm 119:17-24 answers this question. Observe the psalmist's condition: He is blinded by his own sin and lack of understanding (18). He is a stranger (19), crushed (20), plagued with reproach and contempt (22), and gossiped about (23). When you are broken, when you are hated, when you are gossiped about or filled with reproach and contempt, the temptation to respond sinfully is strong. But every time the psalmist suffered, he fled to the Word of God. In Psalm 119:17-24 we find three routes for running to the refuge of God's Word when you suffer.

1. Elevate the Word as your purpose for living (vss 17-18).

DEAL BOUNTIFULLY WITH YOUR SERVANT, THAT I MAY LIVE AND KEEP YOUR WORD. OPEN MY EYES, THAT I MAY BEHOLD WONDERFUL THINGS FROM YOUR LAW (119:17-18).

The psalmist makes two requests in these verses: deal bountifully (vs 17) and open my eyes (18). Bountifully means plenteously, fully, generously or abundantly. The palmist is asking for the full force of God's perfect blessing. Why? So that "I may live and keep Your Word!"

This request for blessing is not for some grandiose, self-gratifying, pleasure-seeking fantasy. Lord, make me a millionaire! Lord, make me the best looking person on the planet. Lord make me the most athletic person in the Olympics! Not at all.

The psalmist wishes for the simple necessities of life, blessings without which no one could live. The psalmist is so intense about keeping God's Word that he prays that God will keep him alive just so that he can keep it!

Perhaps you've heard the wise proverb: "Eat to live, don't live to eat." The psalmist doesn't just keep God's Word to live, he lives just to keep it! The psalmist would rather die and be laid in his grave than live a life of disobedience to His God.

When was the last time you prayed:

"God, give me food that I may have energy to get up and obey your commandments!"
"Give me water that my tongue may be loosed to speak of your truths!"
"Give me a house that I may have other believers over for dinner!"
"Give me a car that I may drive to church meetings!"
"Give me work that I may feed my family and witness to the people I work with!"

Of course, all of these things you probably already have; but when was the last time you saw them as an avenue through which you can keep God's Word? If the first request is "keep me alive," then the second is "enlighten my understanding."

In verse 18 he prays, "Open my eyes." The word "open" literally means "to uncover." In other words, "Remove the obstacle and make me understand." What one thing blocks man's vision to understand and feed upon the Word of God? Sin.

Sin blinds us. If you were to stand in a dark cave with a flashlight, all it would take is the palm of your hand to cover that flashlight and make the entire cave pitch black. That's what sin does to your understanding of God's Word. It blocks out the light. This is why the writers of the New Testament emphasized the vital importance of removing sin before you receive God's Word.

> Therefore putting aside all filthiness and all that remains of wickedness, in humility receive the Word implanted which is able to save your souls (James 1:21).

> Therefore, putting aside all malice and all deceit and hypocrisy and envy and all slander, like newborn babies, long for the pure milk of the word, so that by it you may grow in respect to salvation, if you have tasted the kindness of the Lord (1 Pet 2:1-3).

But why does the psalmist want opened eyes? "That I may behold [literally "look upon"] wonderful[1] things from Your law" (vs 18). You could summarize his two requests like this:

Keep me alive (vs 17)
Focus my vision (vs 18).

Two obstacles keep men from obeying God's Word: death and sin. In verse 17 he prays that God would bless him abundantly that he may live, and in verse 18 he prays that God would remove his blindness caused by his own sin and mortality. But why was the psalmist so set on God removing death and blindness so that he could keep God's Word? Because obeying the Word of God was his purpose for living.

2. Trust in the Word as your comfort in sorrow (vss 19-22).

Many of us confide in people when we are sad. We look to vacation. We seek refuge in the TV. Yet the only thing that can bring true comfort and true healing is the Word of God! Look at the sources of the psalmist's sorrow: In verse 19 he is a stranger. In verse 20 he is crushed. In verse 21 he is perturbed by those who abhor God. And in verse 22 he is covered in reproach and contempt.

That's one sorrowful man! And what does he do? He prays to God!

I AM A STRANGER IN THE EARTH;
DO NOT HIDE YOUR COMMANDMENTS FROM ME (119:19).

People sold out for Christ can be lonely people. They are made from a different fabric than this world. They are unique because they are more sad about sin, more zealous about holiness and more earnest for godliness. They stand alone

---

1   "Wonderful" = surpassing, extraordinary. Comes from a word which means a "wonder." Full of wonder.

because they don't fit the status quo. They are even seen as odd, eccentric and estranged from the world because their minds do not feel at home with earthly things but with Christ above. This world is to them like an airport terminal, just temporary. You will never be a friend with God in heaven until you are a willing to be a stranger here on earth.

But the psalmist pleads with God, "Do not hide your commandments from me." God's Word is the only comfort in his loneliness. He has no friends. He stands alone. He knows that he is different, and God's Word is his comfort.

But would God hide his Word from anyone? Would He blind people from His truth? Paul says in Romans 1:24-26 that God will turn unrepentant homosexuals over to the lusts of their own flesh. He will push them further into their wickedness so that the natural consequences of their own deeds will condemn them. In 2 Thessalonians 2:11 Paul says that God will send a deluding influence upon all those who follow the antichrist. In Isaiah 6:9-10, God makes the ears dull, the eyes dim, and the hearts dense of those Israelites who refuse to repent of their wickedness. In Matthew 13:14-15, Christ applies this prophecy to the Jews who could not understand His parables. *There are times when God punishes those who refuse to hear His Word by not letting them understand His Word (Amos 8:11-12).* God allows the natural consequences of their sin to become punishment for their sin. But the true child of God need not fear this kind of punishment—for God will **never** hide His Word from His own child.

MY SOUL IS CRUSHED WITH LONGING
AFTER YOUR ORDINANCES AT ALL TIMES (119:20).

The psalmist is not crushed with his personal sorrows, not with the death of a loved one, the loss of his job, the breakdown of his car, or the backstab of a friend. He is crushed with a longing to keep God's ordinances.

No one is able to keep God's commandment all the time. Yet the psalmist yearns to obey God perfectly and he longs after God's commandments night and day. Because he fails to keep them as he should, it crushes him.

I listened to an old message from John MacArthur from the 1970's where he made the following statement: "Discontent is the key to godliness." This is patently true if your discontent arises from your lack of sanctification.

The more you long to keep God's Word, the more crushed you will feel when you don't. My soul burns for those who nonchalantly laugh at their own failures. If you love God dearly, day after day you will find yourself tortured with a burning zeal to honor God in all that you do. You will weep over your sins, and you will rejoice in the righteousness of Christ.

Here are a few questions to evaluate how important keeping God's Word is to you:

- What things anger you the most? Things that offend you personally or things that offend God?
- What things do you spend most of your day thinking about?
- What are your last thoughts before you sleep and your first thoughts before you start the day?
- What do you talk about? James, the Lord's brother, tells us that that the words you speak reflect who you are so accurately that if you could perfectly control your tongue you would be a perfect human (James 3:2).
- What do you desire more than anything else? Be honest. "For where your treasure is there will your heart be also" (Matt 6:21)
- What makes you happy? Superficial, immediate gratification, or a soul that rests wholly on Jesus Christ?
- Who are your friends? Are they the type who urge you to be like Christ and aren't afraid to rebuke you when you sin? Or are they just social crutches?

YOU REBUKE THE ARROGANT, THE CURSED,
WHO WANDER FROM YOUR COMMANDMENTS (119:21).

The psalmist has gone from lonely (verse 19), to crushed (verse 20), to indignant (verse 21), yet every emotion is sparked by the same passion: a longing to keep God's Word.

In verse 19, he is lonely but finds company in the presence of God's commandments. In verse 20, he is crushed with longing to keep God's commandments. And now in verse 21, he is indignant toward those who reject God's commandments. The psalmist's love for keeping God's Word is as intense as God's burning wrath toward those who reject it.

TAKE AWAY REPROACH AND CONTEMPT FROM ME,
FOR I OBSERVE YOUR TESTIMONIES (119:22).

The psalmist pleads for God to remove his scorn, his shame and his disgrace caused by his own sin. This phrase "Take away" literally means to "roll away." "God," he cries out, "Roll away all my shame and disgrace!" The psalmist would not ask this if He did not understand that God is gracious!

God would not only do this because He is gracious but also because the psalmist is humbly admitting his sinfulness. The psalmist prays in the same breath, "for I observe Your testimonies" (vs 22b).

The psalmist wants to be right with God. A man who does not realize his need for forgiveness will not be forgiven just as a drowning swimmer will not grab the lifeline until he admits that he is drowning. Conversely, God will not allow the stigma of shame and disgrace to rest forever on the one who keeps His commands. God always rewards pride with humiliation, and humility with exaltation.

3. Flee to the Word as your refuge in affliction (vss 23-24).

Every Christian is called to be a fugitive. The term fugitive comes from a Latin word meaning "to flee." This does not mean that we are to flee with no direction. We flee to the Word of God! We are not running from the suffering but rather from self-pity, giving up, complaining, and all the other sinful escape routes we like to seek when going through pain.

> EVEN THOUGH PRINCES SIT AND TALK AGAINST ME,
> YOUR SERVANT MEDITATES ON YOUR STATUTES (119:23).

Observe his resolute will to continue in obedience! Even the greatest of men do not intimidate him from seeking God. As sinful creatures, what do we like to do when we find out that people are talking badly about us? Talk about them. Return evil with evil. This indicates a pitiful devotion to revenge and vindication.

Instead, forget what they say—it does not matter—and go to God boldly! The more they attack the more you must flee to God's Word as your refuge in affliction.

This world is full of escapes. Some escape reality through drugs, others through alcohol or sexual sin and others through working longer and later hours. But there is only one proper escape, and it's the only escape that makes you face your trials boldly: The Word of God.

The palmist says that he "meditates." Meditate means "to muse, to think on and mull over and constantly immerse oneself in." Instead of letting his mind be filled with thoughts about those who are talking against him, the psalmist fills his mind with God's Word. "The hopes of a kingdom," said Basil, "should carry a Christian cheerfully through all labors and sufferings."[2]

> YOUR TESTIMONIES ALSO ARE MY DELIGHT;
> THEY ARE MY COUNSELORS (119:24).

Notice that the psalmist's joy does not come from the way people treat him, but what God says in His Word. To flee to the Word you must be able to separate yourself from the world, from those who mock you and those who hate you.

---

2   Watson, 47.

You must remove all personal offense, give up your anger, quit thinking about the offense and turn to God.

The psalmist has moved from loneliness, a crushed heart, reproach, contempt and the pain of being gossiped about to sheer delight! Why such joy, such happiness, such wiping away of tears? Because he took refuge in God's precious Word!

From Psalm 119:17-24, we have laid out three routes for running to the refuge of God's Word when you suffer.

1. Elevate the Word as your purpose for living (vss 17-18).
2. Trust in the Word as your comfort in sorrow (vss 19-22).
3. Flee to the Word as your refuge in affliction (vss 23-24).

During the life of John Calvin, the governing authorities arrested five Christian men and sentenced them to death for their faith. Many friends tried courageously to deliver them but failed. Calvin finally wrote the five prisoners a letter, acknowledging that many had tried to rescue them but that "God has stopped it."

The five men were finally led out to be burned to death. As they went out, they sang Psalm 68 until the guards cut out their tongues. These five courageous men endured their suffering with joy because they took refuge in God's precious Word!

Is it true oh Christ in heaven that the highest suffer the most?
That the strongest wander furthest and most?
Hopelessly are lost?
That the mark of rank in nature is capacity for pain?
That the anguish of the singer makes the sweetness of the strain?
~ John Milton[3] ~

---

3   John Milton quoted by J. Oswald Chambers, *Intimacy With God* (Grand Rapids: Discovery House Publishers, 2000), 54.

QUESTIONS FOR CONTEMPLATION

1. Write down all the emotions you see the psalmist experiencing as he writes this section.

2. List all of the psalmist's requests in this passage. What do all these requests have in common?

3. In this section, what does God's Word do for the psalmist?

4. In this passage, to where does the psalmist turn when he is in trouble?

5. What does the psalmist love and what does he detest?

6. Summarizing this section, explain how this passage applies to you. Where does it convict you and why? How can it help you to love God's Word more?

C H A P T E R

20

How to Remember God's Word
When You Suffer the Attacks of Your Enemies
Psalm 119:49-56

During the Gulf War of the 1990's, I read of a soldier who hit the eject button when his plane went into a tail-spin. Landing in the middle of a desert, hundreds of miles from food or water, he began to walk. Minutes turned into hours, and hours into days. His thirst grew so great that he could not speak. The fatigue tempted him to lie down and die, but one memory kept renewing his courage— a school teacher. His mind raced back to the elementary classroom where he raised his hand and requested to get a drink, but the teacher made him wait. She taught him the power of self discipline and the memory of this single incident kept him going until he was finally rescued. Remembering the right thing at the right time can save your life and that is what happened to the psalmist.

In Psalm 119:49-56, the psalmist suffers the affliction (50) and derision (51) of his enemies. His enemies hate him for what he stands for (God's holiness) and they despise him for what he stands against (sin). A quick reading of this passage reveals the strenuous pain in his prayers as he cries out day and night. But the one thing that keeps him going is remembering God's Word!

But what is it about God's Word that brings him such great hope? From this passage, we find eight reasons we should remember God's Word when suffering the attacks of our enemies.

1. Remember the Word because the Word gives you hope (vs 49).

> REMEMBER THE WORD TO YOUR SERVANT,
> IN WHICH YOU HAVE MADE ME HOPE (119:49).

Typically, we pray that God would help us to remember His Word. But the psalmist turns the tables and asks God to remember His own Word. Many servants do not wish for their masters to remember the words the master has spoken to them. Most would prefer that they forget because masters can be cruel, but not the psalmist's Master. All of His Master's words are good and gracious. Not one of them causes the psalmist anguish.

Notice how the psalmist calls upon the faithfulness of God. He obligates God to Himself. When a man cannot win a court case he may appeal to the higher law of the Supreme Court to retry his case. When a sergeant threatens to punish a private, the private may be given acquittal by order of the sergeant's superior. When a governor tries to pass a new state law, the higher law of the Constitution can stop it. In the psalmist's case, however, there is no higher standard than God Himself. Therefore, the psalmist calls upon God to keep His own promise, binding God to Himself.

Learn to plead the promises of God! Remind Him of them, tell Him about them, and ask Him to fulfill them. As Richard Sibbes put it, "God's promises are his bonds. Sue Him on his bond."[1]

At first this may seem irreverent but it is just the opposite. The psalmist is not mocking the omniscience of God but honoring Him by calling upon God's Word instead of the psalmist's own opinions. Those who ask the question "How could God still be loving if He allows little children to die and suffer?" reveal that they have created a God in their own image whose greatest priority is to relieve suffering on earth. But that is not His greatest priority. God's chief end is to glorify Himself. God placed the tree of the knowledge of good and evil in the middle of the garden, yet, even with Adam and Eve's sin, God will be most glorified in the end when He pours wrath on the unrepentant and sheds mercy on all who turn to Him for salvation. Though He allows evil and suffering now, God will be most glorified when He consummates all things in the future, punishing every evil act and rewarding every righteous deed. The psalmist understands this. God's greatest commitment is to Himself, thus, when He makes a promise, He must be faithful to His own promise, otherwise He would be a deceptive God, powerless to fulfill His own Word.

The psalmist asks God to remember His Word because it has given him hope. When every worldly light has gone out, one candle of hope still remains which will never be snuffed—the Word of God. All hopes but the Word of God are empty promises. Spurgeon once compared genuine and false hopes to two men floating down a dangerous river. One man finds the bank and pulls himself to safety. The other finds a floating log which makes him feel safe, but because the log is not fixed to something more stable, it goes down the waterfall with him. Likewise, many things in your life—your family, your skills, your training, your house, your job, your possessions—will tempt you to trust them, but they are temporary. God is our only reliable hope.

---

1   Richard Sibbes quoted by Spurgeon, 244.

The passage which says, "In which you have made me hope" is literally "On which you have made me hope" in the original language. The Word is like a rock above quicksand, not some distant, abstract idea that he recalls to memory. It is a platform of strength, a foundation of security upon which his very feet can rest. All the ground around him may crumble, but the Word of God upon which he stands is the unbreakable boulder.

2. Remember the Word because the Word gives you life (vs 50).

THIS IS MY COMFORT IN MY AFFLICTION,
THAT YOUR WORD HAS REVIVED ME (119:50).

The psalmist boasts of one comfort in the midst of his affliction: that God's Word has revived him. To revive means to make alive again. The weight of persecution threatens to kill the psalmist's soul. The pain and suffering is so deep that he feels that he may die. But when he remembers God's Word, he is resuscitated.

It is no wonder the author of Hebrews calls God's Word the "living sword," or that Stephen the martyr called the Old Testament laws of God "living oracles" (Acts 7:38). The Word of Life (Phil 2:16) is the source of life to every withered and dying soul, and in this book alone will you find revival in the midst of persecution.

This comfort is very personal; the psalmist calls it "my comfort." He has possessed, claimed and owned the comfort of the Word. People seek comfort in sex, food, sleep, money, possessions, vacations or children, but none of these will bring comfort any more than a single matchstick would warm you at the north pole or lightning would help you see during a storm. Only in the Word will you find true and lasting comfort. Spurgeon wrote,

> The worldling clutches his money-bag, and says, "This is my comfort;" the spendthrift points to his gaiety and shouts, "this is my comfort;" the drunkard lifts his glass and sings, "this is my comfort"; but the man whose hope comes from God feels the life-giving power of the word of the Lord, and he testifies, "this is my comfort."[2]

3. Remember the Word because the Word gives you focus (vs 51).

THE ARROGANT UTTERLY DERIDE ME,
YET I DO NOT TURN ASIDE FROM YOUR LAW (119:51).

The arrogant scorn the psalmist. They make fun of him, mock him and degrade him because they hate everything he stands for. Cruel persecution of innocent

---

2   Spurgeon, 240.

men is common. The ungodly did it to all the prophets (2 Chron 36:16), they did it to Christ (Is 53:7-8), they did it to Christ's followers (Acts 5:40), and they will do to you if you live for the Lord. They called Joseph the dreamer (Gen 37:19), Paul the babbler (Acts 17:18), and Christ the devil (Matt 9:34). Paul the apostle wrote, "Indeed, all who desire to live godly in Christ Jesus will be persecuted" (2 Tim 3:12) and John the apostle penned, "Do not be surprised, brethren, if the world hates you" (1 John 3:13). Just hours before His death Christ warned His disciples,

> If the world hates you, you know that it has hated Me before it hated you. If you were of the world, the world would love its own; but because you are not of the world, but I chose you out of the world, because of this the world hates you. Remember the word that I said to you, "A slave is not greater than his master." If they persecuted Me, they will also persecute you; if they kept My word, they will keep yours also. But all these things they will do to you for My name's sake, because they do not know the One who sent Me (John 15:18-21).

Persecution is a natural consequence of obedience to God. But do not be discouraged; Peter the apostle calls it a blessing and a privilege. In 1 Peter 3:14 he says, "But even if you should suffer for the sake of righteousness, you are blessed," and again in 4:14 and 16, "If you are reviled for the name of Christ, you are blessed, because the Spirit of glory and of God rests on you...but if anyone suffers as a Christian, he is not to be ashamed, but is to glorify God in this name" (cf. Matt 5:11). Expect it, endure it, and thank God for it.

Many humans crumble under trial when things get rough. Men and women experience unfaithful spouses, fatal diseases, loss of posessions and unjust accusations. Trials may cause some believers distress which results in their bodies becoming emaciated and diseased. The psalmist suffers unjust slander and attacks from his enemies, yet he does not turn away from the holy law of God! In the middle of a storm, he finds ability to focus on God's precious Book. Let life's tornadoes spin and hurricanes blow but he will not turn his eyes from his only hope.

Any person who puts his hope in anything but the Word of God finds himself hopeless with the next change of wind. The author of Hebrews alludes to this concept in Hebrews 12:1-12:

> Therefore, since we have so great a cloud of witnesses surrounding us, let us also lay aside every encumbrance and the sin which so easily entangles us, and let us run with endurance the race that is set before us, fixing our eyes on Jesus, the author and perfecter of faith, who for

the joy set before Him endured the cross, despising the shame, and has sat down at the right hand of the throne of God.

A runner cannot focus until he has fixed his eyes upon one thing that will not move. He must ignore all things around him. He must not respond to those who mock him or be swayed by things that tempt him. As Spurgeon says, "Their unhallowed mirth will not harm us if we pay no attention to it, even as the moon suffers nothing from the dogs that bay at her."[3]

When I taught tap dance, a common question from new students was "How do you spin without getting dizzy?" The answer is "spotting." By fixing your eyes on one object in the room, you stare at that object as you spin for as long as possible until your head must turn, and then it swings back the other direction to look at it as quickly as possible. By fixing your eyes on an immovable object, your spinning body feels no dizzier then if you were standing perfectly still.

Likewise, every believer must fix his hope on the immovable, unchanging Bible, keeping his eyes on the Word of God who is Christ, so that no matter what persecution bombs are dropped in his lap, he will not lose focus.

4. Remember the Word because the Word gives you comfort (vs 52).

I HAVE REMEMBERED YOUR ORDINANCES FROM OF OLD,
O LORD, AND COMFORT MYSELF (119:52).

This young psalmist (Ps 119:9-10) remembers the ancient Word which brings him deep comfort. Just as old men often have greater wisdom, so God's Word has proven itself through thousands of years. It never changes, never sways, and never lies. It always speaks truth. A young soldier finds far more solace fighting alongside a seasoned general than a private. A broken-hearted teenager will feel more consolation in the counsel of her father than her little brother. Years tend to produce wisdom and nothing is older or wiser than the Word of God. The same Word that brought great comfort to King Edward VI and Robert, king of Sicily, is the same Word that comforts a believer in his trials today.

The psalmist emphasizes that he uses the Word to comfort himself. He knows that ultimate comfort will be found nowhere else. This comfort is not a psychological wish void of substance, but a true comfort that yields what it promises. Trials and persecutions rip the believer from his earthly crutches and force him to rest on God's Word alone.

5. Remember the Word because the Word gives you perspective (vs 53).

---

3   Spurgeon, 241.

BURNING INDIGNATION HAS SEIZED ME
BECAUSE OF THE WICKED, WHO FORSAKE YOUR LAW (119:53).

The psalmist is hot with wrath. This word "burning indignation" means "raging heat" and is translated as "burning wind" in Psalm 11:6. The Hebrews understood hot weather. Desert winds and a glaring sun that baked the land was an accurate comparison to the psalmist's indignation. One translator translated this phrase as, "a burning horror hath seized me!"[4] The psalmist is much more than disturbed!

This burning anger is a holy anger. Instead of protesting or grumbling about the offense and discomfort they have put him through, the psalmist burns with holy anger because the wicked have forsaken God's law. The Word of God makes the Christian so unaffected by the mockery of the wicked that the evil actions of the ungodly move him to hate their conduct rather than to tempt him to join them in their evil. Believers under persecution are tempted to grow bitter and resentful toward their persecutors, but it is not so with the psalmist. He is consumed with God's righteousness and glory and he is concerned about a much higher good than his own welfare.

Nineteenth century theologian John Brown said, "Holiness does not consist in mystic speculations, enthusiastic fervors, or uncommanded austerities; it consists in thinking as God thinks, and willing as God wills." It is a hard thing to keep a biblical, non-self-consumed perspective when others cause you to suffer for doing what is right. We live in the age of vindication and revenge, where every man and woman stands up for his rights and has legal right to turn into a monster if he is mistreated. But the psalmist is humble enough to know that any persecution God brings will be for his own good, and he is holy enough to be more concerned about God's glory than his own ease.

Holy men and women never become accustomed to the world's wickedness. It continues to bother them because God's holiness continues to pervade them. John Gill notes, "And often so it is, that good men tremble more for the wicked than they do for themselves."[5] Do not grow callous to the world's wickedness and impervious to the world's blasphemies. Do not lose the ability to blush at sin.

However, those most indignant toward the ungodly should also be the most compassionate when they consider their doom. As Spurgeon says, "Compassion is far better shown in trying to save sinners than in trying to make things pleasant all around."[6] Witnessing makes unbelievers uncomfortable and the believer nervous, but a little discomfort with deliverance from an eternity in

---

4   Thomas Manton quoted by Spurgeon, 248.
5   John Gill quoted by Spurgeon, 248.
6   Spurgeon, 241.

the burning lake of fire is far better than comfort now and damnation later. We do not witness like we should because our compassion for the destiny of ungodly people is cold and we are not angered as we should be because our passion for God's holiness is weak. The more you let God's holiness become your own, the more you will compassionately witness to the lost and be righteously angered by their evil. This is the paradox of Christian living.

6. Remember the Word because the Word gives you joy (vs 54).

YOUR STATUTES ARE MY SONGS
IN THE HOUSE OF MY PILGRIMAGE (119:54).

Christians are happy people. Far from being miserable, over-burdened legalists, God's people have always been known as the happiest people in the world. Dr. Martyn Lloyd-Jones, the great preacher from Wales and successor of G. Campbell Morgan said, "If you were to ask me to give a definition of a Christian I should say that he is one who, since believing in Christ, feels himself to be the happiest man in the world and longs for everybody else to be equally happy!"[7]

But what makes Christians so happy? Beside the fact that they have an eternity to look forward to of perfect happiness and peace, and that they have power over sin, adoption into the family of God, and perfect comfort in tribulation, Christians have the Word of God. The psalmist in this passage literally sings God's Word! He is not far from Paul's exhortation to speak to one another in "psalms and hymns and spiritual songs, singing and making melody with your heart to the Lord" (Eph 5:19; cf. Col 3:16). Far from home as a pilgrim[8] in a foreign land, the psalmist does not mourn homesickness but sings God's Word with explosive joy. Men and women sing what is on their heart and in their mind. Their song comes from their passion. How many students sing calculus formulas or the second law of thermodynamics? How many scientists sing songs about carbon 14 dating methods or the anatomy of the armadillo? We like to sing those things that are dear to our heart and move our emotions. The Word of God is not like facts and figures of mathematical formulas in the head of the psalmist. It is what he loves and breathes, that which stirs his affections and moves his actions. Though he travels in a foreign land, the Word is at home in the house of his heart.

7. Remember the Word because the Word gives you companionship (vs 55).

O LORD I REMEMBER YOUR NAME IN THE NIGHT,
AND KEEP YOUR LAW (119:55).

---

7   Ian Murray, 56.
8   The word for "pilgrimage" in Psalm 119:54 is plural, thus, "pilgrimages," so the psalmist is referring not to one specific trip, but all his trips in general.

We live in a world of lonely people. Single Japanese ladies have become so lonely that they can now buy "Boyfriend's Arm Pillows," a pillow with a stuffed arm that curls around her while sleeping. The pillow costs $80 and comes with a shirt-sleeve to go over the pillow making it seem authentic. Radio DJ, Junko Suzuki, said of the pillow: "I like to sleep holding hands, and this pillow makes me feel relaxed because I can hold the arm and feel something warm at my side."[9]

In a cold world of loneliness, every believer has a truer companion than life itself. God will be your companion longer than your body lives. In verse 55, God is close to the psalmist's heart and constantly with him no matter what hour of the day. He has become his truest companion and dearest friend. How do you know a true friend? He is one who will stay with you in suffering and pain. God never leaves the psalmist. Through fiery trials—be it flood or famine, persecution or death—God stays with the psalmist even in the darkest hour.

The psalmist mentions the "night" because this is the most unlikely time to remember something. At night people sleep. At night people are tired. Night comes at the end of a full day and is time for winding down, but when it comes to God, the psalmist remembers Him just as much at midnight as at noon. He cherishes the Lord's presence more than his personal rest

The psalmist makes a point of remembering God's name in the night. It is impossible to obey a law that one does not remember. Ignorance produces disobedience but memory produces faithfulness. "It is the remembrance of God that leads to the keeping of his laws, as it is forgetfulness of God that fosters every species of transgression."[10] Over and over again, Moses exhorted the Israelites to "remember" God's mighty acts, for one cannot obey that which he does not remember (Deut 4:10; 5:15; 7:18; 8:2, 18; 9:7; 15:15; 16:3, 12; 24:9, 18, 22; 25:17; 32:7).

Satan wants believers to remain ignorant. In ancient Rome, "a proposal in the senate that slaves be required to wear a distinctive dress was defeated lest the slaves learn how numerous they were."[11] Likewise, Satan will aim all his missiles at wiping out knowledge of God's Word, for without it, no one can honor God. "If we do not keep the name of God in our memory we shall not keep the law of God in our conduct...if we do not think of [God] secretly we shall not obey him openly."[12]

8. Remember the Word because the Word gives you identity (vs 56).

---

9   World Magazine (October, 10, 2004): 11.
10   John Morison quoted by Spurgeon, 251.
11   Ferguson, 59.
12   Spurgeon, 242.

THIS HAS BECOME MINE,
THAT I OBSERVE YOUR PRECEPTS (119:56).

The Word of God is not a book of isolated facts for decorating bookshelves. It has become the psalmist's personal possession. He owns it. His own identity and personality have been shaped by his commitment to God's Word, and he finds his single security in it.

Men find identity in their jobs, women in their looks, teenagers in their friends, athletes in their strength and students in their grades. But the true believer finds his most prized possession and source of confidence in something that will not change with years or fade with time: the Word of God. The very Word that spurs his enemies' hate is the same Word that shapes his thinking, builds his character and defines who he is. If the believer can say any one thing at the end of his life, let it be this: This has become mine: that I obey God's precious Word!

From Psalm 119:49-56, we have found eight reasons you should remember God's Word when suffering the attacks of your enemies:

1. The Word gives you Hope (vs 49).
2. The Word gives you Life (vs 50).
3. The Word gives you Focus (vs 51).
4. The Word gives you Comfort (vs 52).
5. The Word gives you Perspective (vs 53).
6. The Word gives you Joy (vs 54).
7. The Word gives you Companionship (vs 55).
8. The Word gives you Identity (vs 56).

In A.D. 303, the wicked emperor of Rome, Diocletian, ordered every Bible to be burned to ash. But Diocletian died and the Bible lives on. Thousand more like him attacked the Bible both by pen and fire, but their efforts died with them and the Bible still stands true. God has preserved His Word to give every believer all that he needs for enduring every kind of persecution. The inscription of the monument to the Huguenots of Paris rings like a bell, testifying to the enduring nature of God's Word: "Hammer away ye hostile hands, your hammers break; God's anvil stands."[13]

---

13   Jerry Vines and Jim Shaddix, *Power in the Pulpit* (Chicago: Moody, 1999), 55.

QUESTIONS FOR CONTEMPLATION

1. Why does the psalmist find comfort in God's Word? What is bothering him?

2. How can someone have burning indignation toward the ungodly without being sinful (vs 53)?

3. What does God's Word specifically do for the psalmist?

4. How do you typically respond to persecution from those who do not love God? What reactions need to change so that you can find your hope in God's Word?

C H A P T E R

21

Are You Qualified for Divine Deliverance?
Psalm 119:121-128

A man goes fishing. As his boat drifts out into the lake, a barracuda fish leaps from the water and bites his hand, lacerating one finger.

A man purchases a pet bird. After arriving home, it flies off and settles on a power line. High voltage shoots through the bird's body which bursts into flames. The blazing featherball hits the ground, starting a forest fire that destroys over 8,000 acres and several buildings.

A lady sits in her house. A sudden explosion fills the room with dust. She looks under the TV table to find a meteorite the size of a football that flew from outer space into the earth's atmosphere, through her roof, and bounced off her couch.

These are crazy but true stories, yet each story illustrates that no matter where we are, anything can happen. Without the daily protection of God, we would be like a child without parents. And only those who are living in God's will can truly understand the comfort of knowing God's shielding hand of safety day by day.

Have you ever wondered where God is in the midst of pain or fear? Do you find yourself lonely, afraid, or deeply insecure at times, worried about the future? From Psalm 119:121-128, we see the psalmist is very confident that God delivers His people, even when they can't hear or see Him. In these verses, the psalmist gives the reader three reasons why God must deliver His people.

1. God must deliver the believer because of his personal character before God (vss 121-122).

These verses are two out of only three in the entire chapter of Psalm 119 that do not mention the Word of God. The psalmist's persecution has become so intense that he temporarily does not mention God's Word, but instead pleads for help.

I HAVE DONE JUSTICE AND RIGHTEOUSNESS (119:121A).

The psalmist has performed what is fair and what is right, what is just and what is holy. The two terms, justice and righteousness, are similar yet distinct. They are frequently used in Scripture to reflect God's evenhanded dealings with the righteous and the wicked. A man who possesses these qualities will not exhibit partiality, prejudice, or bias; rather honesty, integrity, and fairness.

Using these two terms, the psalmist affirms a high standard of his ethical behavior, which reflects the very character of God Himself. If the psalmist lives in a way that reflects God's morality, he shows he belongs to God and is worthy of God's deliverance.

Is this self righteous? Is the psalmist tooting a horn of pride? On the contrary, the psalmist humbly recognizes his utter incapability to deliver himself from harm. He calls upon God for help. If he was addressing his sin, his tone would be different; but here we have godless men on the blood trail for a godly man who is pleading God for deliverance. And he can do it with boldness because his conscience is clear.

A life of righteousness gives the afflicted believer great boldness in appealing to the Righteous Judge for deliverance. But a man living in guilt and hidden sin will have no stand when he pleads the help of the Righteous One. The apostle John tells us, "Beloved, if our heart does not condemn us, we have confidence before God" (1 John 3:21).

The psalmist follows his affirmation with three requests.

...DO NOT LEAVE ME TO MY OPPRESSORS (119:121B).
BE SURETY FOR YOUR SERVANT FOR GOOD... (122A).
...DO NOT LET THE ARROGANT OPPRESS ME (122B).

These wicked men are not just known as oppressors (verse 121b) but do the act of oppressing (verse 122b). They are arrogant men (122b) who trust in their skills and worldly knowledge, but the psalmist is God's humble "servant," a legitimate cause for supplicating God's help.

"Surety" in verse 122 is a very interesting word. It means to "take a pledge" or "give in exchange." In Old Testament times, if someone borrowed from a lender, the borrower would give the lender an item of lesser value as a guarantee that he would pay his debt. This little piece of collateral—whether it be a coat, ring, or weapon—was the borrower's pledge that he would pay back what he owed, and the item would be returned to him only after he paid his debt in full.

Just as Judah was a surety for Benjamin (Gen 43:9), and just as Christ is eternal surety for the Christian (John 6:37-39), so the psalmist asks that God be surety to his own safety. When God stands by your side, no enemy can assault

ARE YOU QUALIFIED FOR DIVINE DELIVERANCE?

you. He stands like a fierce bulldog, an armored warrior, or a colossal giant. Persecution is good for it moves us to our knees that we may feel our daily dependence on God's protection.

Knowing that Christ has stood between you and your powerful enemy, Satan, when He went to the cross, why would you doubt God's intention to stand between you and permanent harm in other areas? If God saved you, He will continue to keep you.

2. God must deliver the believer because of his personal relationship with God (vss 123-125).

MY EYES FAIL WITH LONGING FOR YOUR SALVATION AND FOR YOUR RIGHTEOUS WORD (119:123).

The word "fail" means to be "at its end" or "completely spent." The psalmist aches for God's deliverance and the Word so deeply that his eyes fail with longing. He has wept them dry. He has strained his eyes to catch even a glimpse of God's help to the point that his eyes falter in strength.

The eyes communicate the anguish or joy of a heart like no other member of the body. Even frowning lips cannot betray joyful eyes. Red eyes can show show someone lacks sleep or drinks heavily. The eyes of the psalmist communicate an impoverished soul, starving for God's deliverance and God's words.

We often suffer infirmities for desiring sinful things, but the psalmist's suffering is caused by yearning for good things. When was the last time you longed for God so much that it hurt?

And notice that he calls it the righteous Word. A pure and holy Word. A spotless Word. A Word void of fault or error. A Word of holiness and truth. A Word that never lies and never fails. That's something worth pining for!

Spurgeon wrote, "The Bible is a vein of pure gold, unalloyed by quartz, or any earthly substance. This is a star without speck; a sun without a blot; a light without darkness; a moon without its paleness; a glory without dimness."

Why would a man suffer so dreadfully just to have a sip of God's presence? Because he understands how good God is! Sometimes, persecution and trials are exactly what the believer needs to make him realize how much he needs God. Thomas Watson understood this when he wrote:

God is the summum bonum, the chief good. There is enough in God to satisfy the immense desire of the angels. He is omnimode dulcis, the quintessence of sweetness. In Him all perfections are centered: wisdom, holiness, goodness. He has rivers of pleasure where the soul shall bathe itself forever with infinite delight (Ps 36). Thus, here is ground sufficient for our drawing near to God. He is the chief good.[1]

This psalmist could sing with the sweet Psalmist of Israel, "O taste and see that the Lord is good! How blessed are all who take refuge in Him!" (Ps 34:8).

If you were stranded on an island for two weeks, think of how you would suffer. No shower. No hot water. No cooked meals. No hairbrush, toothbrush, fresh deodorant, clean clothing, soft bed, DVD players, or plush office chairs. But the native tribesmen on this island would not suffer as you do because they have not experienced all the luxuries of civilized living. It is my conviction that the reason more believers do not suffer and yearn and ache in their longing for God is because they have never really tasted the goodness of His person. They have not relished the heavenly joys and rapturous peace of intimate fellowship with God. The more you delight in God, the more it will hurt when you do not sense His presence.

DEAL WITH YOUR SERVANT ACCORDING TO YOUR LOVINGKINDNESS AND TEACH ME YOUR STATUTES (119:124).

The psalmist does not ask to be dealt with according to God's justice because then he'd be asking for terrifying wrath and punishment. Every human is a sinner worthy of God's fierce judgment and the eternal flames of hell. The psalmist knows that God is holy and righteous and that the psalmist is but a dry leaf in the wind deserving the burning furnace.

The psalmist also knows that God is full of lovingkindness, that God is compassionate and gracious, slow to anger and fast to forgive. He even reminds God that he is God's "servant."

The psalmist does not just ask for mercy but also for knowledge. "...and teach me your statutes" (vs 124b). He is as hungry to learn as he is thirsty for mercy. And now under the attack of persecutors, he needs it like never before.

I AM YOUR SERVANT; GIVE ME UNDERSTANDING, THAT I MAY KNOW YOUR TESTIMONIES (119:125).

In verse 122,, the psalmist called himself "Your servant." In verse 124, he called himself "Your servant." But here in verse 125, the psalmist states it simply and boldly, "I am Your servant." He knows that being God's servant is motivation for God to teach him His statutes.

A parent's responsibility toward his own child is far greater than his responsibility to other children. In the same way, God's responsibility toward His children is faithful and relentless. We can not obligate or require God to do anything, but God's own nature has obligated Himself for it is in the very nature

---

[1]   Watson, 106-107.

of God to love His children and to teach them His will. Thus, the psalmist calls upon God's own attribute of love to ensure his learning of God's Word.

The psalmist needs practical wisdom for responding to persecution. It is incredible that he asks for understanding before he asks for knowledge. He first says "give me understanding," then, "that I may know..." Knowledge is a dangerous weapon in a heart that does not understand. A surgical knife in the hand of an untrained doctor is a lethal weapon while in the skilled hands of a trained surgeon it may save many lives. Great amounts of knowledge have become deadly stumbling blocks to those who lack a heart of understanding. Many good-intentioned men have made themselves great fools with a head of knowledge but no heart to understand it.

The attacks of the psalmist's enemies have driven him to hunger for just one thing: to learn God's Word. Instead of responding in bitterness or revenge, he simply turns to the Word with more fervency, with more passion, and with a greater zeal to learn more than he ever knew.

In his biography on the life of Theodore Roosevelt, Edmund Morris writes that before Roosevelt was president, he was such an avid reader that after his breakfasts the hotel waiters had to clear away piles of ravaged newspapers as high as his table![2] If Christians' hunger for the Word was even half the hunger news lovers have for the paper or sports fans have for the NBA, the church might resurrect from her state of shallow consumerism.

3) God must deliver the believer because of his personal zeal for God (vss 126-128).

IT IS TIME FOR THE LORD TO ACT,
FOR THEY HAVE BROKEN YOUR LAW (119:126).

Again we see the psalmist's zeal for God's holiness. The wicked have gone far enough. Their black souls are ripe for judgment. They have broken God's law, a crime worthy of the Lawgiver's punishment.

But the psalmist calls only upon the Lord because he knows that only God can bring justice and create peace. Negotiations of world leaders, relief funds for the poor, improved school systems and moral legislation will not ultimately solve the wrongs of this world. Vindicating injustice, eradicating war, and rewarding the faithful are jobs that only God can do, and He will do them in His good time.

See how the psalmist refuses to mention himself when he calls upon God to judge the wicked. He does not say, "Lord, they have wronged me so please take revenge!" No. The psalmist knows the root of their sin is not in their affliction of

---

2   Edmund Morris, *Theodore Rex* (New York: The Modern Library, 2002), 178.

the psalmist, but in their disobedience towards God. The psalmist never allows himself to be so consumed with his own sufferings and afflictions that he forgets where the real problem lies: the unbelievers' relationship with God. How can he stay so focused upon God's outlook and not his own? Because zeal for God consumes him! George Webbe shared this spirit when he wrote, "The cry of our sins is exceedingly grievous, the clamours of them pierce the skies, and with a loud voice roar, saying: 'How long, Lord, holy and true? How long ere though come to avenge thyself on such a nation as this?"[3] Christ expressed the same zeal when He drove the swindling moneychangers out of the temple and pronounced, "Zeal for Your house has consumed me!" In this expression He quoted David from Psalm 69:9. If you continue to read this Psalm you find that David says, "And the reproaches of those who reproach You have fallen on me" (Ps 69:9b). David is so close to His great Shepherd that to insult Him is to insult David! That is God-driven zeal.

Zeal will never be found in the heart of a man who is more concerned about his personal comfort than God's glory. We often pray, "Lord help sick Aunt Suzie to feel better. Lord please keep my dog from dying. Lord please give me understanding for my final exam." These are valid and good prayer requests. But when was the last time you prayed, "Lord, your kingdom come! Lord, complete on earth what you have already finished in heaven! Lord, bring Christ back to judge the wicked and save the righteous! Lord vindicate your holy name! Lord, produce a revival throughout our country!"

THEREFORE I LOVE YOUR COMMANDMENTS ABOVE GOLD, YES, ABOVE FINE GOLD (119:127).

Why does the psalmist say, "Therefore?" This word points back to the reason that he cherishes God's commandments above fine gold. The previous verse says: "It is time for the LORD to act, for they have broken Your law." The wicked have broken God's holy law, therefore, the time has come for God to punish them. God's law hates evil and relishes good. It assaults sin and defends righteousness. That's holy zeal.

In order to accurately express his deep affection for God's Word, the psalmist picks the most precious earthly valuable and says the Word is a much better. Men will live for gold, die for gold, and sell their own souls for gold. The death of millions, the founding of nations and the crash or rise of empires have been caused by man's lust for money. A man deeply in love with gold might kill his own father or mother rather than forsake his sparkling metal. But when it comes to God's Word, it stands with no comparison.

---

3   George Webbe quoted by Spurgeon, 375.

Just in case he didn't make the point clear enough, he reaffirms, "Yes! Above fine gold!" This term "fine gold" means pure gold, gold refined of even the smallest impurities, heated over and over again so that only pure solid gold is left. The repeated purification increases its value. The psalmist does not just pick the most valuable metal in existence, but the purest and most refined gold possible and says, "Even this is far less valuable than the holy Word of God!"

THEREFORE I ESTEEM RIGHT ALL YOUR PRECEPTS
CONCERNING EVERYTHING, I HATE EVERY FALSE WAY (119:128).

The psalmist esteems all of God's precepts and hates evil because God's Word is infinitely precious. You cannot measure it or assign a value to it. The only way to describe it is to say it is far more precious than man's most prized earthly treasures. The Word which he dearly loves (vs 127), he also highly esteems (vs 128). The Word which he treasures, he also exalts. The psalmist uses no half-hearted language here.

Men hate anything in God's Word that contradicts their own opinions. As Calvin said, "There is nothing to which we are naturally more inclined than to despise or reject whatever in God's law is not agreeable to us."[4] The psalmist is so sold out for God, so zealous for God's glory, that he gives every single precept, every single command equal value and honor.

Pastor Charles Simeon, who lived in the 1800's, once said, "Of this [I am] sure that there is not a decided Calvinist or Arminian in the world who equally approves of the whole of Scripture."[5] Verse 128 is the test of every Christian's biblical fidelity. We find great comfort in identifying ourselves as Baptists, or Reformed, or Dispensationals, or even with high profile Christian leaders. With the advantages of attaching oneself to a doctrinal system, denomination, or Christian leader comes the temptation to esteem the system higher than the Bible. We often become better defenders of our traditional heritage than God's holy Word. Here is the litmus test: Do you equally value all parts of God's Word, instead of favoring some passages more agreeable to your likings, while avoiding those that don't complement your personality, denomination, or traditional heritage? The psalmist loves every word of the Book.

---

4   John Calvin, *Calvin's Commentaries*, electronic ed. (Garland: Galaxie Software, 2000), n. p.
5   Quoted from John Piper's sermon: "Life of Charles Simeon."

From Psalm 119:121-128, we have looked at three reasons God will deliver the psalmist:

1. God must deliver him because of his personal character before God (vss 121-122).
2. God must deliver him because of his personal relationship with God (vss 123-125).
3. God must deliver him because of his personal zeal for God (vss 126-128).

You may still be asking, "Are these qualities true of me? Am I qualified for deliverance?" There is a simple answer to that question, and the answer is found in a true story:

Dr. Simpson was asked to go to England to preach one sermon in a Bible conference on sanctification. But there was one challenge: The two men to preach before him were preaching on the same subject. The first teacher preached that sanctification is suppressing the old man. The second teacher preached that sanctification is eradicating the old man.

And finally it was Dr. Simpson's turn. He stepped to the podium. What would he preach? With deep trembling he used just one word for his text, *Himself.* By "Himself" Dr. Simpson referred to Christ. He then gave testimony of how all his life he tried to be sanctified, and the moment he caught it he would lose it. He tried and tried again, but kept losing grip.

Then he made this statement, "What a blessedness when I came to the knowledge that I had been looking in the wrong place, when I found that victory, sanctification, deliverance, purity, holiness—all must be found in Jesus Christ Himself, not in some formula."

Out of that knowledge, Dr. Simpson wrote these words to a hymn:

> *Once it was the blessing, now it is the Lord.*
> *Once His gift I wanted, now Himself alone.*[6]

If that is true of you, then you are qualified for divine deliverance.

---

6   Tozer, *Essays*, 53.

QUESTIONS FOR CONTEMPLATION

1. Look at verse 121a. Is this prideful? Why or why not? Why does he say this?

2. What is the psalmist requesting in verse 122a? Surety for what?

3. How intense is the psalmist's desire for salvation in verse 123?

4. Make a list of all the psalmist's requests and all the psalmist's affirmations in this passage. Use that to prepare your own study on this passage.

Resolve to Live God's Word Now and Forever
Psalm 119:9-16, 41-48, 57-64

Some years ago a movie hit the theatres called "Get Rich or Die Tryin'." The movie's title speaks volumes of a person's dedication when something matters to him. How much truer this should be for the believer! For him it should be, "Obey God or Die Tryin'."

God wants obedience, not the rule-driven formality of a legalist, but the attitude of the early Roman Christians who, "became obedient from the heart" (Rom 6:17). This is obedience that flows from a sincere desire to please God and outward actions become the living illustration of the heart condition.

Obedience is not easy. Consider for a moment the odds against you. The devil and all his demons hate you and will do everything they can to tempt you into sin (1 Pet 5:8-9). The world around you is filled with tempting pleasures that will constantly strive to drag you down (1 John 2:16). And if these outward attacks are not enough, your own heart is prone to evil (Rom 7:14-25). God knew that obedience would be so difficult for the believer that he would need supernatural help. That's why He sent His Holy Spirit to strengthen, encourage, comfort, and convict you as you wage this spiritual war (John 14:16; Gal 5:18-25). Apart from the Spirit you can do nothing that pleases God (Rom 8:6-9).

Yet, having the Spirit is not a perfect guarantee of undistracted obedience. Paul warned the Thessalonian Christians to not "quench the Spirit" (1 Thess 5:19), an indication that the believer can resist the Spirit's help. The ancient adage still stands true, "He who stands for nothing will fall for anything." As a true believer in Christ and as a recipient of the Holy Spirit you must still choose to follow God. If this "choosing" waits until the enemy attacks, you will quickly become another Christian casualty. A soldier who has not made up his mind to fight will be fatally wounded when the attack comes unexpectedly. You must resolve to obey. In our seventh and final strategy to slaying Bible apathy, we will look at three passages that show how to resolve to obey God's Word: Resolve to Apply (Psalm 119:9-16), the Paradox of Obedience (119:41-48), and Eight Resolutions of the Man or Woman of God (119:57-64).

C H A P T E R

22

Resolve to Apply
Psalm 119:9-16

In October of 2004, at a "Get Motivated" seminar at The Staples Center in Los Angeles, CA, Dr. Earl Mindell, Ph.D gave 15,000 people a load of advice on what not to eat. And then he made this statement: "If you forget everything I've told you so far, then remember this rule of thumb and you'll be much healthier: Eat nothing advertised on TV." Who would expect that the media's strongest tool of persuasion—your TV set—would advise you to eat the most deadly foods in the marketplace?

Satan does the same thing spiritually. He makes bad things look good. He wants to feed you junk so that you will think and act "junk" and someday die an ungodly miserable soul.

This junk can come through your TV set, radio, a novel, a magazine, or even the latest newspaper. It could be your friend's conversation or advice. All spiritual junk food has one thing in common: it tastes like candy and goes down smoothly; but in reality, it is poison.

Who is to blame? Some people blame the medium of communication. "The TV set is evil! Since Satan is the prince of the power of the air, and since radio is transmitted via air waves, radio is demonic!" Some would say the same about the internet.

There is nothing sinful about the electromagnetic field of radio waves. There is nothing evil about luminance, chrominance, and synchronization signals on your television set. These were ultimately made by God, and every time God created something, Genesis 1 says, "And God saw that it was good." God has actually used these media of communication for great good just as Satan has used them for great evil. Thousands have been saved, brought to repentance, encouraged and comforted through them.

People who accuse the medium of communication are missing the source of the problem. Paul addresses this issue when Gentiles converted from idol-worshipping paganism to Christ and took great offense at a Christian brother eating meat that had been offered to an idol:

> Therefore concerning the eating of things sacrificed to idols, we know that there is no such thing as an idol in the world, and that there is no God but one. For even if there are so-called gods whether in heaven or on earth, as indeed there are many gods and many lords, yet for us there is but one God, the Father, from whom are all things and we exist for Him; and one Lord, Jesus Christ, by whom are all things, and we exist through Him...But food will not commend us to God; we are neither the worse if we do not eat, nor the better if we do eat (1 Cor 8:4-6).

Just as the meat was not the problem, but rather the heart of the one eating it, so the televison set, radio waves and internet are no more inherently evil than a rock in your back yard. The question is, how are they being used?

Everyone carries an appetite for evil at some level (Rom 7:14-25). Man's biggest problem is not outside of him but inside of him, his heart. This is why Solomon warned his son in Proverbs 4:23, "Watch over your heart with all diligence, for from it flow the springs of life." The term "watch over" means "to guard." Guard your heart like a warrior guards his family or a watchman guards a city. We must watch the desires that come from our hearts as well as what we pour into our hearts. Because the heart is the control center of every human, keeping it pure and protected is absolutely vital. An evil heart will automatically reap a sinful life.

Psalm 119:9-16 shows us exactly how to feed upon the Word of God. This eight verse passage teaches us specifically how to apply the Word to key issues that we encounter every day. These key issues come in three areas:

- *How do I defeat my sin?*
- *How do I learn God's Word?*
- *How do I love God intimately?*

From Psalm 119:9-16 we will find three ways we can resolve to apply the Word in our daily walk:

1. Apply the Word as a weapon against sin (vss 9-11).

The psalmist gives practical tips of applying the Word as a weapon against sin. The first is:

- Follow the Word faithfully

HOW CAN A YOUNG MAN KEEP HIS WAY PURE?
BY KEEPING IT ACCORDING TO YOUR WORD (119:9).

The psalmist asks a question and then answers it, "How am I to be set apart from the evil of this world?" *By living according to God's Word.*

He does not answer the question, "By being pure" or "By being holy." That would be like asking, "How do I tap dance?" and getting the answer, "By tap dancing!" The answer to a "how" question should not simply repeat the question but provide further explanation. And so the psalmist answers, "The only way to live a pure and holy life is by living it in obedience to the Word of God."

Notice that the man under discussion is not just any man. He is a "young" man. I believe he is referring to himself. Notice how he continues in verse 10, making himself the person under discussion: "With all my heart I have sought You; do not let me wander..."

It would be most odd for the psalmist to be so intensely concerned about a young man keeping pure if he himself were an old man. Psalm 119 is not about an older wise man instructing a younger, less wise man like the book of Proverbs. Psalm 119 is a man's personal testimony of his own love for God's Word and his desire to keep it. He writes about himself and his personal convictions.

There is another reason he mentions the "young man." The passions of the flesh burn deep in young men. This does not mean that elderly men do not experience fleshly desires, but the passions of the flesh come upon a young man unexpectedly and he sometimes finds sin harder to cope with than an older man of more wisdom. Death's gunshot seems farther away so he fears the consequences much less than an elderly man closer to expiration. His vigor and strength make sin more desirable and intense than it would in a feeble elderly man. The young man often only sees the sin cased in sparkling packages and adorned with the seductions of lust, whereas the old man's experience has taught him to spot the traps hidden in those sparkling packages, ready to knife his soul.

This is not to imply that old men do not struggle with sin—they do! But Satan knows that the naïve, uncontrolled passions and arrogant pride of a young man will bring him down quickly, and if he can get him to fall hard, he can more easily keep him there.

If you are a young man, let me speak to you for a moment. If you choose now to live a life kept clean by the Word of God, the rest of your life will be easier to maintain. Take heed of Solomon's exhortation in Ecclesiastes 12:1, "Remember also your Creator in the days of your youth, before the evil days come and the years draw near when you will say, 'I have no delight in them.'" If you run well now, you will finish well later.

The longer a man has been a Christian, the more godly one would expect him to be. It is a discredit to an elderly Christian who has known the Word of

God for years, but makes no resolution to be pure and set apart for God. He is like an old pipe that once flowed with crystal fresh water, but is now corroded with rust and clogged with rotten debris. But there is something sweet and refreshing about a young man on fire for the Word, applying it daily as he encounters all sorts of temptations and attacks from the flesh. And there is something even sweeter about a young man living this way into his elderly years.

In his first letter, the apostle John turns his pen to his readers who are young men and says, "I am writing to you, young men, because you have overcome the evil one....I have written to you young men, because you are strong, and the Word of God abides in you, and you have overcome the evil one" (1 John 2:13, 14). Notice the key: "The word of God abides in you." You cannot be strong and overcome Satan if the Word of God is not your daily food and drink.

If you pursue holiness down any road other than the Word of God, that road will take you down the path of evil. Christ told His disciples in John 15:3, "You are already clean because of the Word which I have spoken to you." In John 17 He prayed to the Father, "Sanctify them in the truth, Your Word is truth" (John 17:17). In Ephesians 5:26, Christ sanctifies His church "By the washing of water with the Word." The Word works like soap on the bacteria of the human heart. John Calvin wrote, "There is nothing pure in [a man's] life until [he has] made a complete surrender of [himself] to the word of the Lord.[1]

• Pursue God avidly

WITH ALL MY HEART I HAVE SOUGHT YOU...(119:10A).
"With all my heart" means his entire being. This is the Psalm 119 version of the greatest commandment, "You shall love the LORD your God with all your heart, and with all your soul, and with all your mind, and with all your strength" (Mark 12:30). There is no room for idols. No room for second thoughts. No room for looking back.

The believer who pursues God avidly is like the hunter who wounds a deer and finds a trail of blood. He will stop at nothing until he finds that deer. May we pray as one anonymous saint of old prayed,

Oh God, under whom all hearts be open, and unto whom all will speaketh, and unto whom no privy thing is hid, I beseech Thee, so for to cleanse the intent of my heart with the unspeakable gift of Thy grace, that I may perfectly love Thee and worthily praise Thee![2]

Pastor Richard Wurmbrand, the author of *Tortured for Christ*, tells how his underground church in Romania was discovered by the Russian Communists.

---

1   Calvin, n. p.
2   Tozer, 14.

He was sent to prison where he suffered fourteen years of almost unbearable torture. As he wrote of his persecutions, he made this statement: "Christians are often half-heartedly on the side of the whole truth. Communists are whole-heartedly on the other side."[3]

The materialist is often more avid about making wealth then the believer is about saving souls. The Olympics trainer is often more disciplined in his daily routines then the believer is in the simple exercises of reading the Word, praying to God, and witnessing to the lost. If the demons wholeheartedly hate God, should we not love Him twice as much?

• Humbly recognize your weakness

...DO NOT LET ME WANDER
FROM YOUR COMMANDMENTS (119:10B).

As committed as he is to seeking God with his whole heart, the psalmist recognizes that he is weak and unable to do it without the strength of God's help. He is as wise as he is passionate; as humble as he is devoted.

A man who pursues God with his whole heart but does not recognize his weakness will fall hard and fast on his face. Pride is his stumbling block. He is like the arrogant commander who rushes unprepared into battle only to be mowed down by the enemy.

On the other hand, the man who recognizes that he is weak but never pursues God with his whole heart will live like a wounded animal, constantly moaning but never "doing." Doubt and trembling faith are his stumbling blocks. He is like the commander who continually plans an attack but never acts. He retreats constantly until the enemy is in his own country and forces him to take down his flag. You must have both wholehearted devotion to God and humble recognition of your weakness.

Notice that the psalmist does not want to "wander" or "go astray." In Ezekiel 34:6, God uses this word to describe his flock who has wandered astray. Rarely does a believer run full speed away from God's Word screaming, "I hate you God!" No, drifting believers are more like a swimmer on a raft about twenty yards from the shore, on a perfect day. The sun is warm, the breeze is just right. One hour passes by, and then another. He looks back to the shore and things look different. He doesn't remember that white house. He doesn't remember that bending oak tree, and where did the big red umbrella go? And that "No swimming. Beware of sharks!" sign is not familiar either.

A little decision here, a little decision there, slowly but surely the straying believer surrenders his soul to his flesh and the world until he has drifted far

---
3   Wurmbrand, 78.

from God and closer to danger. This will not happen if you recognize your weaknesses humbly.

• Treasure the Word dearly

YOUR WORD I HAVE TREASURED IN MY HEART... (119:11).
This term "treasure" is used to depict something similar to precious diamonds or jewels. God's Word is more precious than any jewel and is to be stored in our hearts so that we can retrieve it at any time.

God's Word will not help you until it is within you. Fill your house with a thousand Christian books and Bibles, and it won't do you an ounce of good until its truth is soaking your mind.

When I lived as a bachelor with my brother, we purchased large loaves of bread and stored them in our cupboard. But we were not alone in this 100 year old house. One bitterly cold night as I lay in my sleeping bag on the living room floor near the fire stove, I awakened to a strange sound. Rats were making their way over my sleeping bag, delivering pieces of our fresh bread to their home beneath the house. The next day we had to throw the loaves away. Because we could no longer eat the bread, it was worthless to us. Keeping it was pointless because if we could not use the bread inside our bodies, it would do us no good. Likewise, the Word will not be of use until you get it inside you and treasure it dearly. Living in a house stacked with unused Bibles is no better than living in a house with no Bibles at all.

Memorization of Scripture is important provided the motive is right. In verse 11, the psalmist has "treasured God's Word in his heart." Notice that he does not memorize Scripture for the simple sake of regurgitation, for the purpose of impressing other believers, or out of obligation because his pastor or teacher told him to. A proper motive for memory of God's Word is to correctly apply the Word as a weapon against sin.

• Face your sin honestly

...THAT I MAY NOT SIN AGAINST YOU (119:11B).
If you memorize the entire Bible, word for word, it does you no good unless you use this knowledge to destroy sin and promote righteousness in your heart. The psalmist realizes that sin is not just bad, wrong, or law-breaking; it is rebellion against God. The same God He does not want to sin against is the God whom he asks to keep him from sinning. The One he does not want to offend is the only One who can keep him from offending!

The psalmist understands how evil sin is. We like to dress sin up. We don't want to admit how ugly it really is. Thomas Watson wrote, "If only people meditated on the damnableness of sin, if they only thought when they meddle with it that there is a rope at the end of it which will hang them eternally in hell, they would break off the course of sinning and become new creatures."[4]

Puritan author, Ralph Venning, wrote a book entitled *The Sinfulness of Sin*. In this book he delivers a graphic definition of sin. He writes, "*[Sin] is deicide, God-murder.*"[5]

> Sin is worse than affliction, than death, than Devil, than Hell. Affliction is not so afflictive, death is not so deadly, the Devil not so devilish, Hell not so hellish as sin is.[6]
>
> [Sin] attempts nothing less than the dethroning and un-godding of God Himself. It has made man a fool, a beast, a devil, subjected him to the wrath of God, and made him liable to eternal damnation. It has made men deny that "God is" or affirm that He is like themselves. It has put the Lord of Life to death and shamefully crucified the Lord of Glory. It is always resisting the Holy Ghost. It is continually practicing the defiling, the dishonor, the deceiving and the destruction of all men. What a prodigious, monstrous, devilish thing is sin![7]
>
> Sin is likened to the most loathsome diseases and to the uttermost loathsome things there are. It is likened to the blood in which infants are born which is loathsome (Ez 16:5, 6), it is likened to mire and dung, to the very excrements that lie in ditches, in sewers, in which sows and swine wallow, and even to the vomit of dogs (2 Pet 2:22). It is compared to the putrefaction of graves and sepulchers (Matt 23:27-28) which stink as Martha said of Lazarus...it is also likened to poison (Rom 3:13).[8]

Peter, the head apostle, the man to whom Christ gave the keys of the kingdom once made this statement, "Go away from me, Lord, for I am a sinful man!" (Luke 5:8). Paul, the apostle of the Gentiles, the apostle who wrote more books of the New Testament than any other man and the apostle who planted churches across the world of his day could boldly say, "For I am the least of the apostles, and not fit to be called an apostle, because I persecuted the church of God" (1 Cor 15:9).

Why is it hard for men and women to apply the Word as a weapon against sin? If we are honest with ourselves, we will admit that it's laziness. When a man lacks discipline in his study, he lacks discipline in the hour of temptation. Christ

---

4   Watson, 29.
5   Ralph Venning, *The Sinfulness of Sin* (Carlisle: The Banner of Truth Trust, 1965), 194.
6   Ibid., 177.
7   Ibid., 172.
8   Ibid., 161.

had the strength to resist Satan's brutal temptation in the wilderness because He knew God's Word! R. C. Sproul said it well,

> Here, then, is the real problem of our negligence. We fail in our duty to study God's Word not so much because it is difficult to understand, not so much because it is dull and boring, but because it is work. Our problem is not a lack of intelligence or a lack of passion. Our problem is that we are lazy.

Make the Word your first priority of every morning. Be more sure that you will pour God's Word into your mind every morning than you will find the sun rising in the east. When you must close the Bible and go to work, do not leave the Bible on your desk, but carry it with you in your mind and heart the rest of the day.

When you go to work you walk on a battlefield. When you go to school, on vacation or even to church, you are on a battlefield. The battlefield is at your desk early in the morning or late at night. The battlefield is in your car when you drive, on the field when you play, in the gym when you run, or in bed before you sleep. You cannot escape the battlefield because the battlefield is in your heart. Satan does not want your money. What use would that be to him? He does not want your fame, your talents, or your looks. What benefit could he find with these? Satan wants just one thing: your soul. If you are washed by the blood of the lamb and sealed in Christ Jesus, then he knows he cannot take your soul so he will tempt you to defile it. He wants to see you fall, to see you curse God, to see you give up, lose heart, or forsake all that you know to be true. You must bring your weapon, the Sword of the Spirit, with you wherever you go. The boxer doesn't use his boxing gloves in the training room and remove them for the fight. The soldier doesn't practice his aim on the firing range but leave his weapon behind when the enemy attacks. You need the Word of God *most* when you encounter temptation.

Perhaps you need God's Word most when you are on the internet, or watching TV. Maybe you need it most when you are in the company of unbelievers, driving in traffic or disciplining your children. Perhaps you need it most when you are eating a meal or when the morning alarm goes off. No matter where you are, apply God's Book as a weapon against sin, or sin will be used as a weapon against you.

Thomas Watson instructs, "Look upon the Word as a spiritual magazine out of which you fetch all your weapons to fight against sin and Satan."[9]

9　　　Watson, 13.

2. Receive the Word as a book of instruction (vss 12-13).

BLESSED ARE YOU, O LORD; TEACH ME YOUR STATUTES.
WITH MY LIPS I HAVE TOLD OF ALL THE ORDINANCES
OF YOUR MOUTH (119:12-13).

The psalmist begins this section with a cry of praise: "Blessed are You, O LORD!" The psalmist is so full of God's Word that he can hardly contain himself. God's Word lifts people's eyes and minds high above the clouds, high above the mountains, into the very courtroom of heaven where Christ sits at the right hand of God.

Then the psalmist says in verse 12, "Teach me Your statutes." Statutes are not the broad commands but God's very specific ones. Here is an attitude of sincere humility, a recognition that he cannot learn God's statutes on his own. The psalmist is saying, "God, teach me those specifics. I need them. I cannot learn without your instruction. Without your teaching I am worse off than a soldier without a gun, or a traveler without a map." Having the Bible is not enough. We need instruction from the God of the Bible!

Notice also that the Psalmist is teachable himself before he teaches others. "With my lips I have told of all the ordinances of Your mouth" (vs 13). A man who is un-teachable, who cannot take loving criticism or finds it very hard to admit he is wrong, disqualifies himself from teaching others. No one can instruct well who cannot learn well. The best teachers have always been, and always will be, the best students.

Nothing will make the Word more difficult to understand than human pride. We think we can understand it on our own (cf. 1 John 2:27), but the truth is, we cannot and the more you know, the more tempted to pride you will be. A. W. Tozer preached, "You can stand on the outside and have all the information and know all about it and yet not be a true disciple who really knows Christ...You can know the doctrine of justification by faith and take your stand with Luther and the Reformation and be blind inwardly."[10]

Notice also that his teachable spirit is so humble that it is worshipful, "Blessed are You, O LORD!" (vs 12a). He is not just ready to learn from God, but he worships God. This is the one Teacher you may worship.

3. Revel in the Word as a letter of love (vss 14-16).

When someone tells me that God's Word is boring, he's really telling me how he feels about God. If a woman's husband left the country to go to war and he sent her a letter, would she not read this letter over and over again until its

---

10   A. W. Tozer, Ten Sermons From the Gospel of John in *The Tozer Pulpit*, vol. 1, edited and compiled by Gerald B. Smith (Camp Hill: Christian Publications), 22.

edges were worn? God's Word is the sweetest, most pure, most loving letter ever written. It is not a mushy letter of sentimentalism and flattery. It is a letter of God's revelation of Himself to man, from heaven to earth, from divine to human. In it you find the bleeding Savior and the exalted King of Kings. In it you find the despair of mankind and the hope of Christ, the wrath of God, and His unending grace.

Your response to God's Word is a barometer of your love for God. If you love God, you will love His Word and if you hate God, so you will hate His Word. When a man says he loves God but does not have time to read His Word, he is as convincing as the husband who tells his wife "I love you," but never listens to what she has to say.

You can you revel in the Word by rejoicing in the Word:

I HAVE REJOICED IN THE WAY OF YOUR TESTIMONIES, AS MUCH AS IN ALL RICHES (119:14).

If you won a sweepstakes, you'd be happy. No matter how "spiritual" you thought it was to act sober about it, you'd still be thrilled. And you probably spend many hours planning how you are going to spend it, invest it, or give it away.

Notice how happy the Psalmist is to be in God's Word: "As much as in all riches" (vs 14). Or, more literally, "As over all riches."

Money moves humans to excitement more than anything else. And that is why the Psalmist takes the most joy-producing object he can think of and sees it as packing peanuts compared to the ocean of joy he receives from the Word of God! If you are not bursting with joy when you study God's Word, there is something else in your life stealing that joy. Could it be some idol, some form of sin or lust that is sucking the joy from your heart?

In reading the book of Acts, we find joy is the single attitude that characterized every single Christian conversion. In his first letter to the Thessalonians, Paul beams with happiness as he recalls the Thessalonians' conversions, "You also became imitators of us and of the Lord, having received the word in much tribulation with the joy of the Holy Spirit," (1 Thess 1:6).

I WILL MEDITATE ON YOUR PRECEPTS AND REGARD YOUR WAYS (119:15).

The Hebrew word for "meditate" can be translated as "muse, commune, speak about, ponder, sing, or study." The word "regard" simply means to *look at* or *to not ignore.* Your mind and heart should soak up God's Word like a wool sweater soaks up water. Thomas Watson wrote, "The bee sucks the flower and then works it into the hive and so turns it into honey. By reading we suck the flower of the Word. By meditation we work it into the hive of our mind and so it turns into profit."[11]

Our lives are made up of millions of minute decisions. Every time we stand at a crossroad, we should ask ourselves, "What does God think about this? What does His Word say?" This comes easy if we have been reveling in His Word.

Pastor and preacher Dr. Kent Hughes lamented our lack of meditation with this statement,

> Many of us never experience silence during our waking hours. We wake up to a clock radio, shave to the news, drive through noisy traffic, enter a noisy busy office. We return home listening to the rush hour reports, relax to the TV and drift off to sleep as the house pulsates with the thump-thump of the family stereo.[12]

To meditate does not mean to be idle. You cannot ponder God's Word without exercising your brain. Charles Spurgeon wrote,

> Those who are the most busy are often the very men who do the most meditation, for idleness and meditation are not generally very close companions. An idle man usually has idle thoughts; but the busy man, when he is able to think, thinks busy thoughts that are worth thinking.

One evening, at age fourteen, I had just finished an exhausting workout and sat down to a huge plate of casserole. I was starving. I said a quick prayer and started shoveling it in. Now when you combine a starving person with tasty food, occasionally the eater forgets to swallow. The result was that I cleaned the plate in 120 seconds. Five minutes later my stomach began to ache. I felt like I ate a box of rocks. That's similar to what happens when you read God's Word but fail to meditate on it. Someone rightly said that reading the Bible without meditating on it is like trying to eat without chewing or swallowing.

I SHALL DELIGHT IN YOUR STATUTES... (119:16A).

The psalmist is not just chuckling with joy. He is bursting with delight! God's Word has made him ecstatic. He is delighting in "Your statutes," not his ideas, his plans or successes, but rather in the Lord's instructions.

I worked as an account manager one year and every few months our sales teams came together for the big pow-wows. We'd throw numbers on the wall that marked our successes and when someone's sales indicated extraordinary success, everybody would clap and cheer and holler. Now there is nothing

11   Watson, 118.
12   Hughes, 76.

wrong with celebrating a successful day, but after the meeting, everyone went back to the humdrum of work and we lived as if the success never happened. Let's compare the world's delight to the psalmist's.

The world delights in things that bring attention to people. The believer delights in things that bring glory to God. The world's delight is temporary; in the next day, month, or year, no one cares anymore. But delight in God's Word is eternal. Never will a day pass in eternity that you will not shout with joy at God's very words. The world's delight is selfish—I am happy because I did well and it makes me look good. But the believer's delight in God's Word is not focused on the believer's success but God's faithfulness.

We have seen that you can revel in God's Word as a letter of love by rejoicing in it, meditating on it, and delighting in it. The palmist provides us with one more key for reveling in God's Word: remembering it. If rejoicing in God's Word means you are happy about it, and meditating on God's Word means you are soaked in it, and delighting in God's Word means you are excited about it, then not forgetting His Word means you are thinking about it.

No matter how many times a husband says, "I love you," if he forgets his wedding anniversary, his actions tell his wife that their relationship is not important. People remember things that are important to them. I am sure you remember the date of your mortgage bill. I doubt you'd forget which flight you are taking on your vacation, where to pick up your paycheck, or that you need to brush your hair and shave before going to work. People remember things that are important to them because they think about them! You may find yourself loving a verse so much that you read it, pray about it, remind yourself of it throughout the day, and you've memorized it before you knew it. That's exactly what the psalmist is doing.

I don't think he's saying, "I'm committed to not forgetting this book!" I think he is saying, "This Word which I've been treasuring in my heart (vs 11), this Word which I've been longing to learn (vs 12), teaching others (vs 13), rejoicing, meditating, regarding, and delighting in (vss 14-16), I will never forget!

Before Israel entered the Promised Land, Moses urged the people over and over again to remember all that God had done for them (4:10; 5:15; 7:18; 8:2, 18; 9:7; 15:15; 16:3, 12; 24:9, 18, 22; 32:7) and never to forget it (4:9, 23; 6:12; 8:11, 14, 19; 9:7). When a man forgets the very Word that saved his soul, nourishes him daily, and gives him truth, he is worse off than a sailor who drops his compass in the sea or a desert nomad who forgets to bring his water and will soon lay breathless in the hot dust that burns beneath his feet.[13]

In this section we have three resolves for applying the Word in your daily walk:

1. Apply the Word as a weapon against sin (vss 9-11).
2. Receive the Word as a book of instruction (vss 12-13).
3. Revel in the Word as a letter of love (vss 14-16).

Following are three practical ways you can apply the three points above:

1. Every morning take one verse, learn it well, and then roll it all over your brain like a delicious candy for the rest of the day.
2. Talk about that verse with at least three people. Your spouse. Your son. Someone at church. A co-worker or fellow student.
3. Turn it into a song. And sing it!

---

13   Why is it so hard for Christian men to revel in the Word as a letter of love? Because we let our analytical strengths dominate our passion and tenderness towards God. The Bible becomes like blueprints to a construction building or a riddle to be solved. As much as we need to analyze its truths and solve it riddles, if the Bible is nothing more than this, then we will grow cold towards its Author. It is not unmanly to be emotional about God's Word. It is Christ like.

QUESTIONS FOR CONTEMPLATION

1. Go through each verse and write down what each teaches you about the psalmist.

2. Read through each verse again and write down the traits of the psalmist's attitude.

3. Going through each verse a third time, write down what each verse teaches you about God's Word.

4. In this passage what has the psalmist done and what is he going to do?

5. In this passage how is the psalmist constantly getting God's Word into his brain?

6. Why do you think the psalmist is so passionate and consumed with God's Word in this passage?

7. According to this passage, what are all the things the Word does? Put another way, what are all the ways the Word benefits the psalmist?

8. Which one of these 8 verses really spoke to you? Why? Write down specific steps you will take this week to apply that principle.

CHAPTER

23

The Paradox of Obedience
Psalm 119:41-48

Life is full of paradoxes, but none so great as the Christian paradox. The Bible teaches that apart from God you can do nothing and yet you are fully responsible for serving God with all your heart. So who is responsible? If God alone can bring the change why should I try? Yet the Bible says that I must try, or I will not change. If you do not run the race then you will not win. But if God does not help you win the race, you will never reach the finish line.

It all depends on you and it all depends on God! Martin Luther wisely stated, "Pray like it all depends on God and live like it all depends on you."

The Bible never teaches that a Christian's growth is 50-50, that God meets you halfway. No. God must carry you from step one all the way to the finish line and yet if you do not get up and run from step one to the finish line you will be another casualty of spiritual warfare. Paul wrote to the Philippians,

> So then, my beloved, just as you have always obeyed, not as in my presence only, but now much more in my absence, work out your salvation with fear and trembling; for it is God who is at work in you, both to will and to work for His good pleasure (Philipp 2:12-13).

Paul commands his readers to "complete your salvation" because "God is completing your salvation." The same Son of God who said, "Follow me," also said, "No one comes to the Son lest the Father draw him." The same Paul who said, "Do not quench the Spirit" (1 Thess 5:19) also said, "Faithful is He who calls you and He also will bring it to pass" (1 Thess 5:24). The same author of Hebrews who said "run with endurance the race that is set before you" (Heb 12:1) also said that God works in us "that which is pleasing in His sight" (Heb 13:21).

On one hand the Bible says to keep God's law, to obey His Word and

STRATEGY 7: RESOLVE TO LIVE GOD'S WORD NOW AND FOREVER

seek Him with all your heart. Yet, on the other hand, the Bible says that you cannot lift a finger of good works apart from God's gracious help. It is God who sanctifies and perfects His children. It is God who receives all the glory for your growth. Which is true? Both! But how can this be? Psalm 119:41-48 answers this question.

In the first half of this section (vss 41-43), we see dependence; utter reliance. But in the second half (vss 44-48), we see confidence. We see commitment and relentless resolution.

This is the paradox of Christian living. In the first three verses (41-43), you will find three directives for depending on God.

1. Depend on God for blessings from heaven (vs 41a).

MAY YOUR LOVINGKINDNESSES
ALSO COME TO ME, O LORD... (119:41A).
The psalmist prays for God's lovingkindnesses to shower upon him. Carefully note that "lovingkindnesses" is not singular but plural. The psalmist is not talking about God's generic attitude of love toward his people but God's specific acts of faithful love. The psalmist already knows that God loves him. He already knows that God cares for him. But now he prays for specific expressions of God's tender lovingkindness.

Because God's nature has previously been very loving and faithful toward His people, we can expect Him to treat us in the same way. God delights in blessing and loving His children (Ps 35:27). He shows us His kindness every day. The failure is not His love but our blindness to see it. Our own selfish expectations or distractions blind us from the incredible selfless love God has for us.

The Psalmist can boldly ask for God's lovingkindness without seeming selfish and presumptuous because he knows the character of God. He knows that God is a loving God and that a loving God will delight in loving His children for whom He died. If God's acts of love toward us were paper clips, you could string them together, end to end, from the west coast to the east coast and back again before you had counted all his acts of love towards you. If God's lovingkindnesses were pennies you could fill the ocean with them or stack them from here to the moon.

In the summer of 2003, I felt a conviction that I should take my wife to Florida for a pastor's conference and stay several days longer so we could celebrate our anniversary. But there was just one problem. It didn't fit our budget. There was no way we could afford the $1000 added expense and if we were to go, I needed to buy the tickets right then. After praying about it, and with full conviction that this was God's will, we purchased the airplane tickets and paid the conference fee. One month later, friends who knew nothing about the conference, sent us a $1000 check. That's the lovingkindness of God.

I believe that God receives pleasure in loving us in very unique and personal ways, by providing just the right amount of money, or healing in just the nick of time or by encouraging the broken heart in just the way that was meant for each of His children.

2. Depend on God for deliverance from enemies (vss 41b-42).

...YOUR SALVATION ACCORDING TO YOUR WORD (119:41B).
"Word" could also be translated "promise." It would read like this: "Your salvation according to your promise." God's promise is to rescue His people. The psalmist is not asking for salvation from sin but salvation from his enemies who reproach him (vs 42).

In the first part of verse 41, the psalmist prayed boldly for blessings because he knows God's character. In the second half, he prays boldly because he knows God's Word. The better you know God and His promises, the more boldly you will be able to pray.

Imagine that you are a fisherman and you walk into a fishing shop to buy worms. You ask the store owner, "I only have enough money to buy twenty worms but I need twenty-five. Will you give me the extra five?"

He may give you the deal and he may not. But let's say there's a sign on the counter that says, "Buy twenty worms get five free." Now you can ask with boldness, "Here's money for the twenty worms and please give me the five free ones." What caused you to have boldness in the second situation that you lacked in the first? Information. In the second scene you knew the deal, therefore you could ask boldly. In the first scene you had no such confidence. Feeble study in the Word will yield a crop of weak and uncertain prayers, but he who is intimate with the Word will be bold in prayer.

Now that he has cried out in bold prayer, the psalmist delivers the result of this prayer:

SO I WILL HAVE AN ANSWER FOR HIM WHO REPROACHES ME,
FOR I TRUST IN YOUR WORD (119:42).
Instead of fighting back, slandering his enemy, despising him, or fuming with anger, the psalmist turns to God's Word and finds the answer. He does not resort to revenge nor does he recoil in cowardice. Instead, he boldly answers his enemy, "Reproach me as you wish, but my trust is in the God of heaven and earth. You can do nothing without His permission and I solely trust in His ability

to deliver and vindicate me!"

The only way you can respond to unjust or cruel criticism with patience and humility is when your identity—your self worth—does not come from this world. A mother who finds her self worth in raising her children will become miserable or hostile when someone criticizes her ability to raise children. The pastor who finds his self worth in his ministry will become distraught when someone mocks his ability as a pastor or preacher. But when your self worth grows from God's enduring Word, no matter what someone says, it matters not, for you rest solely in the Lord Jesus Christ.

3. Depend on God for boldness in witnessing (vs 43).

AND DO NOT TAKE THE WORD OF TRUTH UTTERLY OUT OF MY MOUTH, FOR I WAIT FOR YOUR ORDINANCES (119:43).

The psalmist fears that under the pressure and slander of his enemies he may shudder in fear and lose his ability to boldly give them the Word of God.

But would God take His truth out of His own servant's mouth? Of course not. The psalmist is simply recognizing that God is sovereign, and that the God who spoke His Word is the God who can give the psalmist boldness to proclaim His Word. The psalmist's request is a request for courage in proclaiming the Word of God.

The term "ordinances" can be translated as "judgments." Instead of keeping his mouth shut in disgrace, the psalmist tells his persecutors the Word of truth and then patiently waits on God's righteous and perfect judgments to be rendered against all who reproach him. He does not want personal justice but God's justice.

When persecution from unbelievers becomes unbearable, remember that God will render righteous judgment on the final day. Take hope that God will someday make everything right. See how the psalmist is patient. He does not need vindication right now, because he knows that a day is coming when God will judge every man for his deeds (Eccl 12:14).

Many believers cower when they have opportunities to share the gospel with unbelievers because they are more concerned with their immediate comfort than God's coming justice. Instead of boldly giving the gospel and letting God take care of the persecutors, they close their mouths in shame. Rather than suffer persecution for Christ they'd rather live comfortably and have people like them.

The psalmist's willingness to wait on God's judgments shows his high reverence for God's Word. We wait upon things that we revere. Imagine the President asked to see you and you showed up at the Oval Office. After sitting in the waiting room for five minutes, would you get up and say to the secretary, "Sorry, but I have to get going. Could you tell the President to give me a call sometime this week to reschedule?"

The first three verses of this passage record the psalmist's dependence on God and the 2nd section records the psalmist's commitment to God. In the first part we found his prayers of dependence, but in the second part we find his resolutions of commitment.

Comparing the psalmist's statements of confession with his statements of commitment, Spurgeon noted,

> Both were sincere, both accurate. Experience makes many a paradox plain, and this is one. Before God we may be clear of open fault and yet at the same time mourn over a thousand heart-wanderings which need his restoring hand.[1]

In verses 44-48 you will find three calls of commitment to God:

1. Commit to keeping God's Word eternally (vss 44-45).

SO I WILL KEEP YOUR LAW CONTINUALLY,
FOREVER AND EVER (119:44).

It is appropriate that many translators inscribe this first word in verse 44 as "so." It could be translated as "and" but the word "so" shows the relationship between the psalmist's dependence and his commitment. "So, because I know that only You can bless me, deliver me from my enemies, and give me boldness in witnessing, because of all this, now I choose to follow You with all my heart!" Facing your dependence on God is the first step you must take if you are going to commit to obey Him. An attitude of dependence produces an attitude of commitment.

New Year's resolutions are usually made to cover a year or sometimes even a few months. Even then, most people rarely keep their resolutions half the time they promised. But not so for the psalmist. The psalmist's mind and heart are set on eternity. Obeying God for a lifetime does not match the worthiness of God's precious Word. The psalmist resolves to keep God's law forever. The next verse describes the result of keeping God's law forever.

AND I WILL WALK AT LIBERTY, FOR I SEEK YOUR PRECEPTS (119:45).
The psalmist walks in liberty from sin. He is free from the prison of evil. No longer is he shackled to wickedness and tied down by his lusts. He is free to do exactly what he desires the most: to obey God.

---

1   Spurgeon, 425.

He is free because he seeks God's precepts (vs 45b). Pursuit of God's commands is the only road to emancipation from spiritual slavery. Spurgeon said "The way of holiness is not a track for slaves, but the King's highway for freemen."[2]

2. Commit to proclaiming God's acts boldly (vs 46).

I WILL ALSO SPEAK OF YOUR TESTIMONIES BEFORE KINGS
AND SHALL NOT BE ASHAMED (119:46).

When was the last time you saw evangelism as proclamation of God's person? The difference between a cult missionary and a Christian missionary is that a cult missionary tries to convert the prospect to his system of beliefs, but the Christian missionary does more than try to convert his prospect. He proclaims God's acts of glory, His purity of character. He does not confront the unbeliever with a system, but with a Person. He is not as concerned about getting a new member in his church as he is with seeing a new sinner go to heaven. He confronts the pagan with the nature and character of God. Thus, when the unbeliever rejects the gospel, he is not rejecting an optional religion but the Almighty Creator and Judge of creation.

But notice before whom the psalmist speaks God's testimonies: kings. Of all the positions of power in the psalmist's day, none came close to the power of a king. The higher one's status, the more intimidating it becomes to share the gospel. But the psalmist is so saturated with God's Word, so caught up in God's glory, that even the greatest of men will not make him flinch.

Have you spoken the gospel to someone and later felt shame? Don't let this thinking plague you. There is nothing shameful about speaking God's Word. It is your duty and privilege. And remember what Luke said of Peter and the apostles after they were lacerated with whips by the high priest council, "So they went on their way from the presence of the Council, rejoicing that they had been considered worthy to suffer shame for His name." (Acts 5:41)

3. Commit to delighting in God's commandments affectionately (vss 47-48).

I SHALL DELIGHT IN YOUR COMMANDMENTS,
WHICH I LOVE. AND I SHALL LIFT UP MY HANDS TO
YOUR COMMANDMENTS, WHICH I LOVE;
AND I WILL MEDITATE ON YOUR STATUTES (119:47-48).

These verses have a repeated theme, "which I love." Many believe that for loving affection to be real, it must be spontaneous. They may be reacting to an artificially concocted affection which is not affection at all. But this does not negate the

---

2   Spurgeon, 228.

need to commit to delighting in God's commandments affectionately.

Since you committed to follow God's commands the moment you became saved, why not delight in them and enjoy the life God has given you today? His commands are not restricting, depressing or discouraging (1 John 5:3). There is no such thing as an unhappy obedient Christian.

Loving God's Word will not always come naturally because we still battle our old nature. But we can commit to loving God's Word and make it our delight as the psalmist says, "I shall delight in Your commandments." The word "delight" is reflexive. Used here it literally means, "I shall delight myself in Your commandments." He does not delight in God's commandments from a long ways away or from a cold heart. He personally delights himself in them. He chooses to let them capture his affections and steal his devotion. This is an effective strategy against sin.

The psalmist continues, "I shall lift up my hands to Your commandments" (vs 48). He does not worship God's commandments (that would be bibliolatry). Instead, the psalmist expresses a deep-rooted desire to know and obey God's Word. It is so great that he lifts his hands in the air as an expression of deep affection for God's holy Word.

And what is the only appropriate response to his great affection for God's Word? "And I will meditate on Your statutes" (vs 48). The things we spend most time thinking about are the things we love the most. Christ said, "For where your treasure is there will your heart be also" (Matt 6:21).

From Psalm 119:41-43, we found three directives for depending on God:

1. Depend on God for blessings from heaven (vs 41a).
2. Depend on God for deliverance from enemies (vss 41b-42).
3. Depend on God for boldness in witnessing (vs 43).

From verses 44-48, we looked at three calls of commitment to God:
1. Commit to keeping God's Word eternally (vss 44-45).
2. Commit to proclaiming God's acts boldly (vs 46).
3. Commit to delighting in God's commandments affectionately (vss 47-48).

Remember Sampson? Consider the last day of his life. There he stood. A blind laughingstock. The trophy of the Philistine's victory. The man who tried it by himself all his life.

But this time things were different. Samson had a change of heart. For the first time in his life, he realized that no matter how faithful he tried to keep his Nazirite vow, he failed miserably. For the first time Samson realized that he desperately needed God's help. The strongman was weak without the strength of the Almighty One.

As the Philistines mocked and jeered at their trophy, blind Samson turned to a little boy and said, "Let me feel the pillars on which the house rests, that I may lean against them" (Judges 16:26). These pillars supported a roof of 3,000 wicked Philistines. Turning his heart toward God, Sampson prayed his final prayer: "O LORD God, please remember me and please strengthen me just this time, O God, that I may at once be avenged of the Philistines for my two eyes" (Judges 16:28). The Lord answered that request.

Popular Sunday school storybooks for children like to sketch Sampson as big and muscular. They make him look like he was born in a 24 Hour Fitness gym, giving him the pre-California governor physique. But I do not believe that Samson was extraordinarily buff because then people would give glory to Samson's muscles and not to God for his incredible strength.

On several occasions when Samson performed a deed of miraculous strength, the text says that, "The Spirit of the Lord came upon him mightily" (Judges 14:6, 19; 15:14). When he divulged his secret and his hair was cut, the text says that "He did not know that the LORD had departed from him" (Judges 16:20) and for that reason he could no longer fight off the Philistines who captured him and gouged out his eyes. It was not long hair nor big muscles that empowered Samson with supernatural power, but the Holy Spirit of God.

And why did Samson go down into history as a Bible hero? Because he surrendered to God and resolved to obey! In the last hour of his life, he saw his dependence and made a commitment (Judges 16:28-31). It is my prayer that you will do the same.

QUESTIONS FOR CONTEMPLATION

1. In verse 45 what is the promise from God that the psalmist sees?

2. How are we to respond to unbelievers who persecute us? Give examples of what this response should look like.

3. Look at each verse and write down what the psalmist says about the importance of God's Word. How do each of these apply to you in a practical way?

4. If you had 15 minutes to share something form this section that would change the heart of your child or close friend for the Lord, what would that be?

CHAPTER

24

8 Resolutions of the Man or Woman of God
Psalm 119:57-64

People who make resolutions value life. People who make resolutions prove that how they live matters greatly to them. People who make resolutions prove that they have considered their short time on this tiny globe and want to live life to its fullest. This was the heart of Jonathan Edwards and this is why he wrote no fewer than 70 resolutions by which he strove to live.

Face the vapor of your life (James 4:14) and maximize it fully. Life on earth in light of eternity can be compared to a husband taken captive by guerillas. For 20 years he cannot see his wife. Finally, she receives a phone call informing her that she may see him for just five minutes and after this, she will never see him again. If this were you, what would you do during those five minutes? Those 300 seconds would be the most precious moments of your life. All humans have been given their five minutes–their life on this earth. Only on this side of eternity do you have the freedom to choose your life to count or to squander. From psalm 119:57-64, we find eight resolutions of the man or woman of God:

1. The man or woman of God is resolved to keep the Word (vs 57).

THE LORD IS MY PORTION;
I HAVE PROMISED TO KEEP YOUR WORDS (119:57).

This is the greatest resolution from which all other resolutions flow. Until one is ready to commit himself to complete obedience to God's Word, he cannot grow in Him.

The psalmist begins by saying, "The Lord is my portion" (vs 57a). When the psalmist's lived, if an army was conquered, soldiers either died by the sword or fled for their lives with no time to bring their food, camels, tents, pottery, or weapons. Often their wives and children were left behind as well. The victorious army plundered anything left behind and portioned them off to the warriors and commanders as a reward for victory.

A man's portion today is often his paycheck, commission or the proceeds from his stocks and bonds. But the godly man knows these things will never satisfy–not that check he yearns for every Friday, not his family, his wife or his house. His portion is the Lord! It is God Himself! In the Lord you will never suffer want, nor lack a single good thing. Let Him be your portion!

Can you say, "God is my inheritance. He is my food and my drink. He is my happiness. He is my fulfillment. He is my identity. He is everything that matters and all that I could ever need!"? In Spurgeon's words, "There is no possession like Jehovah himself."[1] No treasure of this world compares to the eternal treasure of knowing God! When you find yourself complaining about your finances, your family problems, or your withering health, turn and thank God that you have far more than this world could ever give, for you have God Himself! To have everything but God is to have nothing. To have nothing but God is to have everything.

But how does the first part of the verse, "having God as my portion" relate with the second, "keeping God's words?" Investors don't buy land they know will plummet in value. Stockbrokers don't purchase stock from a company that is going out of business. Before investing in something, one must see its value. The psalmist is no fool. He invests his life into this LORD who is his portion, who is his life, his joy, his happiness, his purpose for living. He invests in this One whose commands he obeys.

When people make promises which they later lose interest in keeping, they soothe their consciences by forgetting the oath. But the psalmist knows nothing of this. He keeps himself accountable to his own words by reminding both himself and God that he "promised to keep Your words." Indeed, this is an oath worthy to keep, even at the cost of his own life!

2. The man or woman of God is resolved to seek God's mercy (vs 58).

I SOUGHT YOUR FAVOR WITH ALL MY HEART;
BE GRACIOUS TO ME ACCORDING TO YOUR WORD" (119:58).
The independent, I-can-do-it-myself mentality of today's world is foreign to humility and is the enemy of godliness. The psalmist prays as a broken man who rests his credit on God's mercy alone. This man of God seeks God's grace because he knows that he will never earn God's acceptance by his own merit. He asks God to be gracious "according to Your Word" because he knows that the Word teaches God's grace. Without this truth of God's Word, the psalmist would be distraught and hopeless and his prayer would be anemic.

---

1   Spurgeon, 254.

The psalmist seeks God's favor with all his heart. Seventy five percent commitment is not good enough. Ninety eight percent will not do. Every cell in his body yearns for God. He holds nothing back. His resolution reflects Solomon's words in Ecclesiastes 9:10, "Whatever your hand finds to do, do it with all your might; for there is no activity or planning or knowledge or wisdom in Sheol where you are going." Life is terribly short, and once we die, our opportunity is gone—at least on this side of eternity. Therefore, everything we do, must be done wholeheartedly. We believers should treat God's favor as we would beg for our own life. What greater happiness can a person feel than to know that God's favor is upon him (Ps 147:11)?

3. The man or woman of God is resolved to change (vs 59).

I CONSIDERED MY WAYS AND TURNED
MY FEET TO YOUR TESTIMONIES (119:59).

Notice the order of events in this verse. *First* he reflects, *then* he turns. Thoughtful reflection must precede godly conversion. A godly man spends more time evaluating what God sees in his heart than what others think of his actions. Many men hate to consider their ways because the consideration is unbearable, so they walk on like the man who forgets his own face in James 1:23-24. We must search our hearts before we can turn down the right path, just as a sailor must check his compass before he sets his sails. Spurgeon writes, "Action without thought is folly, and thought without action is sloth: to think carefully and then to act promptly is a happy combination."[2]

4. The man or woman of God is resolved to act now (vs 60).

I HASTENED AND DID NOT DELAY
TO KEEP YOUR COMMANDMENTS (119:60).

He who hesitates has already lost. Postponed obedience is disobedience. If you always choose to obey later, you will never obey because later never arrives. You cannot obey before because before already was. The right time to obey will always be now.

Our haste to obey a manager or honor a superior is shameful when compared to our negligence and sluggardliness in obeying the Lord. But this reveals fear of man and flippancy towards God. We should follow the motto of General Thomas Jonathan (Stonewall) Jackson of the south during the Civil War who said, "Duty is ours, the consequences are God's."

---

2   Spurgeon, 255.

5. The man or woman of God is resolved to remember (vs 61).

THE CORDS OF THE WICKED HAVE ENCIRCLED ME,
BUT I HAVE NOT FORGOTTEN YOUR LAW (119:61).

Often the hardest time to remember God's law is when the cords of one's enemies are wrapped around his throat and threaten death. Even when trapped and held hostage by his bitter enemies, the psalmist remembers the only thing that will bring him comfort, God's Word. The psalmist can remain resolute because his enemies cannot rob him of his greatest treasure, the Word of God.[3]

6. The man or woman of God is resolved to inconvenience himself (vs 62).

AT MIDNIGHT I SHALL RISE TO GIVE THANKS TO YOU
BECAUSE OF YOUR RIGHTEOUS ORDINANCES (119:62).

This man of God does not care what time of the day it is—never is any time of the day so important that he cannot make room to give thanks to God. He picks the most unlikely time of giving thanks—the middle of the night. And he inconveniently rises up from his warm, cozy bed, falls on his knees, and gives thanks to God in the dead of night. Through his actions he says, *Thanksgiving to God is more important than my sleep.* By picking the most inconvenient time of the day to thank God, he makes a strong statement that humble recognition of God's goodness is far more important than the most urgent, time sensitive activities of our hectic lives. Spurgeon notes, "Midnight ends one day and begins another, it was therefore meet to give the solemn moments to communion with the Lord."[4]

He gives thanks because of "Your righteous ordinances." Ordinances can be translated as judgments. In this context he is suffering the strangling cords of the wicked (vs 61), but instead of moping, complaining or fighting back, he thanks God for His righteous judgments. God's judgments do not strike fear into the heart of the psalmist for he rests in the mercy of God, safe from God's wrath.

7. The man or woman of God is resolved to befriend the godly (vs 63).

I AM A COMPANION OF ALL THOSE WHO FEAR YOU,
AND OF THOSE WHO KEEP YOUR PRECEPTS (119:63).

This man of God is a wise man. He befriends "all those who fear" God. A God-fearing person likes to spend time with God-fearing people. He does not want to be influenced by the attitude of those who fear people, or worse, those

---

3   Cf. Spurgeon, 256.
4   Spurgeon, 256.

who live lives of wickedness. The standard for the psalmist's company is *God-fearing*. We often pick friends based on likable personalities, similarity in tastes, or matching trades. But these are shaky grounds for lasting friendships. The only foundation for friendship that transcends all temporary matters and will last into eternity is the friendship molded in a relationship with God Himself.

These companions do not just fear God, for even the demons fear God and shudder. These companions prove their God-fearing life by keeping "God's precepts." They love God's instructions and demonstrate this love by obeying them. These people have an intimate fear of God.

Recently, I attended a wedding of friends at our church. As I greeted the man next to me at the dining table, I quickly discovered that this man claimed Christianity but never attended church and rarely spent time with other believers. After asking him a series of questions about his beliefs and reasons for such strange convictions, I asked him, "You said you worked for the city?"

"Yes."

"Did you ever spend time with your fellow co-workers outside of your job?" I asked.

"Why, of course," he responded.

"Why?"

"Because we knew each other—worked at the same job, had lots in common," he replied.

"Then why is it that you think you could be a Christian but not desire to be with other Christians at church? If you truly were saved, then you would desire the company of others who are saved." It is only natural to desire the company of those who have been saved from the same hell, by the same Christ, and for the same destiny of eternal glory.

8. The man or woman of God is resolved to hunger (vs 64).

THE EARTH IS FULL OF YOUR LOVINGKINDNESS, O LORD;
TEACH ME YOUR STATUTES (119:64).

Some believers legitimately chide those pastors who plague their people with an anorexic diet that emaciates their spiritual health. Sheep need a healthy, seven course diet of the Word of God. But just like a physical diet, no matter how good you eat, if you don't exercise your body, you'll likely gain weight and lose health.

I've heard ministers say that sheep should be fat. But I don't see a fat sheep in this psalm. I see a hungry, healthy sheep. Fat sheep don't need more food, they need to start using the food they already have. Many believers are content to sit and soak and learn until gradually their appetite grows dull and sluggish.

They never get up and live out what they have been fed.

But not the psalmist. He witnesses the great lovingkindness of God all throughout the whole earth—he sees the rain that waters humanity, beast, and plant. He witnesses the warm sun that grows flowers and warms cold bodies. He sees the wind blowing seed to continue the cycle of life in God's creation. He experiences God's mercies day by day everywhere, through people, through creation, and especially through His Word. And what does this do? It gives him an appetite. There is no better way to know God than to feast upon His statutes and live them out with all your heart.

In this final section of the last step we have looked at eight resolutions of the man or woman of the Word:

1. The man or woman of God is resolved to keep the Word (vs 57).
2. The man or woman of God is resolved to seek God's mercy (vs 58).
3. The man or woman of God is resolved to change (vs 59).
4. The man or woman of God is resolved to act now (vs 60).
5. The man or woman of God is resolved to remember (vs 61).
6. The man or woman of God is resolved to inconvenience himself (vs 62).
7. The man or woman of God is resolved to befriend the godly (vs 63).
8. The man or woman of God is resolved to hunger (vs 64).

The consulting firm, Coopers & Lybrand, placed a series of print ads featuring a large picture of an ancient Chinese sword. The ad's caption read, "Does your consultant quote The Art of War but shy away from battle?'"[5] The same question needs to be asked of every believer: Do you quote God's Word, but shy away from obeying it? Make it your life resolve to cherish the precious Word of God, and for all eternity you'll praise God that you did!

---

5   Jerry Stapleton, *From Vendor to Business Resource* (Fort Collins: Summa Business Books, 2002), 150.

QUESTIONS FOR CONTEMPLATION

1. What is everything that the psalmist promises to do in this passage?

2. Why is it significant that he "considers his ways" in verse 59 before he turns his feet to God's testimonies?

3. Why does he say, "At midnight I shall rise to give thanks to You..." in verse 62?

4. Explain the significance of verse 63.

5. Construct an outline for this passage entitled: "The Characteristics of a Believer Who Loves God's Word." Study each point and ask how you are applying this to your walk with Christ.

A FINAL WORD FROM THE AUTHOR

Dear Reader,

Search every book in every library on every continent and you will not find one so deep, so rich, so powerful and so worthy of your affection as the Word of God. Would the richest man give all his possessions for this Book, he still could not find a price high enough to match its endless worth. This Bible you read comes from the lips of God, the Creator of the universe.

Let it be your joy in sorrow, your strength in weakness, your confidence in fear, your health in sickness and the very breath of life to your soul.

Commit yourself to a lifelong love of God's Word, and then you can say with Simon Peter, "Lord, to whom shall we go? You have words of eternal life." (John 6:68)

Seth Kniep

T. S. Kniep

Loving God's Word
Twenty-five lesson outlines for preachers,
teachers, and small group leaders

◆ Preface
◆ Introduction: Precious as Gold—Practical as Tools

PART ONE: MOTIVES, STUMBLING BLOCKS, TOOLS AND QUESTIONS

◆ Chapter 1: Why Love God's Word?
- ❖ Wrong Motives
  - ⇨ Duteous obligation.
  - ⇨ Arrogant ambition
  - ⇨ Personal selfishness
- ❖ Psalm 119: Thirty-three Actions in Loving God's Word
- ❖ A Well of Refreshment
- ❖ Stumbling Blocks to Loving God's Word
  - ⇨ Temptations distract it
  - ⇨ Junk food de-flavors it
  - ⇨ False doctrines muddle it
  - ⇨ Modern culture belittles it
  - ⇨ Time strangles it
- ❖ Three Tools for Loving God's Word
  - ⇨ The Holy Spirit in your heart
  - ⇨ The Word of God in your mind
  - ⇨ A broken heart before the Lord
◆ Chapter 2: Four Questions for the Lover of the Word
- ❖ Do I Make God's Word My Priority?
- ❖ Do I Put God's Word in My Memory?
- ❖ Do I Love God's Word Dearly?
- ❖ Do I Face God's Person Seriously?

PART TWO: SEVEN STRATEGIES FOR SLAYING BIBLE APATHY FROM PSALM 119

Strategy 1: Embark on God's Word as the Path to Knowing God

◆ Chapter 3: How to Be a Lover of the Word
- ❖ Walk as a Believer of the Word with Devotion (vss 1-3)
  - ⇨ Blameless in reputation
  - ⇨ Active in obedience
  - ⇨ Protective of Scripture
  - ⇨ Superlative in devotion
- ❖ Embrace the Purpose of the Word with Conviction (vss 4-5)
- ❖ Receive the Blessings of the Word with Thanksgiving (vss 6-7)
- ❖ Ask God to Help you Obey the Word with Resolve (vs 8)
◆ Chapter 4: The Bible Zealot
- ❖ Three Sketches of a Bible Zealot
  - ⇨ Deeply desires God's holiness (vss 113, 115, 118, 119)
  - ⇨ Rests in God's protection (vss 114, 116, 117)
  - ⇨ Shudders in God's presence (vs 120)
◆ Chapter 5: Fresh Ground or Instant—Experiencing the Word of God
- ❖ Three steps to a "Word-soaked soul"
  - ⇨ Embrace the holy character of God (vs 137)
  - ⇨ Revere the perfect deeds of God (vs 138)
  - ⇨ Possess the cherished Word of God (vss 139-144)

Strategy 2: Revere God's Word with Awesome Wonder

◆ Chapter 6: The Magnificent Word of God
- ❖ Seven Reasons Why God's Word is Wonderful
  - ⇨ It revives the dead (vs 25)
  - ⇨ It teaches the ignorant (vs 26)
  - ⇨ It uplifts the downcast (vs 27)
  - ⇨ It strengthens the weak (vs 28)
  - ⇨ It guides the lost (vss 29-30)
  - ⇨ It comforts the discouraged (vs 31)
  - ⇨ It frees the imprisoned (vs 32)

◆   Chapter 7: Mining the Treasure House of Wisdom
  ❖   Two Digging Tools for Mining Wisdom from the Word of God
    ⇨   Dig the right mountain. Get your wisdom from God's Word (vss 98-100)
    ⇨   Mine the right gold. Apply that knowledge to your daily life (vss 97, 101-104)
◆   Chapter 8: What God's Word Will Do to You
  ❖   It Will Produce Supreme Happiness (vss 129-131)
  ❖   It Will Produce Dogged Purpose (vss 132-135)
  ❖   It Will Produce Sacred Sadness (vs 136)

Strategy 3: Cling to God's Word Like a Rock in a Storm

◆   Chapter 9: What to Do When Suffering is Unbearable
  ❖   Four Tools for Surviving Suffering
    ⇨   Face your suffering (vss 81-87)
    ⇨   Talk to God about your suffering (vss 81-87)
    ⇨   View your suffering in light of the Word of God (vss 81, 83, 86, 87)
    ⇨   Live to keep the Word of God (vs 88)
◆   Chapter 10: The Word: Your Survival Kit for Staying Alive
  ❖   Two reasons the believer needs God's Word
    ⇨   The Word is a shouting testimony to God's faithfulness (vss 89-91)
    ⇨   The Word is a nutritious feast for the believer's soul (vss 92-96)
◆   Chapter 11: What to Do When You Need Help from God
  ❖   Three Prayers based on His Promises
    ⇨   Oh God, deliver me, for I am your child! (vss 153, 155, 157, 158)
    ⇨   Oh God, deliver me, for Your Word promises deliverance! (vss 154, 156, 160)
    ⇨   Oh God, deliver me, for You delight in delivering! (vs 159).

Strategy 4: Follow God's Word As a Guide in Prayer

◆   Chapter 12: How God Can Help You Keep His Word
  ❖   Ask For Help to Obey His Word
    ⇨   Ask to learn the Word with a motive of obedience (vss 33-34)
    ⇨   Ask to obey the Word with a heart of delight (vs 35)
    ⇨   Ask to love the Word with an abhorrence for sin (vss 36-37)
    ⇨   Ask to be grounded in the Word with an attitude of reverence (vs 38)
    ⇨   Ask to take in the Word with a clear conscience (vs 39)
    ⇨   Ask to hunger for the Word with a craving appetite (vs 40)
◆   Chapter 13: How to Pray Using God's Word
  ❖   Prayers That Will Solidify a Biblical Prayer Life
    ⇨   Pray for the ingenuity of God's Word to cultivate your character (vss 73, 80)
    ⇨   Pray for the competence of God's Word to shape your testimony (vss 74, 79)
    ⇨   Pray for the vigor of God's Word to endure your trials (vss 75, 78).
    ⇨   Pray for the pledge of God's Word to receive God's compassion (vss 76, 77)
◆   Chapter 14: Divine Instant Messaging
  ❖   Three Patterns for Prayer
    ⇨   Pattern #1: Pray in dependence (vss 145-147)
    ⇨   Pattern #2: Pray with resolve (vss 145-147)
    ⇨   Pattern #3: Pray with understanding (vss 148-152)

Strategy 5: Shine God's Word on Your Heart and Life

◆   Chapter 15: Enter the College of Christian Living
  ❖   Four Tests for Spiritual Growth
    ⇨   Accept God's loving discipline (vss 65, 67, 71)
    ⇨   Realize your need to learn from God (vss 66, 68)
    ⇨   Respond to persecution by running to the Word (vss 69, 70)
    ⇨   Prize God's Word above all earthly treasures (vs 72)
◆   Chapter 16: How to Be Dominated by the Word of God
  ❖   Four Areas of Our Lives That God's Word Should Dominate
    ⇨   The Word is to dominate your choices (vss 105, 106, 112)
    ⇨   The Word is to dominate your suffering (vss 107, 109, 110)
    ⇨   The Word is to dominate your worship (verse 108)
    ⇨   The Word is to dominate your attitude (vs 111)

◆ Chapter 17: Dead Orthodoxy or Living Truth: The Importance of the Affections
  ❖ Seven Traits of Affection for God's Word
    ⇨ The believer who loves God's Word is struck with awe (vs 161)
    ⇨ The believer who loves God's Word is filled with joy (vs 162)
    ⇨ The believer who loves God's Word is roused with hate (vs 163a)
    ⇨ The believer who loves God's Word is captivated with love (vs 163b)
    ⇨ The believer who loves God's Word is flooded with praise (vs 164)
    ⇨ The believer who loves God's Word is wrapped in peace (vs 165)
    ⇨ The believer who loves God's Word is committed to obedience (vss 166-168)
◆ Chapter 18: How to Worship a Holy God in an Unholy World
  ❖ Worship God by Turning to His Grace (vss 169a, 170a, 171a, 172a)
  ❖ Worship God by Submitting to His Teaching (vss 169b, 171b, 172b, 174b)
  ❖ Worship God by Relying on His Strength (vss 170b, 173, 174, 175, 176)

Strategy 6: Flee to God's Word As a Refuge from Persecution

◆ Chapter 19: God's Word–a Refuge for the Broken-hearted
  ❖ Three Routes for Running to the Refuge of God's Word When You Suffer
    ⇨ Elevate the Word as your purpose for living (vss 17-18)
    ⇨ Trust in the Word as your comfort in sorrow (vss 19-22)
    ⇨ Flee to the Word as your refuge in affliction (vss 23-24)
◆ Chapter 20: How to Remember God's Word When You Suffer the Attacks of Your Enemies
  ❖ Eight Reasons to Remember God's Word
    ⇨ The Word gives you hope (vs 49)
    ⇨ The Word gives you life (vs 50)
    ⇨ The Word gives you focus (vs 51)
    ⇨ The Word gives you comfort (vs 52)
    ⇨ The Word gives you perspective (vs 53)
    ⇨ The Word gives you joy (vs 54)
    ⇨ The Word gives you companionship (vs 55)
    ⇨ The Word gives you identity (vs 56)
◆ Chapter 21: Are You Qualified for Divine Deliverance?
  ❖ Three Reasons That God Will Deliver The Believer
    ⇨ His personal character before God (vss 121-122)
    ⇨ His personal relationship with God (vss 123-125)
    ⇨ His personal zeal for God (vss 126-128)

Strategy 7: Resolve to Live God's Word Now and Forever

◆ Chapter 22: Resolve to Apply
  ❖ Three Resolves for Applying the Word in Your Daily Walk
    ⇨ Apply the Word as a weapon against sin (vss 9-11)
    ⇨ Receive the Word as a book of instruction (vss 12-13)
    ⇨ Revel in the Word as a letter of love (vss 14-16)
◆ Chapter 23: The Paradox of Obedience
  ❖ Three Directives for Depending on God
    ⇨ Depend on God for blessings from heaven (vs 41a)
    ⇨ Depend on God for deliverance from enemies (vss 41b-42)
    ⇨ Depend on God for boldness in witnessing (vs 43)
  ❖ Three Calls of Commitment to God
    ⇨ Commit to keeping God's Word eternally (vss 44-45)
    ⇨ Commit to proclaiming God's acts boldly (vs 46)
    ⇨ Commit to delighting in God's commandments affectionately (vss 47-48)
◆ Chapter 24: Eight Resolutions of the Man or Woman of God
  ❖ The Man or Woman of God is Resolved to Keep the Word (vs 57)
  ❖ The Man or Woman of God is Resolved to Seek God's Mercy (vs 58)
  ❖ The Man or Woman of God is Resolved to Change (vs 59)
  ❖ The Man or Woman of God is Resolved to Act Now (vs 60)
  ❖ The Man or Woman of God is Resolved to Remember (vs 61)
  ❖ The Man or Woman of God is Resolved to Inconvenience Himself (vs 62)
  ❖ The Man or Woman of God is Resolved to Befriend the Godly (vs 63)
  ❖ The Man or Woman of God is Resolved to Hunger (vs 64)

Meet Pastor Seth Kniep

 Born in Dallas, TX and raised in a Christian home, the influence of the pastorate etched deep as Seth watched his father shepherd a church for ten years. Age five found him praying the sinner's prayer, but the gospel fell like drops of rain on the cold stone of his sin-filled heart. The lust, pride, greed, and selfishness of his sin nature only entangled him deeper as he trusted in the false assurance of his sinner's prayer.

At age twelve God confronted Seth with his desperate wickedness in the book of Romans. Paul's words "There is none righteous, not even one; there is none who understands, there is none who seeks for God" (Rom 3:10-11) pierced his soul like an arrow. Suddenly all his Bible knowledge of Christ's suffering, death, and resurrection moved the greatest distance in the world—from his head to his heart, and he knew that he was redeemed. It was at this moment that Seth turned his back on sin and embraced the gospel. Christ was now more than a Sunday school story. He was his Lord.

After salvation, Seth's heart burned for the lost and he hungered to teach God's Word. He pursued the entertainment business for several years as a magician and tap dancer, but eventually left this to become a pastor and evangelist.

God blessed Seth with an abundance of ministry opportunity. He taught Bible studies, hosted call-in talk radio show, interviewed on TV, launched an evangelistic group that proclaimed the gospel on street corners, and formed a Christian music band. Seth's first preaching experience happened at the Good News Rescue Mission where people attacked him with curses and spittle. He ministered as a lay youth pastor in Cottonwood, California, followed by a part time position in Torrance, California. God then placed Seth for three years as a minister over college, high school, and Jr. High ministries at a church in Thousand Oaks, California, followed by serving as part time pastor for a small congregation in Reseda, California.

In the midst of the jungle of ministry Seth met the loveliest woman on God's earth, Kimberly Joy. On the fifth date she asked Seth what the goal of their relationship was. Upon telling her that he dated to marry and was entering full time ministry, she responded, "Well that's funny, because I always told my Mom that I wanted to marry a pastor." The light could not have been greener and they were married eight months later. One year later Seth started at the Masters Seminary. During those years at school, God packed their quiver with four balls of energy: Audrey, Josiah, Elijah, and Atalie.

As the end of seminary drew near, Seth began searching for more practical ministry training. After serving in a fellowship at *Grace Community Church* of Sun Valley, CA, overseeing the newcomer ministry, follow up ministry, Bible study organization, and launching a weekly prayer meeting, he joined *Calvary Bible Church of Burbank* because of their commitment to expository preaching, an elder-based leadership, and discipleship of men for ministry. For two years he enjoyed the privilege of learning and serving at Calvary as an intern for adult ministries under Dr. Jack Hughes.

While at Calvary, Seth fulfilled multiple aspects of church ministry, launched street evangelism and guest preached at churches throughout southern California. During this time Seth published his first book, *The Truth Behind the Passion Film and How to Respond*. He was later ordained by elders of *Calvary Bible Church* and professors at *The Masters Seminary* in October of 2005.

During this time Seth launched Divide the Word Ministries, a ministry devoted to training believers in the Word and in evangelism (www.dividetheword.com) and providing cutting edge software for Christians. Seth's ministry travels have taken him to Mexico, Ukraine, and Kazakstan.

After serving at Calvary Bible Church of Burbank for two years, God called Seth to Calvary Bible Church of Kalamazoo, Michigan, a multi-staffed church where he now serves as Pastor of college and singles and oversees the church's evangelism.

Seth's life pursuit is to fulfill Paul's final charge to the young pastor Timothy:

"I solemnly charge you in the presence of God and of Christ Jesus, who is to judge the living and the dead, and by His appearing and His kingdom: preach the word; be ready in season and out of season; reprove, rebuke, exhort, with great patience and instruction. For the time will come when they will not endure sound doctrine; but wanting to have their ears tickled, they will accumulate for themselves teachers in accordance to their own desires, and will turn away their ears from the truth and will turn aside to myths" (2 Timothy 4:1-4).

Divide the Word Ministries

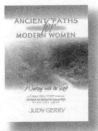

Seth Kniep is a speaker and trainer for Divide the Word Ministries, a ministry devoted to training believers in Bible study, teaching, preaching, discipleship, evangelism, leadership, and prayer. To book him to speak at your church or ministry, contact him at questions@dividetheword.org.

Divide the Word Ministries also provides cutting edge software through the genius of Stuart Zahn, a man devoted to maximizing modern technology for the kingdom of God.

Visit www.dividetheword.com to find out more.

LifeSong Publishers

For Baptism and Communion Preparation

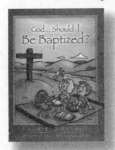  

God... Should I Be Baptized?
ISBN 978-0-9718306-1-5
$10.99 100pp 8.5x11
For children 8-12

God's Plan... My Response
ISBN 978-0-9718306-0-8
$9.99 96pp 6x9
For Jr. Hi/ Hi School

The Lord's Supper...Let's Get Ready!
ISBN 978-0-9718306-6-0
$10.99 100pp 8.5x11
For Ages 8-14

"This is a great effort that I recommend highly for churches that desire to expose their children to solid teaching on the Lord's table..."

John MacArthur, Grace Community Church

Ancient Paths For Modern Women

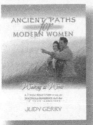 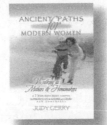 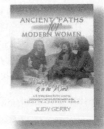

Walking With the Lord
ISBN 0-9718306-2-2
$11.99 100pp 7.5x10

Walking as Wives
ISBN 978-0-9718306-3-9
$11.99 112pp 7.5x10

Walking as Mothers and Homemakers
ISBN 978-0-9718306-4-6
$11.99 110pp 7.5x10

Walking in the Church and in the World
ISBN 978-0-9718306-5-3
$11.99 130pp 7.5x10

"Judy Gerry has dug deeply into the sacred records of the Bible to surface divine guidance for women in every generation. Here is a timely, reassuring and professionally crafted study resource which belongs in every church library and on the study agenda for thinking women..."

Howard G. Hendricks, Distinguished Professor, Dallas Theological Seminary

LifeSong Publishers Order Form

(See website for further description of items)

	Price	Quantity	Total
Loving God's Word (softcover)	$15.99		
Loving God's Word (hardcover)	$20.99		
God... Should I Be Baptized?	$10.99		
The Lord's Supper... Let's Get Ready!	$10.99		
God's Plan My Response	$ 9.99		
Ancient Paths 1- Walking/Lord	$11.99		
Ancient Paths 2- Walking/Wives	$11.99		
Ancient Paths 3- Walking/Mothers/Homemakers	$11.99		
Ancient Paths 4- Walking/Church/World	$11.99		
Ancient Paths Set- (AP 1-4)	$43.16		
Hope When The River Rages	$12.99		

Subtotal of "Total" Columns	
CA Sales Tax (CA Residents Only) 7.25% of subtotal	
Shipping Media Mail- $3.50 or $4.50 for over 3 items (7-10 days)	
Shipping Priority- 7% of total/minimum of $5.00 (3-4 days)	
Total	

Name and/or Church _____

Address_____

City, State, Zip_____

Phone (   )_____

Email_____

This address is my _____ Church _____ Home _____ Other

Make check payable to:

Lifesong Publishers
P.O. Box 183, Somis, CA 93066-0183
Phone: 805-655-5644
www.LifeSongPublishers.com
Email: mailbox@lifesongpublishers.com

To pay by credit card: _____Mastercard _____Visa
Please fill out above address information
Card # _____
Exp. Date_____
Name on Card_____